THE June Masters Bacher COUNTRY COOKBOOK

HARVEST HOUSE PUBLISHERS
Eugene, Oregon 97402

Scripture quotations are from the King James Version of the Bible.

Illustrations by
Sandy Silverthorne

THE JUNE MASTERS BACHER COUNTRY COOKBOOK

Published by Harvest House Publishers
Eugene, Oregon 97402

Bacher, June Masters.
The June Masters Bacher country cookbook.

Revision of: Kitchen delights. c1982.
Includes index.
1. Cookery, American. I. Bacher, June Masters. Kitchen delights.
II. Title. III. Title: Country cookbook.
TX715.B143 1988 641.6 88-16525
ISBN 0-89081-358-2

Printed in the United States of America.

To
wonderful friends,
who over the years have shared with me
their recipes
and life's basic ingredient,
LOVE!

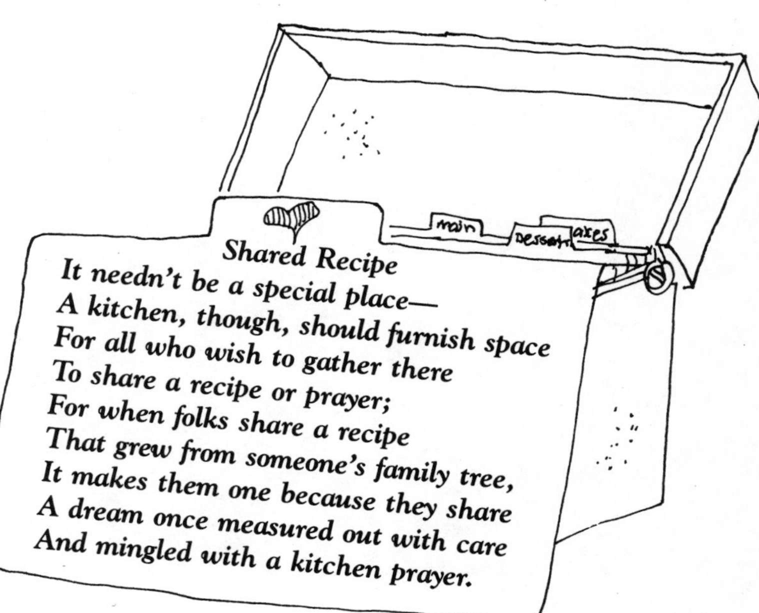
main
Desserts
Cakes
Shared Recipe
It needn't be a special place—
A kitchen, though, should furnish space
For all who wish to gather there
To share a recipe or prayer;
For when folks share a recipe
That grew from someone's family tree,
It makes them one because they share
A dream once measured out with care
And mingled with a kitchen prayer.

CONTENTS

Ancient Art

"Come for coffee . . . come for tea . . .
Just drop your work and share with me."
Some brought sweetenings for the pots:
Molasses cookies, apricots,
Even mending they should do,
For they could work and visit, too.
Where did it go, the ancient art
Of time to share a cup of heart?
The world is too much with us now—
I fear that we've forgotten how,
Until I search old recipes . . .
Then my heart brims with love of these.

OUR HERITAGE

The Lord is my Shepherd; I shall not want (Psalm 23:1).

America! Land of the free, home of the brave. Land of the beautifully diverse people. Give us your tired, your poor, your *hungry*. They came, bringing their hopes, their dreams, their recipes. And in this wonderful new world they dared mingle food of the peasant with that of the king's men. Survival depended on blending all codes, creeds, and colors; on ingenuity; and on sharing. Through a long line of "begats," those ancestors of ours made us one. American cuisine spells out the history of our country—God's "heartland."

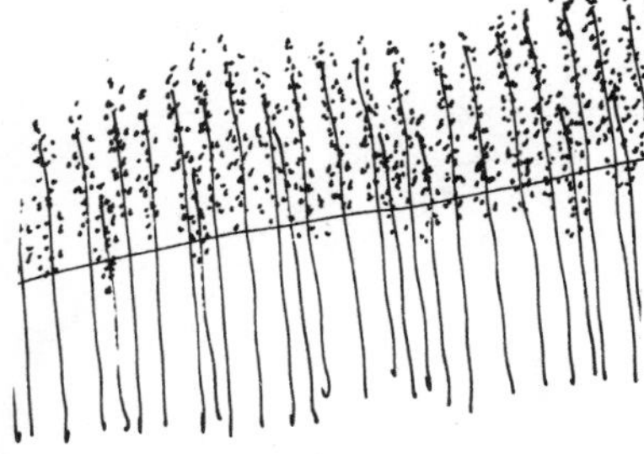

As they learned to live in harmony, we have learned to harmonize our foods, achieving what our Chinese contributors strive for: *balance*, the "yin" and the "yang" of hot, cool, and neutral foods.

The settlers learned to adapt their dishes to accommodate wild game and fish along with the cornmeal ground from what the Indians called maize. From the forests they gleaned fungi which we call mushrooms. The native nuts became a kind of cooking staple (ground between stones, the first gristmill). Hulling the nuts stained hands a dark brown, a stain which only time could remove. But nobody minded; it was manna like God sent to feed the Israelites.

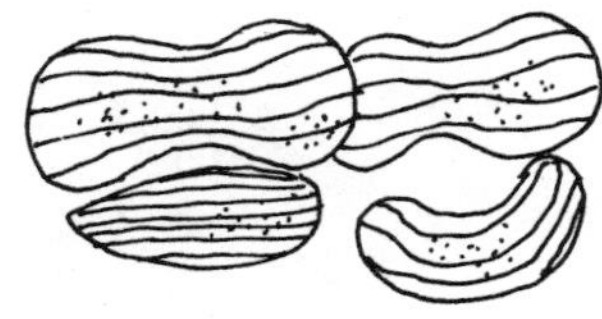

Often hungry, they looked to the hills where the stars lived and knew that one day they would climb to the top where food was plentiful for themselves, for generations to come, and for the whole world. Faith lighted a candle of hope from each star . . . Now those stars shine brilliantly in the flag over this Land of Plenty. And isn't it comforting to know that we have kept their traditions—perhaps more through foods than any other single factor in our classless society? That,

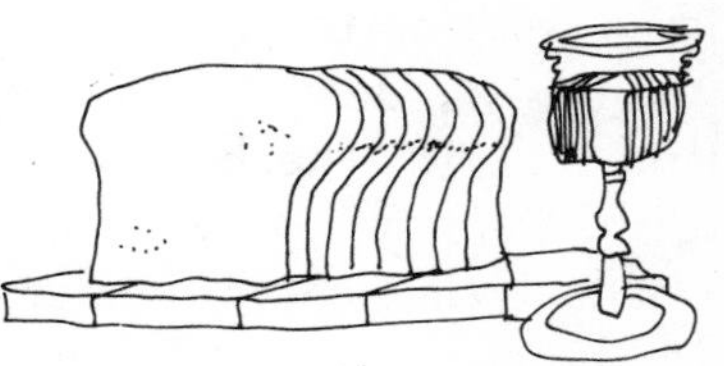

then, is our first definition of COUNTRY COOKING, the firstborn of our diverse lifestyles.

Thou preparest a table before me (Psalm 23:5).

Our second definition is less tangible. It is more of a regional homesickness for which we have no name—a deep yearning for the foods that once comforted when blizzards boxed us in or mumps kept us home from school. No pill was as curative as Mama's chicken soup or Grandmother's frothy custards. No matter what our generation, we have childhood memories which bring us together in a kind of commonality that the early settlers knew. Old recipes

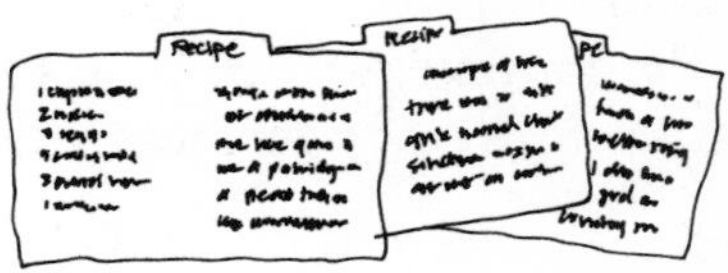

have survived to soothe and reassure through wars, reconstruction periods, depression, and inflation. They have been modified (and often enhanced) but never lost.

Or perhaps you are remembering down-home goodness recalled from an era when there was time to look for buttercups on dewy mornings and relax in the hammock with a frosty glass of lemonade in the heat of the day. Maybe memory goes beyond penicillin, nylon, or credit cards. It could lead to tea cakes after a rousing sermon at a summer revival . . . fruit punch following a traveling tent show . . . or the last drive-in.

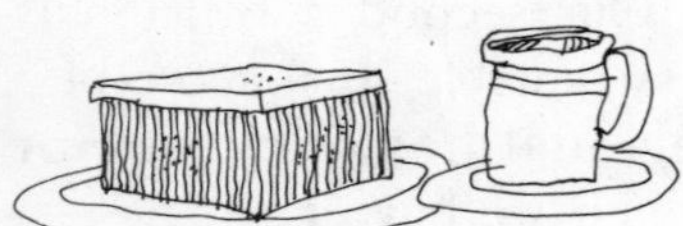

Whenever, it was a time when our world was less urbanized and we lived closer to nature—at least for the summer at Grandpa's farm.

Remember the food? Smell it? *Taste* it? It's COUNTRY COOKING you're missing!

This cookbook is full of recipes collected and cherished, old ways found good and made better—trusted flavors that take us back to our roots converted from yesterday's slow methods to today's "fast foods" to keep in step with our busy lifestyles. They come from other lands and our own . . . from the mountains to the prairies . . . from the orchards, vineyards, gardens, and fields to our own backyards.

So follow the Yellow Brick Road to gentle memories of favorite times—made better! Enchantment and enhancement will be your reward.

INVITATION

If one be gracious to strangers, it shows one is a citizen of the world. The heart is no island, cut off from other islands, but a continent that joins them.
—Bacon

So come on in! We're easy to find. Just follow that "Homemade Goodness" aroma straight into our country kitchen. We will take you back to a more gentle era, when the air was spiced with oven-fresh bread and Grandmother's favorite stew. Be prepared to "dip in" as we combine yesterday's mellow flavors with today's newer and easier methods. It's easier than you think, requiring mostly a sense of adventure, a willingness to experiment, and a hearty helping of imagination.

Our world and our lifestyles change rapidly today, but now, as "back then," dining is a pleasure. "Eating in" is becoming popular again. And the timing is perfect! Now the hostess can make use of the new products available, and—with the experienced know-how shared here—she can relax and enjoy right along with her guests. In fact, she (you!) will undoubtedly be the star because everybody enjoys a "down-home" meal. And (warning!) our approach may very well make the kitchen the heart of the home again—no longer an "island, cut off from other islands, but the continent that joins them."

Everything is "Country" now, so get in step with the music with the simple methods tried and tasted here.

We Promise You...

A delightful surprise with each turn of a page...
Something wonderful for every member of the family...
Recipes as rich and warm as your fondest memories of the past...
And as exciting and full of promises as your brightest hopes for the future...
In this book of favorite shortcuts to cooking success.

Bon Appetit!

Appetizers

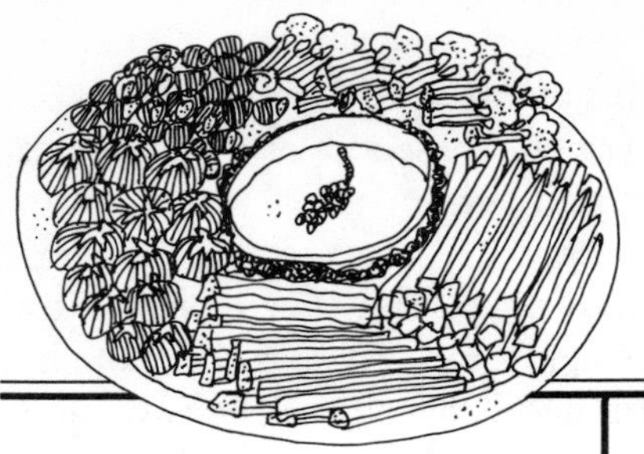

Getting to Know You

Time was when one thought of the "getting-to-know-you" hour as calling for soft music and dress-up clothes, then a lighting of candles as twilight faded. And that is still a lovely way to relax with friends and family—that magical moment when day closes and loved ones close in around a relaxed, confident, and smiling hostess. It's appetizer time!

But time was, too, when neighbors shared the same togetherness before breakfast and after dinner, munching crisp apples and popping corn. Mingling friends, mingling fun recipes, and mingling traditions is something to consider renewing. But what is appropriate for the easy, successful, tasty, and beautiful food tray? Something that goes together with a minimum of work?

Farther on you will find a multitude of recipes that you will want to try. But for the before-or-after-a-meal snack that holds all the answers, there is nothing more acceptable than the age-old fruit-and-cheese tray (more on this in later chapters). As a preview, however (something you can do this very day!), let's talk about the APPETIZER TRAY:

- *Before* the meal, accompany cheeses with crackers and relishes;
- *After* the meal, feature cheeses with apples, pears, and grapes (some sliced—peeled or unpeeled—and others left whole for munching).

Serving cheeses! The favorite *cheddar*, which has a range of flavors from mild to sharp, may be cut in wedges, slices, fingers, or cubes. *Swiss* cheese is always sliced thin; *brick*, cut pretty much as you please. *Camembert* usually comes in neat little triangles, foil-wrapped, which may be left on or removed, as you choose. *Blue* cheese may appear as a wedge as if cut from a wheel ("hoop") of cheese. And do remember *cream* cheese. Serve it in the original loaf form or cut in cubes or fingers.

The pretty little red ball—*Gouda*—is the small cousin of the *Edam*, which you must meet if you haven't already. It may

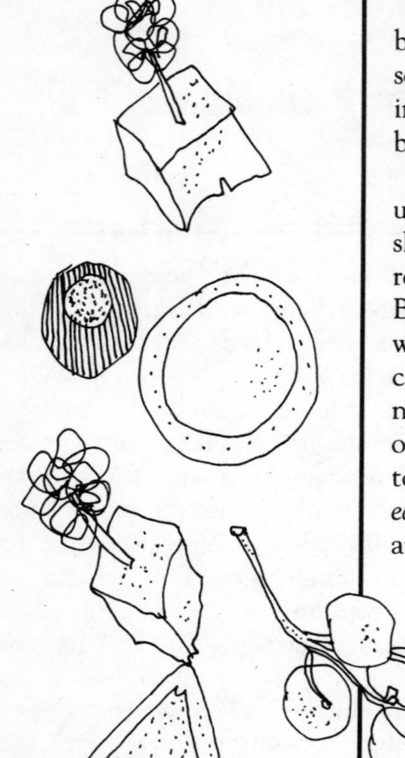

be left whole with the top cut off so the cheese may be scooped out with a teaspoon or cheese scoop, or it may be cut in wedges much the same as an apple. Its color will add a bright note to any cheese tray.

For the Appetizer (before-dinner) Tray, keep everything under control except your imagination. Arrange rows of all-shaped slices and wedges (include cheese balls)—rows and rows of *Swiss, provolone, brick, cheddar, blue,* and *Gouda.* Between the rows, heap black and green olives, then feather with parsley tied with ribbons of pimiento pepper, celery curls alternated with interestingly-carved carrots and turnips, or painted daisies, rosebuds, geraniums, or whatever other flowers you have on hand (making sure that none are toxic). If you really want to be original, garnish the tray with *edible* flowers, such as nasturtiums and rose petals. Now arrange baskets of bread sticks and assorted crackers.

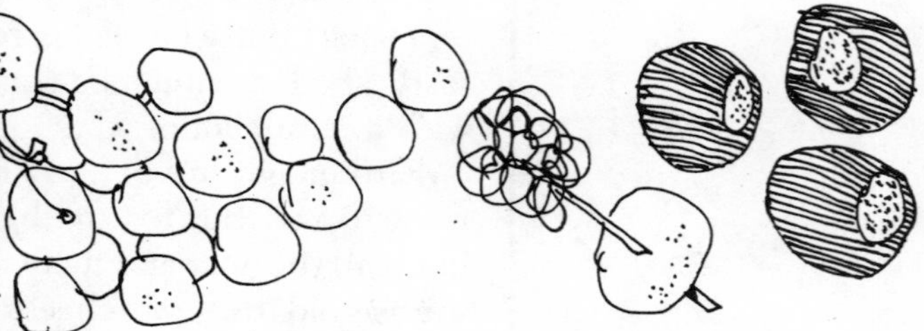

For the Dessert Tray, use the same cheeses (or add to them) and fill the center of the tray with clusters of red and white grapes, bananas, apples, etc. Go tropical and use pineapple fingers, papaya, guavas, mangoes, or whatever else is in season; or else get fancy and make "acorn cups" of figs and fill them with one of the cheese mixes available in jars. Dried prunes (steamed briefly to plump, then seeded) and fresh apricots work equally well. Time permitting, express your individuality by slicing large grapes lengthwise, seeding, spreading with cream cheese, and putting the halves back together in little "sandwiches."

Prepare cheese trays ahead, cover, and refrigerate. Arrange breads on table in advance. Allow yourself time for a shower, and answer the door with a glowing face. After several guests arrive, place cheese trays on the buffet or serving table. Relax! *Simplicity is always in good taste.*

Guests will serve themselves and relax right along with you.

Salads

Fill Your Basket with a Rainbow

Is anything more beautiful to the eye or satisfying to the taste than the bright, crisp colors of fresh vegetables? The copper of carrots . . . sun-yellow of corn . . . deep purple of eggplant . . . and pink blush of radishes—all fluted by leaf-lettuce. Vegetables are as often the artist's "still life" inspiration as fresh fruits. But they go into action when placed within reach at snacktime or mealtime. There is something within us earthlings that makes us love to munch. Remember the surge of victory that came with biting into a tart apple after that liquid diet? Think of them as a centerpiece. Think of them as appetizers and salads. Or go creative! Arrange them into your own work of art—a colorful, beautifully arranged centerpiece to be eaten.

Frugality may be termed the daughter of prudence, the sister of temperance, and the parent of liberty. One who is extravagant soon will become poor, and poverty will enforce dependence and invite corruption.

—*Johnson*

Canned, frozen, or dried vegetables are good stand-ins for garden-fresh products. A lot of fun and food value come from the starchy vegetables and the lesser-known varieties.

Dried beans and peas, white potatoes, sweet potatoes, pumpkin, and hard-skinned squash are among the more hearty vegetables that are often included in main-dish salads. And the imaginative cook (with an eye on the clock, budget, and nutritional value of salads) will want to experiment with eggplant, endives, fennel, kohlrabi, leeks, okra (for "soul foods"), rutabaga, and maybe bean sprouts and alfalfa sprouts.

For maximum food value and eye appeal, serve vegetables in salads in the raw. When cooking is essential, keep it to a minimum and skimp on the water. In most cases it is sufficient to bring vegetables to a boil, then turn off the heat and allow them to stand (covered) until cool. Drain and chill, reserving liquid for soups or gravies.

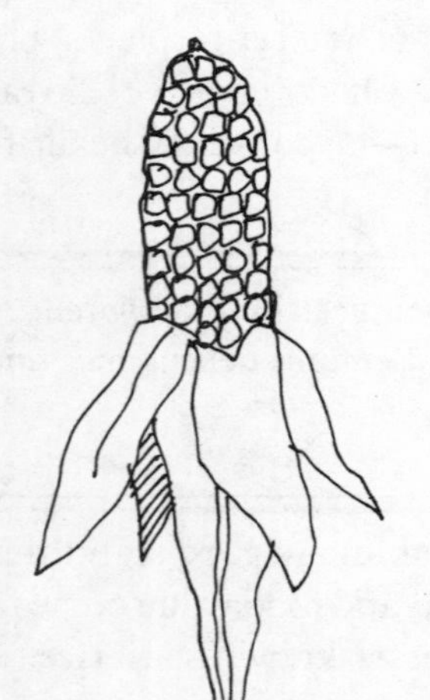

VEGETABLES
Availability and Cost

Artichokes: All year. Cheapest at peak of crop, March-May.

Asparagus: March-July (sometimes early fall). Cheapest in summer months.

Beans (fresh): All year. Cheapest in midsummer.

Beans (lima): All year. Cheapest August-September.

Broccoli: All year. Plentiful September-May; hence cheaper.

Brussels Sprouts: Same as above.

Cabbage: All year.

Carrots: All year.

Cauliflower: All year. Plentiful October-November; hence cheaper.

Celery: All year.

Corn: All year. Cheapest May-September.

Cucumbers: All year. Cheapest May-August.

Lettuce (and other leafy greens): All year.

Mushrooms: All year (use cultivated varieties).

Onions: All year. Green onions cheapest in summer months.

Peas: All year. Plentiful January-August; hence cheaper.

Peppers: All year. Cheapest in summer months.

Radishes: All year. Usually cheapest in spring.

Spinach: Same as above.

Summer Squash: All year. Plentiful in summer months; hence cheaper.

Tomatoes: All year. Cheapest in season, May-October.

Turnips: All year.

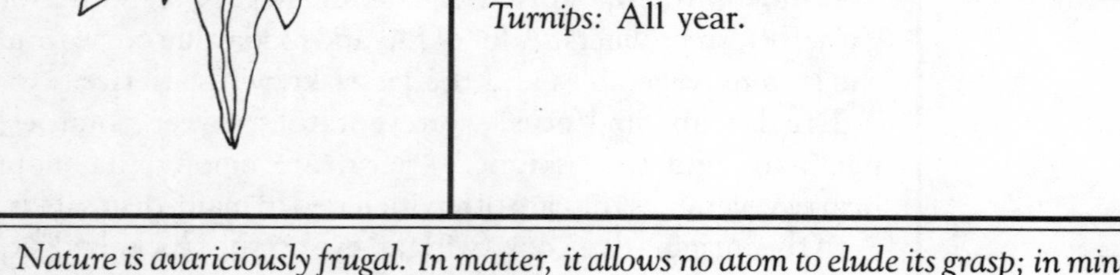

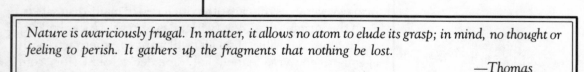

Nature is avariciously frugal. In matter, it allows no atom to elude its grasp; in mind, no thought or feeling to perish. It gathers up the fragments that nothing be lost.

—*Thomas*

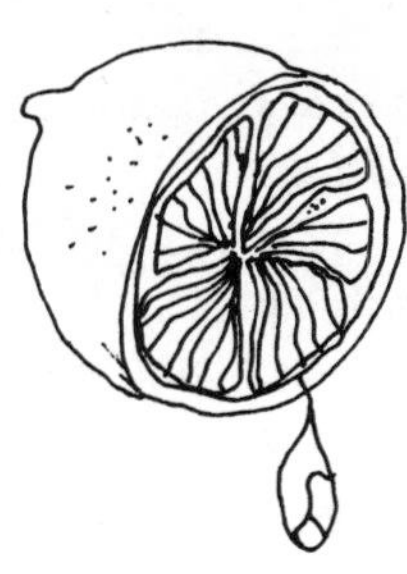

All vegetables are enhanced with seasonings. The amount varies with individual taste. Lemon or lime juice, salt, and often a sprinkle of sugar work well with them all. In addition, experiment with bay leaf, garlic, oregano, allspice, dry mustard, coriander, chili powder, chives, dill, sage, parsley, bacon bits, cloves, nutmeg, celery seed, orange, curry, ginger, mace, marjoram, mint, paprika, rosemary, thyme, basil, tarragon, cayenne, vinegar, sesame seed, black pepper, or 1) a combination of these, 2) a spice of your choice, or 3) a putting-together of several of the chopped vegetables to complement one another.

For added zest, make your own "Secret Spice." The following comes from the traditional French seasoning blend called "Quatre-Epices" (or four spices). Try it, then come up with your own "spin-off."

Four Spices

3 T. ground white pepper
5 T. ground cloves
3 t. ground nutmeg
3 t. ground ginger

Measure into a small jar with a tight-fitting lid. Shake to blend. Use in stews, raisin sauce, or vegetable dips, or blend with salt to taste and shake on broiled meats, fish, or poultry. For a surprising change, try this version of Secret Spice combined with French dressing as a marinade for barbecued meat.

Another combo? We have it for you:

Creole Seasoning

2 T. oregano
1/3 c. salt
2 T. garlic powder (unsalted)
1/4 c. fresh-ground black pepper
1/3 c. cayenne pepper
2 T. thyme
1/3 c. paprika

Pour into large jar and shake. Yields 1 1/2 c. which, covered tightly, will keep indefinitely. For milder flavor, reduce amount of peppers to taste.

Creole cuisine comes from the "Creole State" of Louisiana, where the direct descendants of the original French and Spanish colonists form an important element in the social fabric. We think of New Orleans—cradle of the jazz—and of Basin Street, the Mardi Gras, and paddle wheelers along The Delta. But most of all we think of the famous, incomparable Creole cooking that bites the tongue and sticks to the ribs. The popular dishes are a rare combination of peppery Spanish recipes combined with the mellow touch of the legacy left behind from slavery days and set off by that special flair that French chefs seem to be born with. The hot, humid climate does not alter the demand for "my kind of cookin'." In fact it seems to enhance it. And the climate is perfect for production of the fiery sauce called Tabasco. The liquid fire, distilled from peppers allowed to sun-ripen on the bush and age naturally in wood, develops its own distinct flavor for which Avery Island, Louisiana, is famous. Natives will declare that no kitchen is complete without it; but do use it discreetly. Tabasco sauce, like our concoction of Creole seasoning, adds zest to spaghetti, chili, salad dressings, barbecue sauce, baked beans, gravy, and soups. Or add a "gourmet touch" at the table to hamburgers, eggs (any style), and ice-cold tomato juice. ***Devilishly hot!***

GOOD NEWS IN SALADS!

Whoever said that everything exciting in life is either illegal, sinful, or fattening must have known very little about vegetables! An excellent source of vitamins and minerals that is low in calories and often high in fiber, vegetables have proven themselves as "good medicine." Salads offer a way of serving vegetables at their best—appetizer salads, accompaniment salads, main-dish salads, and dessert salads (which make use of fruits).

Experiment until you find your favorite dressings, then go easy on them. Learn the just-enough amounts. Commercial dressings are expensive and often overly rich, and they tend to make greens wilt.

APPETIZER SALADS

Vegetable Chips and Dips

Arrange the uncooked vegetables in individual dishes, on a glass serving tray, or on a lazy Susan. Use the standbys (cauliflower flowerlets, carrot sticks, celery curls, turnip rings, green onions, rounds of zucchini squash, halved mushrooms, etc.). But be original also and make use of raw peas (strung on toothpicks), tender green beans, cabbage stalks (peeled and marinated in vinegar); radish flowers (made by cutting peels gently with a sharp knife into wedge shapes from the root end halfway to the stem); cherry tomatoes, green pepper rings, avocado fingers, etc. And would you believe Irish potatoes and yams?

For variety, try tenderized green string beans, cabbage roll-ups (tender leaves rolled and secured with toothpicks and dipped in boiling salt water); and whole artichokes (leaves trimmed, boiled whole with lemon and garlic, cooled, and "choke hearts" removed).

Kitchen Advice: If you simply must doubt, doubt your doubts—never your beliefs!

DELICIOUS DIPS FROM CALIFORNIA

Guacamole

4 ripe avocados (peeled, seeded, chopped)
1/2 c. mayonnaise
1/4 c. dry onion (peeled, chopped)
3 T. lime or lemon juice
2 t. chili powder and 1 t. salt, blended
1 t. garlic powder (or 1 clove, chopped)
1/2 t. Tabasco sauce
2 medium tomatoes (peeled, diced)

Mash avocados with fork or puree in blender. Mix remaining ingredients except tomatoes. May be prepared a day in advance. In order to retain color, push at least one avocado seed into dip and cover bowl tightly with plastic wrap. When ready to serve, remove avocado seed, garnish dip with tomatoes, and sprinkle with paprika.

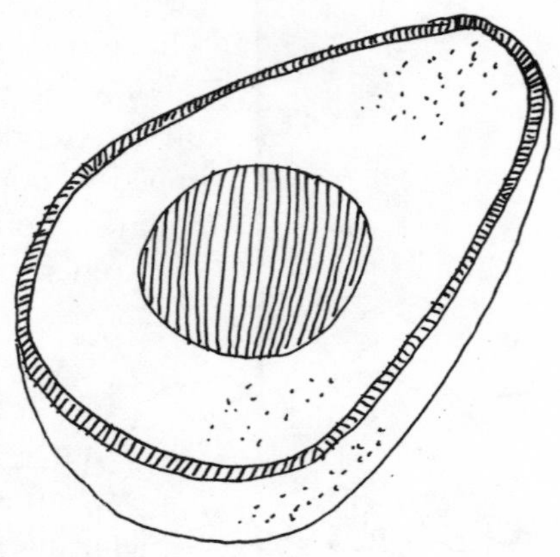

Once considered a delicacy, the avocado is now a basic-good-eating item for all meals and all courses. For breakfast, try avocado mashed and spread on your toast or English muffin instead of butter (lower in calories and rich with Vitamin A). And have you tried peeling and chopping the fruit to be added to scrambled eggs? For lunch, an avocado sandwich is just right—slices of peeled fruit on dark bread, thinly spread with mayonnaise. Or maybe a salad? We have them here for you. Dinner, or course, begins with avocado dip (try ours to get your guests mingling and enjoying a good old-time talk without interruption of television or tape decks). And, yes, avocados are main-dish ingredients. They are also super in breads and desserts. We can thank Mexico and Central America for the magical tree which, properly cultivated and "talked to," yields the year round. The evergreen trees, large and covered with round magnolia-like leaves to protect the young, are parents of the round (often pear-shaped) fruits. Groves of all varieties (producing green, purple, and sometimes red) fruits abound in California and Florida. In fact, their very abundance has made them within the reach of all who enjoy the mild, addictive flavor. And hear this! The healthful pulp, frequently included in cosmetics, is a boon in home hair and skin care! Recipe: ***Rub it in. Let it stand. Wash it out. Then watch your hair glow.***

Quick Onion Dip

1 pt. sour cream
$1^{1}/_{4}$-oz. pkg. dehydrated onion soup mix
chopped pimientos
chopped green or black olives
chopped mushrooms
4 T. finely chopped English walnuts (optional)

Blend together sour cream (or imitation) and dehydrated onion-soup mix. Add pimientos, green or black olives, or mushrooms, according to taste. All should be well-drained before adding to dip. For variety, add English walnuts. Keeps well up to one week in refrigerator. Store covered.

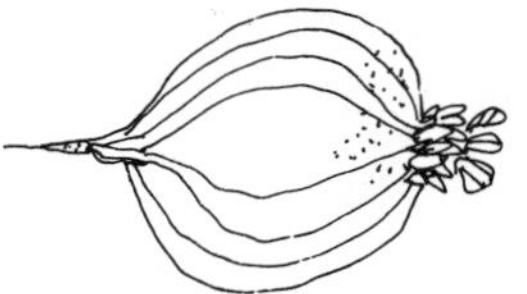

California Gold Dip

$^{1}/_{2}$ c. sour cream
$^{1}/_{2}$ c. mayonnaise
1 t. Worcestershire sauce
$^{1}/_{2}$ t. prepared mustard
$^{1}/_{2}$ t. curry powder
2 T. chopped chives
$^{1}/_{2}$ c. chopped black olives

Blend sour cream with mayonnaise. Add remaining ingredients, folding in olives and chives last. Refrigerate. Keeps well for a week.

Dilly Seafood Dip

one 8-oz. package cream cheese
$^{1}/_{4}$ c. milk
one $4^{1}/_{2}$-oz. can shrimp (rinsed, drained, and diced) or one $6^{1}/_{2}$-oz. can minced clams or tuna (drained)
1 t. lemon juice
1 t. Worcestershire sauce
$^{1}/_{2}$ t. garlic salt
$^{1}/_{4}$ t. dill weed

Soften cheese to room temperature and blend with milk. Stir in seafood and lemon juice. Add remaining ingredients.

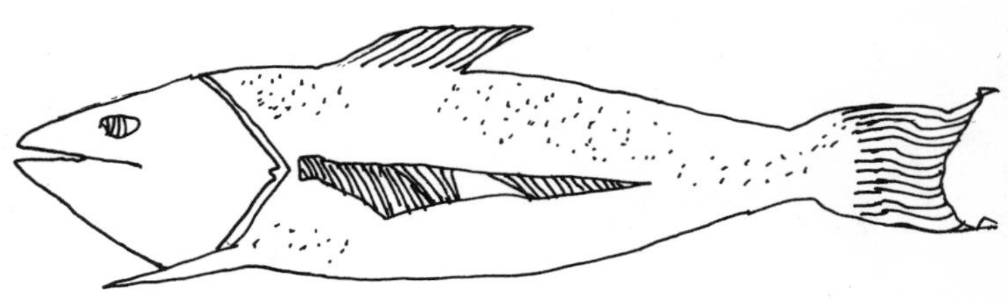

We may live without poetry, music and art;
We may live without friends; we may live without heart;
We may live without conscience; we may live without books;
But civilized men cannot live without cooks.

—Meredith

Creamy Chopped Beef Dip

1 c. creamed cottage cheese
2 T. buttermilk
3 t. horseradish
1 T. minced onion
1 package dried beef (snipped into small pieces with kitchen shears)

Use a blender or mash cottage cheese with a fork. Blend cottage cheese with buttermilk. Whip until creamy. Add remaining ingredients and whip until all is well-blended. Cover and refrigerate. Keeps well for a week.

Some-Like-It-Hot Dip

one 5-oz. jar pimento-and-cheese spread
one 2¼-oz. can deviled ham
¼ c. mayonnaise
2 T. snipped parsley
1 T. minced onion
4-6 drops red-pepper sauce

Beat all ingredients together until creamy. Keeps well when refrigerated.

Olé Dip

one 30-oz. can refried beans
1 small can Ortega chilies (diced)
1 lb. Monterey Jack cheese, grated

Mix beans and chilies together and pour half into 2 qt. baking dish. Cover with half the grated cheese. Repeat layering. Heat in 350° oven only until bubbling. Serve immediately surrounded with crisp, raw vegetables. Store leftovers, as this warms up nicely.

FRUITS
Availability and Cost

Apples: All year. Cheapest in October. Most expensive June-August.

Apricots: Most plentiful in June and July.

Avocados: All year. In-season varieties always cheaper.

Bananas: All year. Sales on overripe fruit offers an opportunity to purchase fruit for freezing (peeled, frozen, bagged, and kept frozen). Thaw for breads, cakes, etc., for fresh eating.

Berries: Strawberries all year. Best supply April-July; hence cheaper. Other berries available generally only June and July.

Cherries: May-August.

Cranberries: September-January. Highest around holidays.

Grapes: All year. Most plentiful July-November. Cheaper during those months.

Grapefruit: All year. Most plentiful October-May; hence cheaper.

Kiwis: June-December. Price seldom varies.

Lemons and Limes: All year.

Loquats: Summer months. Often unavailable in markets.

Mangoes: April-September.

Melons: April-November (depending on variety). Most plentiful in summer months; hence cheaper.

Nectarines: June-September.

Oranges: All year. Most plentiful in winter and spring months; hence cheaper.

Papayas: All year. Watch for special shipments.

Peaches: Spring through fall.

Pears: All year. Most plentiful August-December; hence cheaper.

Pineapples: All year. Watch for specials.

Plums: June-October (depending on variety).

Rhubarb: January-July except in warmer states, where the plant thrives all year.

Tangerines: October-April.

Fruits have their own distinctive flavor and seldom call for anything to enhance it except as the taste buds dictate. Honeydew melon, for instance, takes kindly to a twist of lemon with just a sprinkling of ginger. Avocados enjoy a sprinkle of salt. Apples come alive with cinnamon or a sift of nutmeg. A few fruits like cranberries, gooseberries, and rhubarb demand sugar in order to behave. Pineapple—good though it is in its natural state—is even better when soaked a few minutes in slightly salted ice water and drained before serving. Shredded coconut adds zest to sliced oranges.

Fruit is the perfect light-touch dessert following a heavy meal. It can be the just-right salad to bring out the best in main dishes. It serves willingly as an appetizer. Or, just to show its versatility, fruit qualifies on most diets as a healthful, between-meals snack.

Success is never final and failure never fatal. It's courage that counts.

MORE GOOD NEWS IN SALADS!

We no longer need settle for an apple a day. There is a bountiful supply of fresh fruit (not necessarily in season) as near as the closest supermarket. Fruit is good-tasting and good for us, kind to the figure and the budget (when we watch for the good buys), and acceptable on most diets. In planning a balanced menu, we need to include four daily servings from the fruit-and-vegetable group. It is best to serve citrus fruit or tomatoes (for vitamin C) and at least one additional fruit. If a particular fresh fruit is unavailable, there are frozen fruits and such delicious dried fruits! So slice them, dice them, spice them . . . with one word of caution: Fresh fruit is more perishable than vegetables. Ripen at room temperature; then refrigerate. Citrus fruits are the exception.

Fruit gathers popularity as more and more cooks discover its contribution to the wholesome, well-balanced diet. And it's so versatile! Use it as an appetizer, a soup (yes really!), an accompaniment to or a part of the main dish, or—as always—the perfect finale to the most elegant meal. With a dip, fruit is an appetizer and cheese is a dessert.

The best part of beauty is that which no picture can express.
—Bacon

APPETIZER SALADS

Fruit and Fixings

There is very little you can do that would prevent fruit from being beautiful. So go ahead, be creative! Serve whole green grapes, purple plums, pineapple fingers, and red apple wedges (unpeeled) piled high in coconut shells, scooped-out pineapple halves (lengthwise), or scalloped watermelon-rind bowls. Or use wooden salad bowls to heap colorful arrangements of your favorite fruits. And nothing has more eye-appeal than layers of freshly peeled fruit on crystal trays. Be whimsical (using novelty cookie cutters to shape designs in larger fruits) or keep work to a minimum and simply peel,

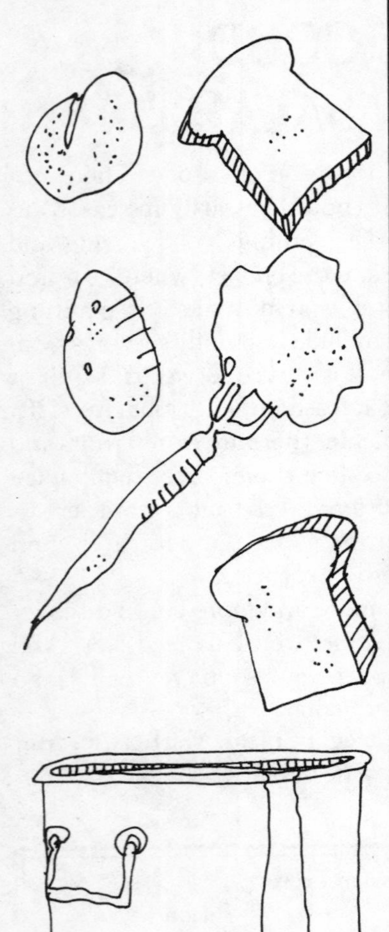

core, and slice fruit. Either way, it makes a good hostess into a great one!

ON-THE-TRAIL DIPS

"Dips," by that name, are relatively new. But they have been around since settlement of the first colony. Dips had other names, of course. There were "dunkers" (homemade doughnuts dunked in milk for children and coffee for adults). There were "soakings." Mothers soaked cold bread in milk as a "weaning food." And then there were "soppin's," the most popular of all among all ages. Large kettles of food centered the family dinner table and diners dipped cornbread sticks (or wedges if "stick pans" were unavailable) into the communal dishes of boiled cabbage, stews, or whatever else was available. There is some thought among historians that the practice inspired the use of bibs for children and the practice of tucking napkins beneath one's chin while dining.

But, for most of us, the phrases are new—or, at best, something we may have observed our great-grandparents doing. We have become too "civilized" for such. And, yet, when Mother poured off the "pot liquor" (juice from the cooked vegetables) and put it into the plates or bowls of the children too small to reach the common pot, she was serving her young the most nutritious part of the dish. It is good that in an entirely different way we have returned to the old. Remember this when you follow the invitation of your host or hostess to "Dip in" (exactly what our forebears would have said!).

Gold Rush Dip

2 T. orange juice
2 T. lemon juice
2 T. honey
1½ t. grated orange rind
½ t. salt
½ t. dry mustard
⅛ t. paprika
1 c. sour cream or yogurt

Blend together citrus juices, honey, orange rind, salt, mustard, and paprika. Fold in sour cream. Cover and chill. Keeps for a week.

Heaven gives us friends to bless the present scene; resumes them to prepare us for the next.
—Young

Sweet Memories Dip

¼ c. powdered sugar
1 c. sour cream or yogurt
1 T. lemon juice

Sift sugar into sour cream alternately with lemon juice. Blend until smooth. Cover and chill. Add a few drops of yellow food coloring if desired, stirring in just before serving.

Apricot Jam Dip

2 c. cottage cheese
¼ c. apricot jam
2 t. lemon juice
½ t. grated lemon rind

Put cottage cheese through sieve or use blender. Beat together (by blender or hand) cottage cheese, jam, lemon juice, and rind. Cover and chill. Keeps well for a week.

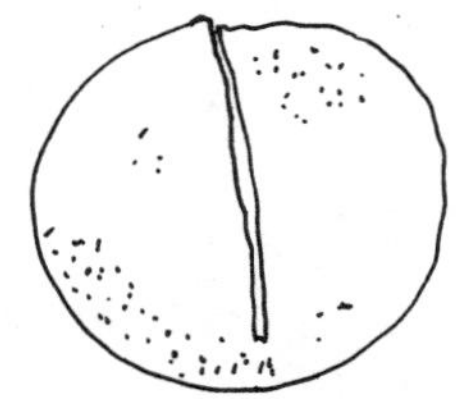

"Old Cheese" Dip

4 oz. blue cheese
2 c. sour cream
1 T. minced onion
few drops Worcestershire sauce

Crumble cheese. In blender or mixer (or in bowl using rotary beater) whip cheese and ¼ c. of the sour cream. Add onion and Worcestershire. Fold in remaining sour cream. Keeps for several weeks when refrigerated. Excellent as dip for fresh fruit, as a "dunk" for breadsticks, or as filling for celery stalks.

What's America eating? Some changes include: 767 percent more broccoli, 198 percent more low-fat milk and yogurt, 120 percent more pasta, and 34 percent more fish. Is the news really so innovative? Remember our rows of the "cabbage family" in the summer and fall garden . . . how "yogurt" would have been Gran's "clabber" . . . and how fish was a staple that everybody enjoyed at the community fish fries?

Adapted from Wild (Fruits and Nuts) Days of Forty-Niners

1 c. fresh strawberries
1/2 c. sour cream or yogurt
1/3 c. milk
1 t. honey
1/2 banana (fresh or frozen)
1/4 c. pistachio nuts

Blend all ingredients together in blender until smooth. If mixing by hand, mash berries before adding other ingredients. Best when made just before serving with any kind of fresh fruit. Especially nice with giant strawberries (wash and leave hulls on for color).

Sunshine Dip

1 c. fresh orange juice
1 t. grated orange rind
1 c. pineapple juice
1 pkg. instant vanilla pudding

Blend juices and rind. Add pudding slowly, thickening to suit taste. Beat well. Cover and store. Keeps well for one week.

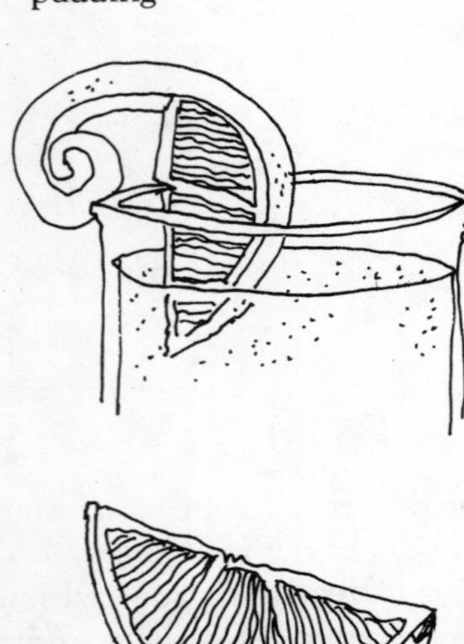

An appealing and low-calorie garnish on the rim of the salad bowl, ice-tea glass, or fish entree is the Lime Curl. Start with a lime slice. Cut out half the pulp (as shown) but leave entire peel attached. Cut remaining peel toward center and hang over rim of bowl, dish, or glass.

The juicy Lime Wedge brings out the natural flavor of many foods (and no sodium). Cut limes into 4 to 6 plump wedges to be squeezed over fresh fruits, vegetables, fish, and chicken entrees.

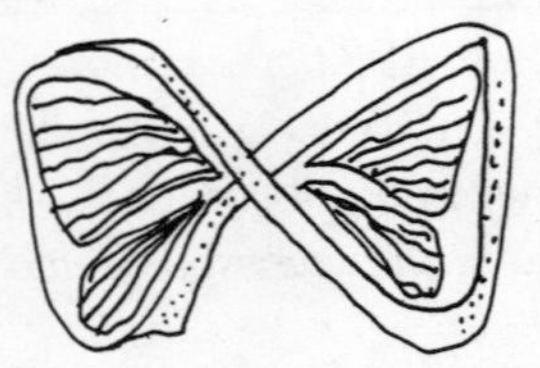

Easy-to-make Lime Cartwheels look glamorous and professional. Start with a lime slice. Make one cut from the center through the peel. Pick up and twist cut ends in opposite directions (gently) to form cartwheel shape. Graceful garnish for hors d'oeuvre trays, salads, entrees, and salads.

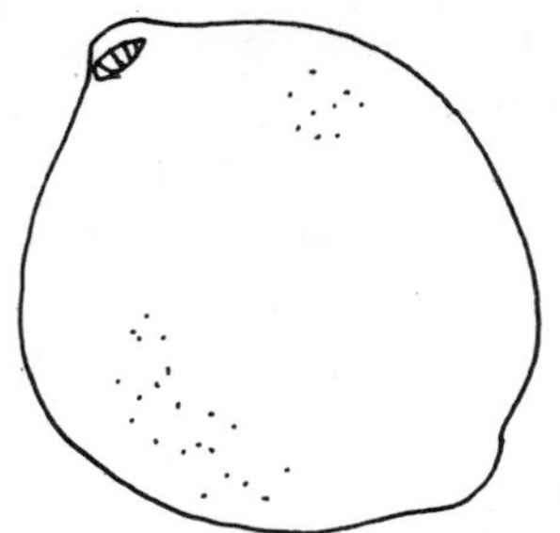

ACCOMPANIMENT SALADS

Accompaniment salads are heartier than appetizer salads (a mixture of shredded greens, never overdressed) or a variety of raw vegetables and fruits with dips. These can consist of a combination of vegetables, fruits, or gelatins, or they can be a putting together of any two—or all three—categories.

A salad should be beautiful—always! Achieve this by serving colorful mixtures on chilled beds of shredded lettuce or in "bowls" you make. For instance, serve a fruit salad in avocado dishes (made of avocado halves, seeded and sprinkled with lemon or lime juice). Serve coleslaw or raw cranberry salad in grapefruit cups (scooped-out halves with saw-toothed edge achieved by use of a sharp knife to create a zigzag). Sawed halves of a coconut make attractive dishes for tropical salads, as do watermelon halves (for large servings, as in a group) pineapple halves, etc.

Garnishes add the finishing touch. Use sweet-pepper rings, purple-onion rings, radish accordions (radishes sliced around almost all the way through from the root to stem end and soaked in ice water), etc. And remember that a sprinkling of sunflower seeds, sesame seeds, chopped nuts helps achieve a balanced diet and gives an added "crunch" to an otherwise ordinary salad.

Happiness is like potato salad. When you share it, it's a picnic.

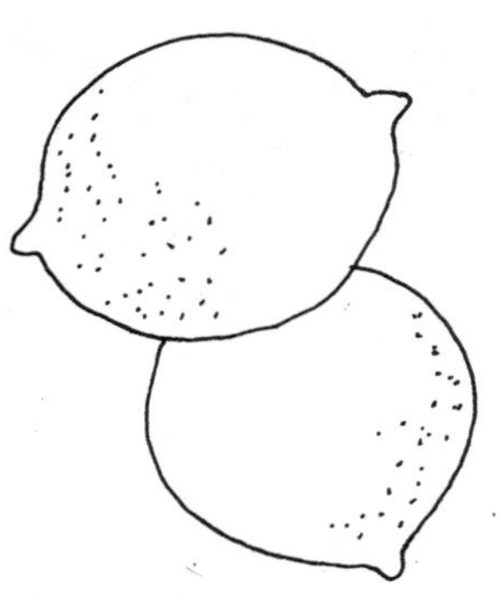

Another new twist (and not so new at all!) is use of the exotic lime. Californians can pluck tasty fruits right from the parent trees. Others should look for limes—firm, smooth, and shiny. Anything lemons can do, limes can do better! And that includes your daily "beauty baths." They are refreshing astringents (be sure to dilute well, adding juice of 1/2 lime to a basin of water). Also, limes will add luster to the hair when added to the final rinse.

Limes are "in" again. Hostesses "in the know" set themselves apart by adding a squeeze of lime to iced water, sparkling water, and tea. Their perky bite adds zest. And the little green citrus fellows are so good for you!

The glossy-leafed fruit is a native of southeastern Asia but has spread to the warmer climes the world over. Once rejected because of its acidity, the lime gained favor in the medical world as far back as the Crimean War. French soldiers and sailors had few fresh vegetables or fruits. An improper diet of salt fish and pork (often tainted) led to an outbreak of scurvy. On some unidentified island, quite by accident the ship's doctor discovered a thicket of wild limes. Hungry for anything fresh, the men readily drank his concoction of limewater—and improved miraculously!

So the generation before us knew what was good for us. They were closer to the earth then, and so right in insisting (in spite of our puckered-up faces) that we gulp a glass of warm water into which was squeezed half a lemon or lime. One word of caution: Avoid contact between the fruit itself and the teeth. Undiluted, both peel and fruit tend to damage enamel on the teeth. Stick with limeade, sipped on the front porch some warm summer afternoon. Your friends will love the cool, old-fashioned refreshment, and it is a good conversation piece now that you are in the know!

BACK-TO-BASICS TOSSED SALADS

What should you include in a tossed salad? *What do you have?* Make use of the usual greens, but get into the habit of experimenting with something a little unusual: Chinese cabbage, endive, leeks, etc.

Try "something old, something new" in the body of the salad, too.

Here are some good combinations making use of vegetables: minced onion added to shredded carrots, thin slices of cucumber, and sliced water chestnuts; beet pickles, onion rings, and drained whole-kernel corn; diced celery, red cabbage, and flaked coconut, etc. Tomatoes add color, zest, and vitamins to any combination.

Since fruit is so compatible it is possible to get by with almost any combination, but here are some favorites: melon balls, tangerine slices, and apricot halves; sliced pears, peaches, and halved and seeded plums; strawberries, pineapple fingers, and bananas. Raspberries or blueberries tossed on top make any fruit combo more exotic and offer a change from the accepted cherry.

Experiment with fruit-and-vegetable combinations: sliced apples, onions, and raisins (which have been dipped in boiling water and drained); cucumber wedges, pineapple fingers, etc. Use avocados when you need a touch of green, and use whole cranberries for a touch of red and a whole new concept. Vary dressings to enjoy a different and exciting tossed salad every day.

Train up a child in the way he should go, and when he is old, he will not depart from it.

—Proverb 22:6

SOME FAVORITE COMBINATIONS

Get-Together Holiday Salad

- 1/4 c. mayonnaise
- 1/2 c. cream cheese
- 1/2 c. blanched almonds
- 1 small can crushed pineapple (drained)
- 1/2 lb. large marshmallows (quartered)
- 2/3 c. nondairy whipped topping
- 1 c. seedless green grapes
- Maraschino cherries

Blend cheese and mayonnaise. Add almonds, pineapple, and marshmallows. Fold in whipped topping and grapes. Cover and refrigerate at least overnight. Top each serving with a cherry. This recipe doubles well. Nice with turkey or ham.

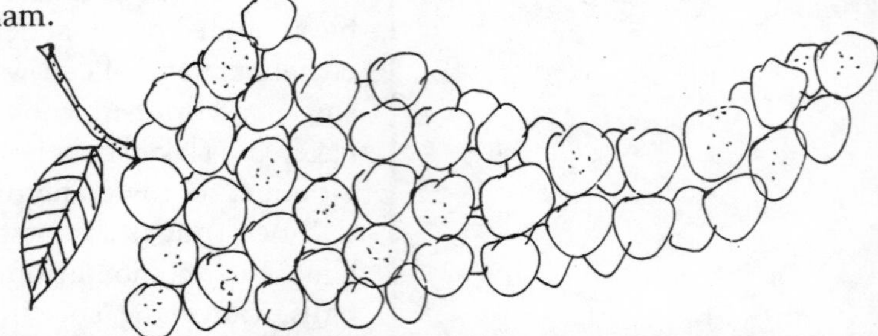

Better is a dinner of herbs where love is than a stalled ox and hatred therewith.

—Proverbs 15:17

Make-Ahead "Sabbath Salad"

- head lettuce
- mango
- celery
- onions
- peas (fresh, frozen, or canned)
- mayonnaise or salad dressing
- cheese
- sunflower seeds
- 2 T. sugar (optional)
- 2 T. milk (optional)

Choose salad dish or bowl. Spread with first layer of finely shredded lettuce. Cover with a second layer of chopped mango fruit (seeded but unpeeled). Add a third layer of chopped celery and a fourth layer of diced onion. Add a fifth layer of peas (can be fresh and uncooked; frozen, cooked, cooled, and drained; or canned and well-drained).

Spread a layer of mayonnaise or salad dressing over the salad and top with a final layer of grated cheese of your choice. Sprinkle with sunflower seeds. Cover and refrigerate several hours or overnight.

Amounts on this salad will vary according to the number to be served. This makes a nice party salad. Plan on about a pint of dressing for a group of 10-12 (2 T. sugar gives a nice tang, and the same amount of milk will make the mixture easier to spread).

California Coleslaw

1 medium head cabbage
1 green pepper (seeded and chopped)
2 large avocados (seeded, peeled, sliced)
1/2 c. chopped dates
1 celery stalk (sliced)
1 large carrot (grated)
1/2 c. walnut halves

Dressing

1/2 c. mayonnaise mixed with:
1 T. milk
1 T. lime juice
1/2 t. sugar
1/4 t. garlic salt
1/8 t. each paprika and black pepper

To make a bowl, carefully pull bottom layer of cabbage downward. Use a sharp knife to remove remaining cabbage. Use cut-out portion in coleslaw recipe. Refrigerate bowl in plastic bag.

Mix together all salad ingredients except walnuts. Add dressing. Toss. Cover and refrigerate until ready to serve (overnight is fine). Heap coleslaw into cabbage-head bowl and top with walnut halves—dropping some of them at random and pushing into mixture.

This is another nice party salad. If preparing an at-home meal, skip the making of the bowl. Or, plan that the following evening will be corned-beef-and-cabbage casserole to make use of the bowl!

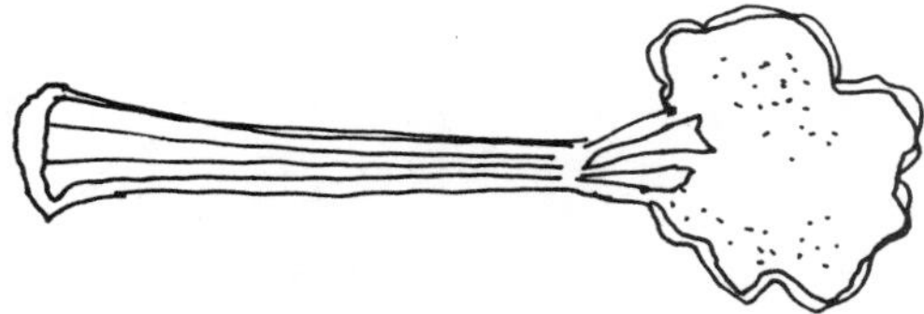

Healthful eating, skillfully engineered, can become a joyful habit which lasts a lifetime. The basic ingredient is a relaxed hostess. Remember the words of Horace Mann: "Habit is a cable. We weave a thread of it every day, and at last we cannot break it."

Minted Bean Salad

one 16-oz. can each: French-sliced green beans, golden wax, and red kidney beans
1 large onion (chopped)
1/3 c. fresh mint leaves

Dressing

1/2 c. sugar
1/2 c. salad oil
1/2 c. vinegar
1 t. salt

Drain beans. Mix with onion and add dressing. Mix well, cover, and refrigerate (will keep a week or longer). When ready to serve, sprinkle top with freshly chopped mint leaves. Especially nice with lamb.

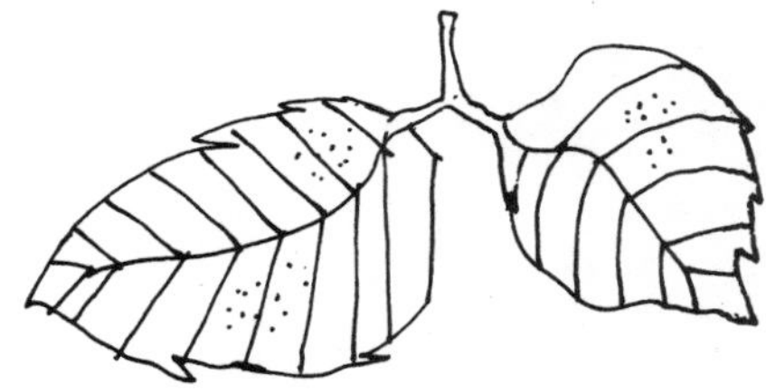

Pickled Kraut Salad

1 c. sugar
1 c. vinegar
one #303 can sauerkraut (drained)
1/2 c. chopped onion
1/2 c. green pepper (chopped)
1 small can chopped pimiento
lettuce
eggs, hard-boiled
green olives, or red apples

Make a syrup of sugar and vinegar boiled together for two minutes. Stir in sauerkraut while syrup is hot. Cool and add green pepper and pimiento. Cover and refrigerate. Dish with slotted spoon onto beds of shredded lettuce. Garnish with sliced boiled eggs and stuffed olives if serving with baked beans. If serving with pork, garnish with slices of red-skinned apple (unpeeled).

"Sail On!" Fruit Boats

1 small pineapple cut into fingers (or 1 large can of chunks)
1 honeydew melon (seeded, peeled, and cubed)
2 oranges (peeled, seeded, and cut into bite sizes)
6 apricots (peeled, seeded, and halved)
4 bananas (peeled, sliced)
1 c. seedless green grapes
2 red plums (seeded, unpeeled, sliced)
juice of 1/2 lime
4-6 papayas
rum flavoring

Mix fruits together gently (except papayas). Squeeze lime juice over the top. Heap fruit into papaya halves (which have been washed, seeded, and lightly laced with rum flavoring). When ready to serve, spoon *No-Cook Syrup* over top (recipe follows on next page).

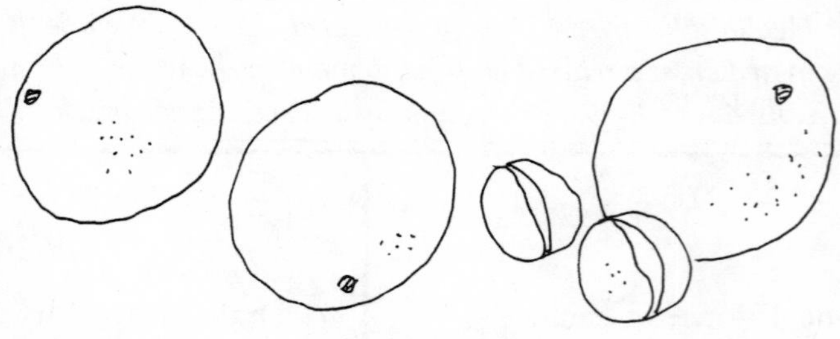

No-Cook Syrup

1/4 c. minced preserved ginger
1/4 c. lime juice
1/4 c. corn syrup
1/8 t. salt
flaked coconut

Mix ingredients together and "mellow" several hours before spooning over top of salad. Sprinkle each serving with flaked coconut. Allow one "fruit boat" per person. Good eating with any pork dish.

Something New

Surprise and delight family and friends! Arrange stuffed dried fruits on a bed of "dressed" greens on individual salad plates. You will need dried figs, dates, and prunes. Stem the fruits and plump the prunes by plunging them into boiling water and draining (those which do not say "ready to eat" will take longer). Figs need only to be stemmed. Dates need no preparation except seeding. Stuff each fruit with a whole almond, a bit of peanut butter, a walnut half, or candied-fruit mix. Roll in finely grated coconut and chill. Then slice in half crosswise. Choose a red-toned salad dressing for the greens and use very sparingly. Heap fruit on top. Nice with fried chicken.

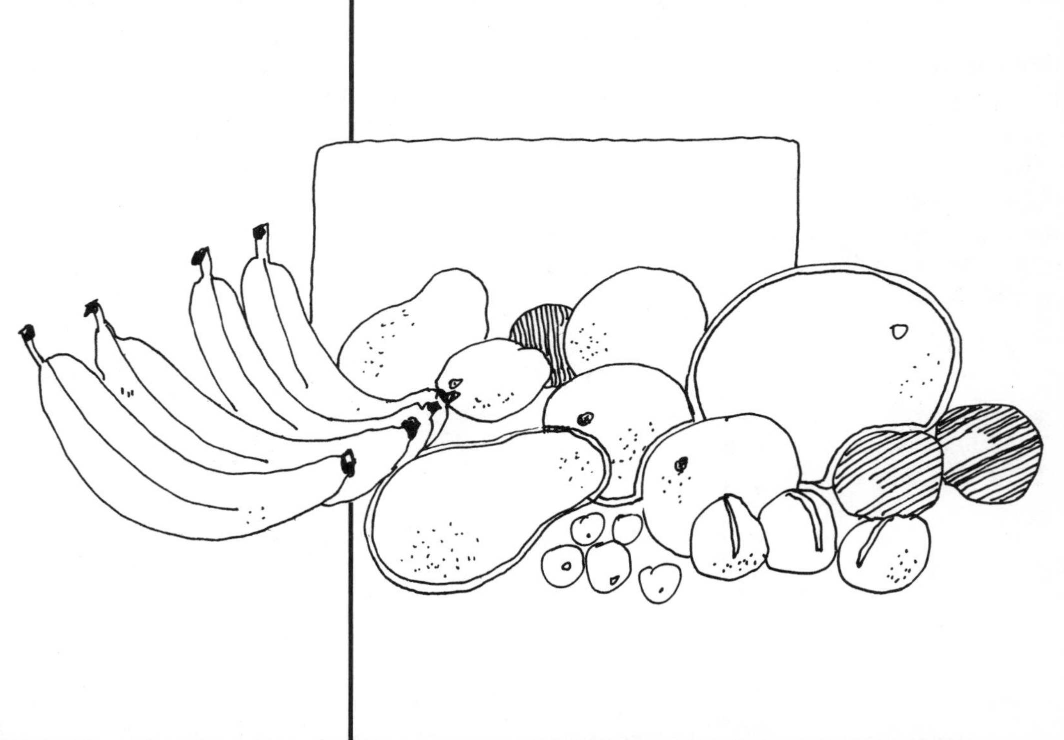

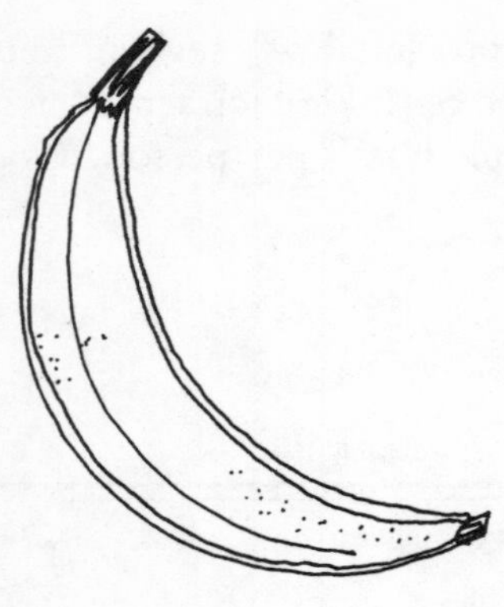

MOLDED SALADS

Molded salads add a special sparkle to the most ordinary bill of fare. Make use of the large, fancy molds for buffets; individual molds for on-the-table salads; or gelatin cubes for hurry-up meals. The latter can have any combination of ingredients or can be made from fruit gelatin (several flavors preferably), chilled in shallow dishes, cut into cubes, and piled on shredded greens and topped with your favorite dressing.

Usually, molded salads are those which accompany main-dish meals. However, with the addition of cheese, poultry, fish, or meat, molded salads can become the main dish of the meal.

Lime Salad
(Good and *so* good for you)

one 6-oz. package lime gelatin
2 c. boiling water
1 doz. large marshmallows (cut)
1 T. lime juice
2 c. chilled ginger ale
1 c. pineapple chunks (drain and save juice)
4 firm bananas (sliced)

Dressing

orange juice
pineapple juice
1 pkg. vanilla instant pudding
lime twist

Dissolve gelatin in water. Add marshmallows and stir until dissolved. Add lime juice, ginger ale, pineapple, and bananas. Refrigerate.

Serve with dressing made by mixing pineapple juice with vanilla instant pudding and enough orange juice to make dressing thick enough to "peak." Top with a twist of lime. Great with fish dishes.

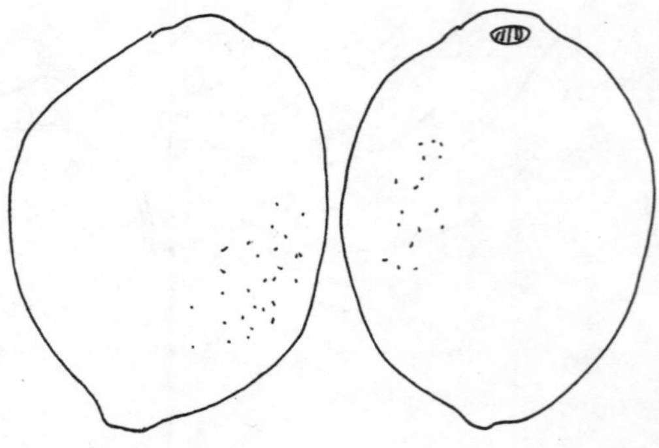

For something entirely different, try this versatile Lime-Pineapple Whip—versatile because of its chameleon personality! Its pleasing color delights the eye as a salad; then, since it changes hues by candlelight, this whip can double for a light dinner dessert. The recipe harks back to when we used unflavored gelatin.

Lime-Pineapple Whip

1 envelope unflavored gelatin
1 1/2 c. unsweetened pineapple juice
1/4 c. sugar
3 T. fresh lime juice
1/4 t. grated fresh lime peel
few drops green food coloring
lettuce, shredded
mayonnaise
lime twists
optional:
fresh or frozen blueberries
1 T. sugar
1 T. lime juice

Soften gelatin in 1/2 c. pineapple juice 5 minutes. Add sugar and heat to dissolve gelatin. Stir in remaining pineapple juice, lime juice, and peel. Chill until slightly thickened, then whip with electric mixer (or rotary hand-beater) until light and fluffy. Pour into flat glass dish (later to be cut into squares) if used for salad. Spoon gently onto salad plates upon which you have made a nest of finely shredded lettuce. Top with mayonnaise and lime twists. If fixing for dessert, pour mixture into clear goblets. Chill until firm and go festive! Delicious and beautiful combined with fresh or frozen blueberries mixed with 1 T. each of sugar and fresh lime juice. Invite the host (or an invited guest) to spoon berries over the top.

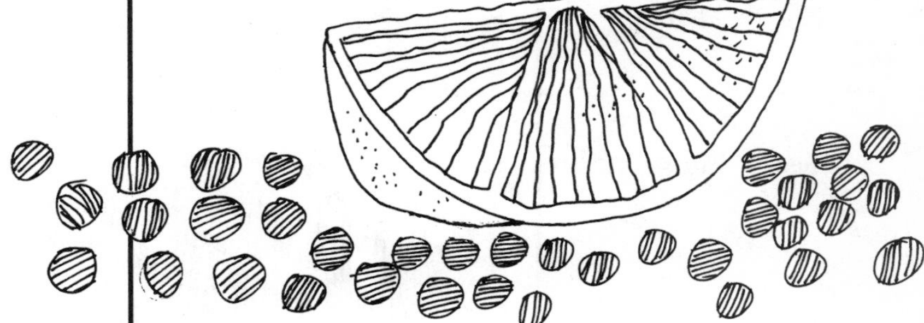

"Apples on Each Branch in Oregon" Shimmering Squares

2 c. canned applesauce
one 6-oz. package lemon gelatin
1/2 c. orange juice
1 c. ginger ale

Bring applesauce to a boil and add gelatin. Stir in orange juice and ginger ale. Chill. Serve in squares. Nice with baked ham.

Three-Minute Tomato Aspic

one 3-oz. package lemon gelatin
1 1/4 c. boiling water
one 8-oz. can tomato sauce
1/4 c. minced onion
1 1/2 T. vinegar
1/2 t. celery salt
dash of black pepper
horseradish to taste
lettuce
green pepper

Dissolve gelatin in water. Add all ingredients except lettuce and green pepper in order given. Pour into ice-cube trays and chill until firm. Serve aspic squares on beds of shredded lettuce and chopped green pepper. Very nice with fish.

Raw Cranberry Salad

one 6-oz. package raspberry gelatin
one 1-lb. package cranberries
4 large apples (peeled and cored)
1 c. orange juice
2 3/4 c. boiling water
1/2 c. chopped walnuts

Stem cranberries, wash, and grind with apples. Cover with orange juice and let stand while dissolving gelatin in water. Combine gelatin mixture with cranberry-apple mix. Add walnuts. Cover and refrigerate. The so-easy and so-good-with-turkey salad!

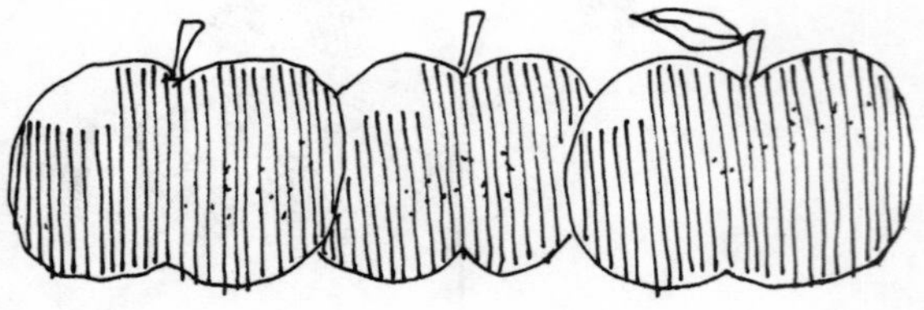

"Shortcut to Jersey" Cream Mold

one 1-lb. (or 14-oz.) can apricot halves
one 3-oz. package orange gelatin
1/2 c. mayonnaise
1 c. nondairy topping
one 3-oz. package orange gelatin
one 3-oz. package lemon gelatin
2 c. boiling water
1 1/4 c. cold ginger ale
1/3 c. toasted slivered almonds
mint leaves

Drain fruit, reserving syrup. Dissolve one 3-oz. package of orange gelatin in 1 c. boiling apricot syrup. Cool gradually and add to mayonnaise. Mix well. Fold in topping and pour into lightly greased 2-quart mold. Chill until almost firm.

In the meantime, dissolve orange and lemon gelatins in boiling water; add ginger ale. Chill until slightly thickened and fold in 1 1/2 c. apricots and almonds. Pour over molded layer. Chill until firm and gently unmold on large salad plate. Surround with clusters of drained apricot halves (placed at random, seed-side down) with mint leaves tucked beneath.

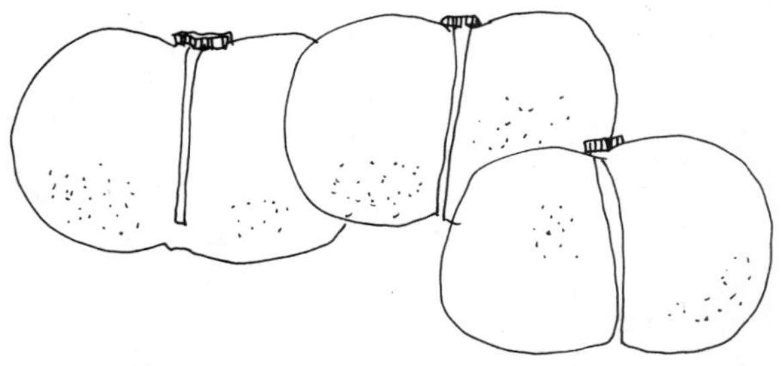

Pineapple-Carrot Whip

1 medium can crushed pineapple
one 3-oz. package lemon gelatin
3 T. sugar
1/2 t. salt
1 T. lemon juice
1 c. carrots, finely grated
1/2 carton nondairy whipped topping
lettuce
chocolate curls

Drain crushed pineapple, reserving syrup. Add enough water to pineapple syrup to make 1 1/2 c. and heat to a boil. Remove from heat and stir in lemon gelatin until dissolved. Add sugar, salt, and lemon juice. Chill until slightly thickened, then whip with electric mixer or rotary hand beater until mixture is meringue-like in texture. Add drained pineapple and finely grated carrots. Fold in nondairy whipped topping.

Chill until firm, then pile in craggy peaks onto lettuce leaves (for individual servings). Top with chocolate curls.

Snow-on-the-Mountain Salad

1 lb. white marshmallows
1/2 c. milk
one 8-oz. package cream cheese
2 c. small curd cottage cheese
one #2 can crushed pineapple
1 carton nondairy topping

Melt marshmallows in milk. Cool. Mix the two cheeses, add pineapple and topping, stir this mixture into the first. Chill until firm. Lovely served on finely shredded purple cabbage.

Main-Dish Salads

Main-dish salads are just what their name implies. They take the place of other main dishes by providing meat, poultry, fish, cheese, eggs (or combination of these high-protein foods) and often making use of starch-foods, such as potatoes, rice, or pastas.

Small wonder these salads are popular! They offer an opportunity for using up leftovers in creative ways. They are great for hurry-up meals. And the main-dish salad can be prepared in advance, allowing host and hostess to visit instead of work when company comes for a meal.

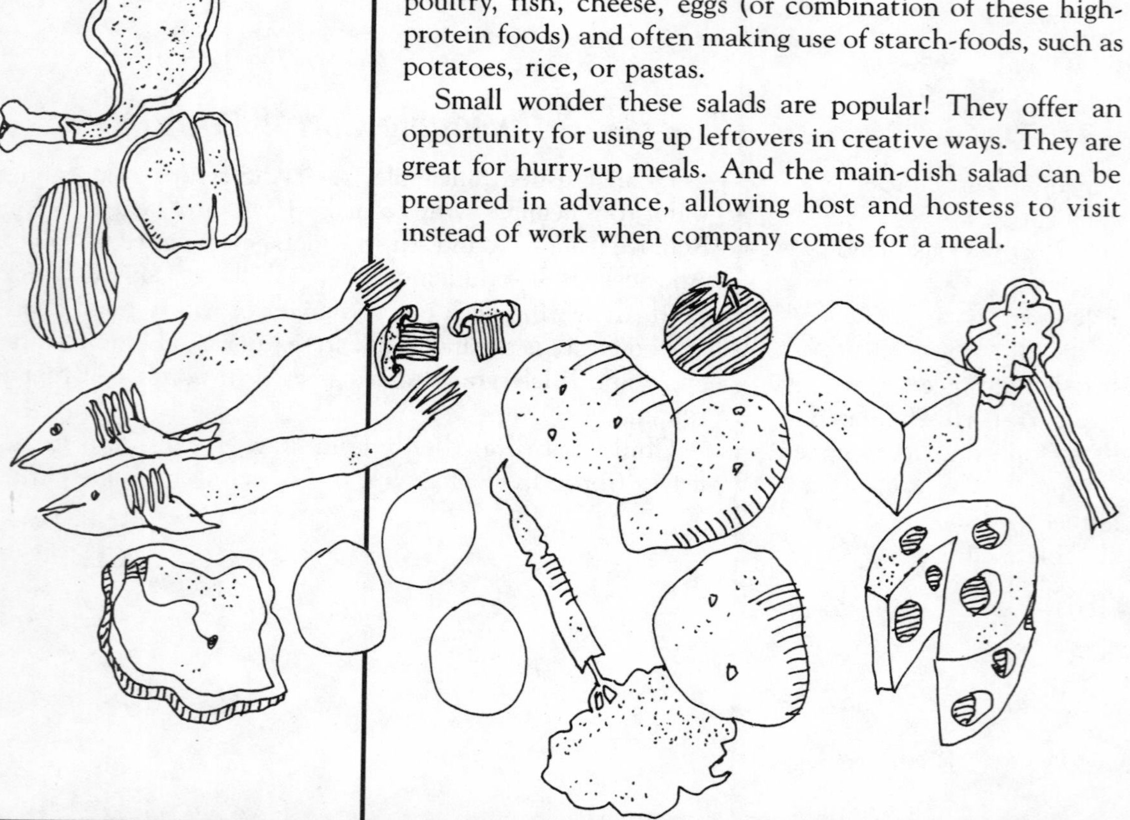

After-the-Holidays Special

2 c. diced turkey
1 c. drained pineapple chunks
1 c. celery (sliced diagonally)
$^{1}/_{2}$ c. sliced green onion
$^{1}/_{4}$ c. dry roasted peanuts
1 c. seedless green grapes
$^{2}/_{3}$ c. mayonnaise
2 T. chopped chutney
2 T. lime juice
$^{1}/_{2}$ t. grated lime rind
$^{1}/_{2}$ t. curry powder
$^{1}/_{4}$ t. salt

Toss together first six ingredients. Combine remaining ingredients to make a dressing. Stir dressing into turkey mixture. Serve on a bed of greens. Serves four. May be doubled or tripled.

Curried Rice and Ham Salad

$1^{1}/_{2}$ c. cooked rice
1 T. oil
2 T. vinegar
1 t. curry powder
$^{1}/_{2}$ t. salt (preferably seasoned)
$^{1}/_{2}$ c. mayonnaise
1 small can peas and carrots (drained)
1 c. chopped ham
lettuce
tomato wedges
black olives

To cooked rice, add oil, vinegar, curry powder, and salt. Mix and chill, then toss with mayonnaise. Fold in peas and carrots and chopped ham. Refrigerate (keeps well for several days). Serve on shredded lettuce topped with tomato wedges and black olives. Bread sticks, apple wedges, and assorted cheeses round out a meal. Serve Key Lime Pie as the perfect finale (recipe in dessert section).

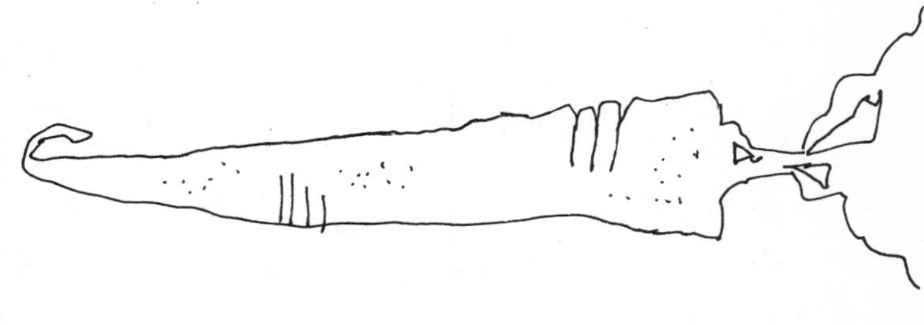

Long-Ago-in-Mexico Seafood Salad

1 small head lettuce
3 large, ripe avocados (seeded, peeled, quartered)
2 T. fresh lime juice
3 seedless oranges (peeled, cut in bite-size pieces)
one 1/2-lb. jicama (peeled and cut into cubes)
1 small can each shrimp, chunk tuna, and crab meat (drained)
pitted black olives
pimento and cheese spread

Shred lettuce. Prepare avocados and pour lime juice over sections. Prepare oranges and jicama. Refrigerate until ready to serve, then arrange in wheel-shape on a large salad plate (with avocados on the outside rim, followed by a ring of oranges and jicama alternated for color). Pile seafood in center. Stuff olives with cheese mixture and reserve until salad is dressed with recipe that follows, then toss olives at random over entire plate.

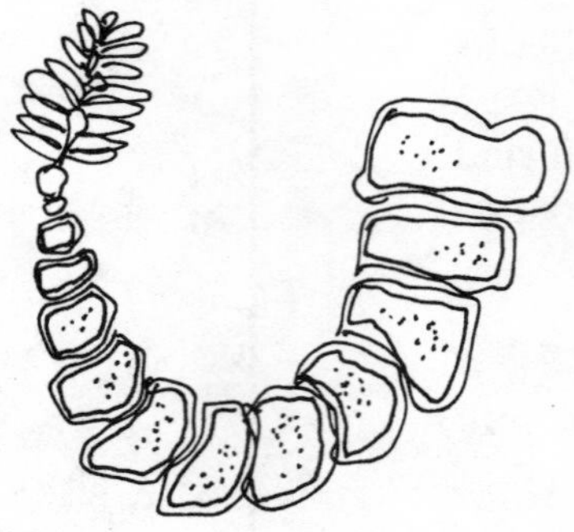

Avocado Dressing

1 large avocado pureed (with blender or mashed with fork)
1/3 c. orange juice
1/4 c. fresh lime juice
2 T. honey

Blend. This will keep for several weeks in refrigerator.

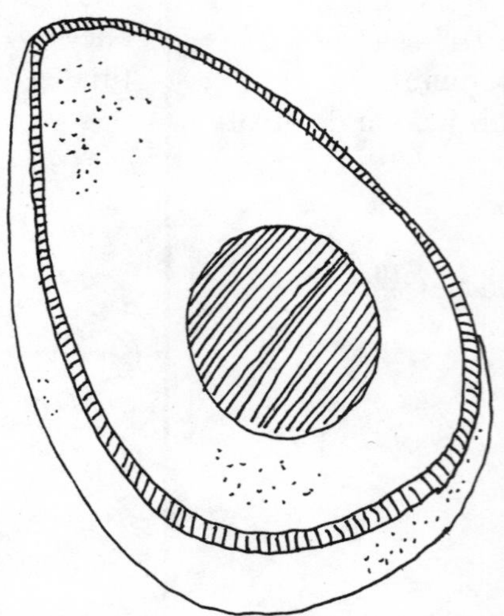

Hot Chicken Salad

4 c. chicken (light and dark) cubed
2 T. lemon juice
1 c. slivered almonds
3/4 c. mayonnaise
1/2 t. salt
2 c. celery (chopped)
4 boiled eggs (peeled and sliced)
3/4 c. cream of chicken soup
1 t. chopped onion
2 pimientos (minced)
1/4 t. sage
dash of Worcestershire sauce
1 c. grated cheese (white or yellow)
1 1/2 c. potato chips (broken)
1 c. black, pitted olives
shredded greens (chilled)

Combine all ingredients by hand except cheese, almonds, potato chips, olives, and greens. Spread in large baking dish and refrigerate overnight. Top with cheese, potato chips, and almonds. Bake at 350° about 30 minutes or until only lightly browned. Serve immediately, scooped onto beds of greens arranged on individual salad plates, topped with olives. Nice accompaniments are hard rolls and cranberry juice on-the-rocks.

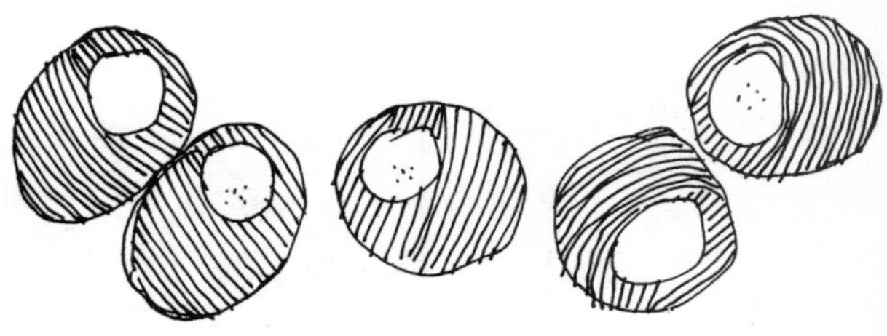

In a hurry? Use the micro. We won't tell!

Vegeroni-Beef Salad

- 3 c. shell macaroni (cooked, drained, rinsed)
- 1 c. shredded carrots
- 1 c. shredded coconut (unsweetened)
- 1 c. shredded red cabbage
- 1 c. shredded green cabbage
- 1/2 c. chopped onion
- 2 c. leftover cubed roast beef
- 1 c. chopped celery
- 1/2 c. mayonnaise
- 1 1/2 t. prepared mustard
- 2 T. sweet relish
- 1/2 t. celery seed
- 1/8 t. coarse black pepper
- 2 hard-boiled eggs
- paprika

Mix together all ingredients except eggs. Refrigerate until ready to serve. Arrange in a large salad dish and surround with a fringe of parsley (sprigs stuck stem-ends down). Peel eggs and slice in rings. Sieve yolks over entire top and toss egg-white rings at random. Sprinkle lightly with paprika. Serve with hot garlic bread and a side dish of chilled fresh fruit. Avocado pie for dessert? Yes!

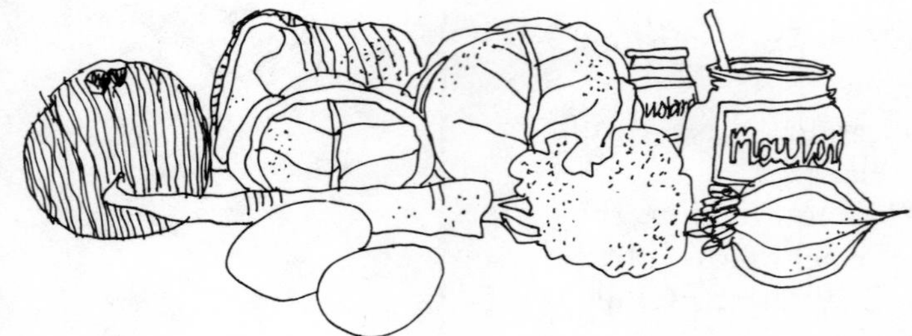

Praise the Lord for dirty dishes! They say the meal went well.

Corned-Beef-'n-Cabbage Mold

one 12-oz. can corned beef
one 3-oz. package lemon gelatin
1 3/4 c. hot water
1 c. mayonnaise
1 c. chopped celery
2 hard-boiled eggs (chopped)
1/4 c. minced onions
1 c. yellow cheese cubes
few drops of Tabasco sauce
shredded lettuce

Flake corned beef and let stand while dissolving gelatin in hot water. Chill gelatin mixture until syrupy. Add mayonnaise and whip until smooth and velvety. Add corned beef and then remaining ingredients. Chill in a square dish until firm, then cut into individual squares. Serve on crisp lettuce. Yummy with buttered lima beans, cornbread sticks, and fresh fruit wedges.

Sweet-Pea Salad

one 17-oz. can peas (drained)
3/4 c. sharp cheddar cheese (cubed)
1/2 c. sweet pickle relish
6 sliced green onions (include blades)
1/2 c. mayonnaise
2 hard-boiled eggs (chopped)
salt and pepper
lettuce
cold, boiled ham

Mix all ingredients except lettuce and ham (adding salt and pepper to taste). Refrigerate until ready to use. Arrange crisp lettuce leaves on a large platter and place a thin slice of cold boiled ham in each. Top with generous scoops of Sweet Pea Salad. Round out menu with vegetable relishes and Orange-Kissed Biscuits (see Quick Monkey Bread).

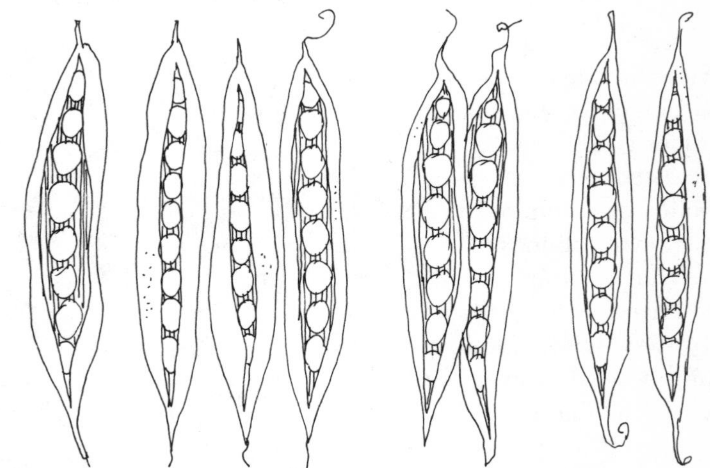

The one ingredient for which there is no substitute: Love.

THE QUEEN IS IN THE PARLOR

Now for the most fun of all: "The queen is in the parlor" salad meals! Here are some ideas which lock in freedom for the hostess and fun for the guests.

African Ground-Nut Meal Shared with Early America

Ground-Nut Gravy:
2 c. milk
2 c. chicken broth
1 c. chunk-style ground-nut butter (peanut butter!)
3 c. cubed chicken
salt
cayenne

Mix milk, broth, and ground-nut butter. Stir over low flame until thick (peanut butter will thicken mixture). Remove from heat, add chicken, salt (if needed), and a dash (about 1/8 t.) cayenne pepper. Refrigerate until ready to serve and then reheat.

Salad:
2 1/2 c. instant rice (uncooked)
2 c. pineapple chunks (canned or fresh)
1 1/2 c. shredded coconut
2 c. grapefruit and orange slices (fresh or canned)
2 c. sliced bananas
6 boiled eggs (chopped)
2 c. tomato chunks
1 1/2 c. diced onion
3 c. mixed melon balls (watermelon, cantaloupe, and honeydew in season)
2 c. avocado chunks
1 c. ground nuts (unsalted peanuts)

When ready to serve meal, heat ground-nut gravy and cook instant rice for six people. For a buffet, place the rice dish where the dining line begins, setting gravy dish and ladle next. Arrange remaining salad ingredients in given order so that guests can "layer" this special salad and end up with a sprinkle of ground nuts! *Guaranteed to please.*

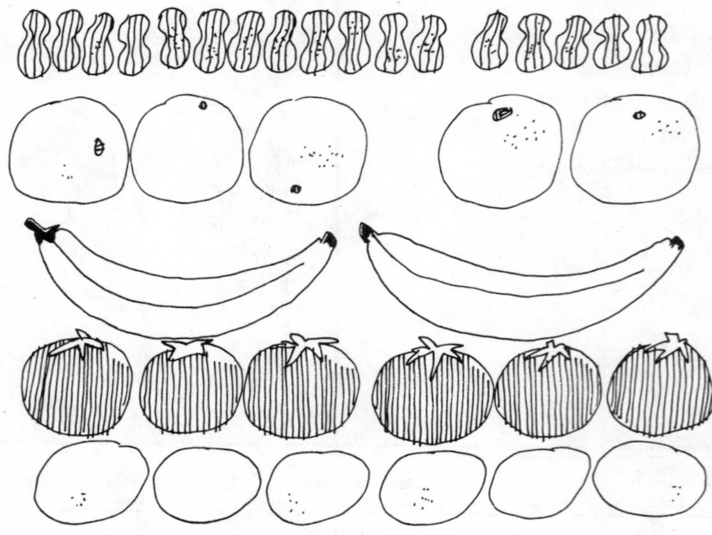

What's the secret ingredient that differentiates between a collection of foods and a meal that evokes whispers of anticipation and lip-licking compliments from an appreciative family or guests? What leads up to a warm after-dinner gathering around the piano to sing familiar songs? One answer is a simple, well-planned meal. Another is a meal which allows self-service (and conversation as diners progress from dish to dish), or, if a "sit-down meal," one which provides for the family-style "pass it on." With dishes prepared in advance, the hostess is truly the "queen in the parlor." And guests will love it!

Americans have progressed to this informal-type dining from the pioneer "dinner-on-the-ground" tradition (tablecloth spread beneath the trees after church or a quilting bee), progressing to the still-popular potluck meal, the block party, and/or the buffet. On what occasion? **Any!** *A time-saver that is good fun is planning ahead with menus for: a Traditional Holiday Dinner, an All-Time Favorite Brunch, a Something-Different Meal (impromptu any time), a Classic Touch Buffet, an Exotic Snack (as a surprise party), a Before-the-Theatre Pow-Wow, an After-Church Meal (why not include the minister and his wife?), a Saturday Night Soiree (just for the fun of it!), a PTA Tonight Hurry-up Supper, an After-the-Shopping-Spree Grill (provide a foot tub for burning feet!), Reunion Time . . . Happy Birthday . . . The Boss is Coming! Keep adding your own original ideas.*

Serve-Yourself Taco Salad

1 family-sized (giant) package tortilla (or Frito) chips
1 large head iceberg lettuce (washed, shredded, and chilled)
6 ripe tomatoes (peeled carefully and sliced)
3 large avocados (peeled, seeded, and sliced lengthwise)
3 large sweet onions cut into rings (if onions are hot, soak in ice water in refrigerator several hours)
1 lb. bean sprouts (washed and drained)
2 cans Mexican-style (hot!) chili with beans
1 lb. grated yellow cheese

Prepare vegetables in advance and refrigerate. When ready to serve, heat chili to boiling point and pour into serving dish. For buffet, set the makings out in order given. Guests help themselves first to a base of chips, followed by a layer of lettuce, etc., ending with hot chili topped with cheese. *Olé!*

Olé! Dish (Our Gift from Mexico After Spanish-American War)

1 lb. ground beef (lean)
1 large onion (chopped)
2 cans refried beans
one 7-oz. can diced green chili pepper
3 c. shredded jack cheese
taco sauce
guacamole
sour cream
black olives
tortilla or corn chips

Brown beef and onion in large skillet. Drain and discard fat. Spread beans in baking dish. Top with meat mixture and sprinkle with peppers, topping with cheese. Drizzle with taco sauce. Place in 350° oven (uncovered) for 20 minutes (or until cheese is melted). Serve at once with side dishes of guacamole, sour cream, taco sauce, and sliced black olives. In another dish arrange heaps of tortilla or Frito chips for guests to use as "dippers." Plan on seconds—and thirds!

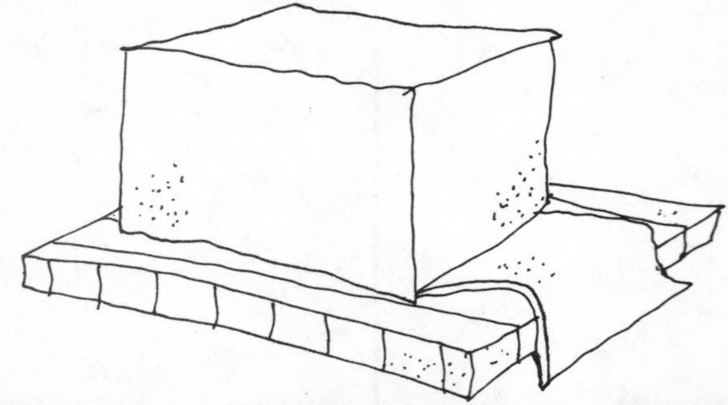

Easiest-Ever Crab Louis

three 6-oz. packages frozen Alaskan king crab (thawed and drained)
3 hard-cooked eggs (sliced)
1 cucumber sliced (not peeled)
2 tomatoes (peeled carefully and sliced)
1 head shredded lettuce
1 medium onion (chopped)
2 bell peppers (chopped)
1 c. celery (diced)
2 c. water chestnuts (drained and chopped)

Dressing
1 c. mayonnaise
3 T. catsup
2 T. green onion (chopped)
1 T. Worcestershire sauce
1 T. red wine vinegar
2 t. lemon or lime juice
1/2 t. salt
1/8 t. white pepper
1 clove garlic

In medium bowl prepare salad dressing and refrigerate at least an hour before using (overnight or longer is better).

In center of one salad platter, pile crab. Encircle with eggs, cucumber, and tomato slices. For buffet, place a large bowl of shredded lettuce at the head of the table, and next to it set the crab platter. Arrange other ingredients in order given—each in a separate bowl, to allow guests to choose favorites. Last, remove the garlic clove from the dressing and place the super-good dressing at the end of the buffet. *Exotic!*

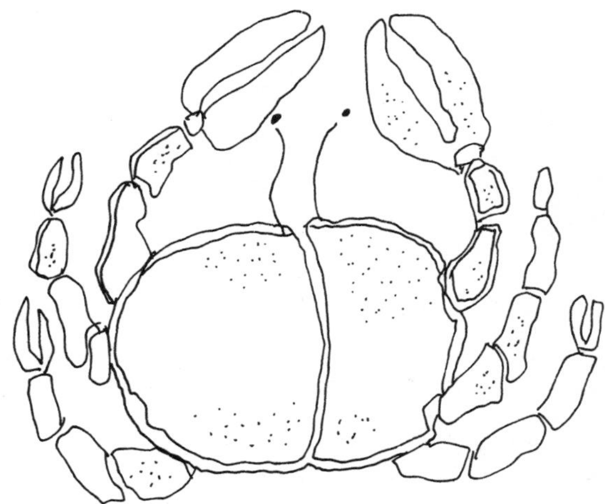

Ready-to-bake pastry squares from your grocer's dairy case become savory salad accompaniments when filled with small sliced sausages and your favorite cheeses.

A Kitchen Prayer

Dear Lord, please bless my
kitchen
And bless this cooking book,
Then bless each busy morning
When I come here to cook.

Make this a friendly kitchen
That smells of gingerbread—
Aroma of sweet spices
Mixed in with prayers said.

Let kettles hum a greeting
While the well-scrubbed floor
Reflects a square of sunshine
Of welcome from the door.

Yes, Lord, please bless my kitchen
And foods I cook within;
May it speak peace and comfort
To all who enter in.

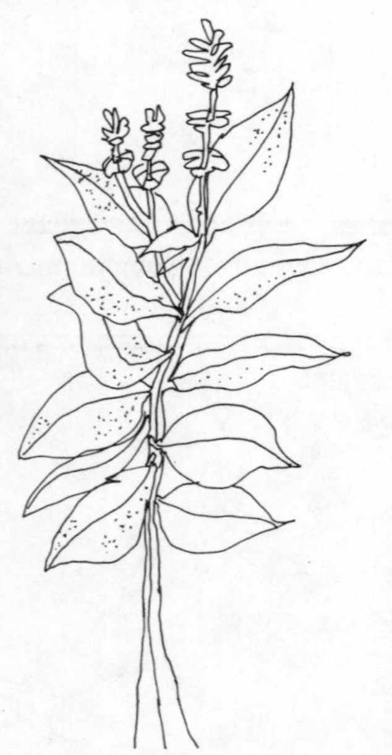

Other Ideas Worth Sharing

There are those who prefer vegetables in salads steamed. There are others who, because of a diet, do not eat raw food. Steamed vegetables can be a delicacy if treated with respect. (A steamer is a good investment for other uses too.) Steaming is a quick process. Steam only until vegetables can be pricked with a fork. The color will remain bright, although the flavor can be a bit boring without help. Try mixing 1 T. prepared mustard with 4 T. butter and add salt and pepper to taste. Toss vegetables lightly with mixture. Sprinkle with coarsely chopped, toasted nuts.

There comes a time when one feels like a change. If you hail from that area of the country from Maine to Florida and westward to Minnesota and Texas, maybe it's poke sallet (pokeweed which grows wild, often around stumps and logs). The young, tender shoots and seedlings (not the berries or roots, as they are poisonous) are good eating—if you were brought up on poke. For those who wish to sample, let us tell you that the shoots taste much like asparagus; the seedlings, like spinach. Prepare poke as you would those two vegetables after parboiling. In Asia, the plant is cultivated commercially.

You would rather play it safe? Then wild mustard is for you, and the edible pest is available almost everywhere. Watch for the bowers of dainty yellow blossoms and learn to recognize the leaves (similar to the turnip). Organize a Mustard Hunt as a spring outing. And why not boil your findings with chunks of ham and enjoy together?

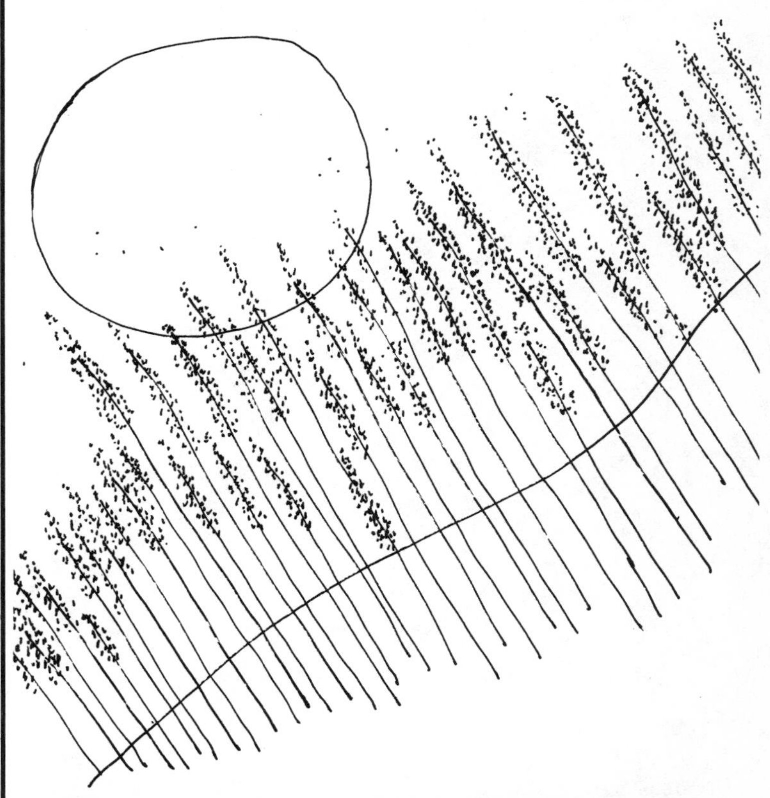

Soups 'n Sandwiches

Two Great American Traditions

Legend has it that Soup Royal began in merry olde England—and nobody knows when. The King, so the story goes, ordered that the Cook prepare a soup with a different flavor every day—never once repeating down through the years. Now the Cook valued his head, so he put it to work. Why not, he asked himself, make use of the abundance of leftovers (secretly, of course, as there were spies on every hand)? And so he did.

Beginning with a fresh, rich broth, the Cook added whatever was left from the royal table—excepting desserts. One could use, he discovered, the buttered vegetables, liver puddings, diced fowl, gravies—why, there was no end to what he could do. And every day, of course, the brew indeed tasted different. The King grew so fond of Royal Soup that he demanded each guest at the palace be served a bowl from the always-steaming pot at tea time.

So much for legend, but it is a matter of record that early American settlers did somewhat the same. Base for the broth came from wild game, and before gardens were producing, there was maize (the Indians' name for corn). Gradually they added to the colony pot, each person contributing every morsel left from the meager fare. Flavor improved as spices became available.

When migration westward began, the practice (which had been all but buried in history) recommenced. Old diaries declare that the rich soups (made from buffalo broth and leftovers cooked over a campfire along the trail) tasted "mighty fine" after periods of near-starvation in which there was no food except Slick-Go-Down (a mixture we would call "flour paste").

Begin with a broth (see directions here) and use fresh vegetables for the "starter." After that . . . well, you know how to proceed. Be a pioneer in your own kitchen. As important as the broth is a sense of adventure. This is basic! It takes courage to dump scrambled eggs, spaghetti and cheese, and candied sweet potatoes into a pot. This is *soup*? Yes, it is soup, and deliciously so. It provides a new surprise daily, too.

Eventually the soup needs to be divided and shared with friends (nice to take to shut-ins, or maybe you'd like to plan an eat-it-all-up party). Still some left? Bring to a rolling boil and use for one more meal. Discard and start anew. Besides the inimitable flavors you come up with, there's another bonus: You will never be caught without a meal should unexpected friends drop by. That's hospitality!

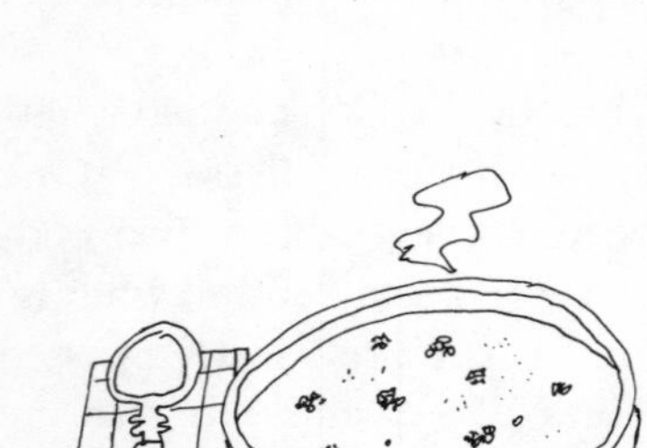

Soup is one of the easiest-on-the-budget of all the menu items. It takes the chill from a winter evening. It has a "healing power" (according to some who agree with Grandmother's theory about chicken soup's curative ingredients). And certainly it can provide the nutrients from all the major food groups. You can add pasta, assorted vegetables, grated cheese—you name it—and come out with a nearly complete meal. Toss a green salad, remove the brown rolls from the oven, and dinner is served!

The secret of flavorful soup is broth. And broth, so easy to make, is one reason why soup is so economical. Just save the beef bones from a roast or the bone from a baked ham, bring to a boil, chill, and skim. What remains is the makings for homemade flavor even if you use a mix or a can of soup. One other idea worth sharing is turkey broth, which comes from what most people discard. When only the carcass remains of the traditional bird—even without a trace of meat—simmer it in enough water to cover it completely. After several hours, discard the bones, chill, and skim. The result is best-ever broth, which seems to taste better day after day, even when soup is warmed over.

Here, then, are three kitchen delights in soup which you are sure to enjoy: one quickie idea with mixes and two soups from scratch.

SOUPS

Instant Soups

Simply substitute broth for water when preparing canned soup. If the freezer offers a selection of flavors, choose ham broth for split-pea soup, turkey soup, or chicken-with-vegetable soup. Take it from there!

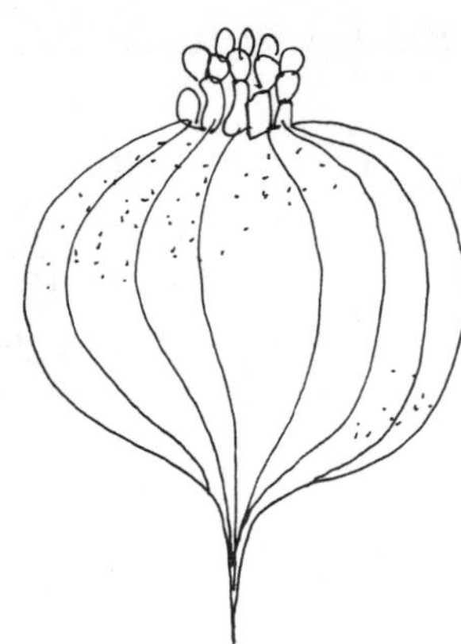

Hamburger Supper Soup

1/2 lb. lean ground meat
1 large onion (sliced)
1 stalk celery (sliced)
3 carrots (scraped and sliced)
1 T. parsley (chopped)
one 6 oz. can tomato paste
2 c. cabbage (chopped)
1 medium potato (peeled, cubed)
4 c. broth (any flavor)
1 1/2 t. salt
1/4 t. sugar
1/2 c. whole-kernel corn
one 10-oz. pkg. frozen peas

Brown meat in heavy skillet with salt and pepper. Drain and add all other ingredients (any order) except peas. Bring to a boil. Reduce heat to simmer and cook (covered) 30 minutes. Add peas. Return cover and cook 10 minutes more. Good tonight, better tomorrow night, and *best* frozen, thawed, and reheated!

Old-Fashioned Chicken Gumbo Soup

- one 2½-lb. chicken (cut as for frying, salt to taste)
- salt (to taste)
- 5 peppercorns
- 2 stalks celery with leaves (sliced)
- 3 sprigs parsley (snipped)
- 1 bay leaf
- ½ c. rice (uncooked)
- ½ t. thyme
- 1 pkg. frozen lima beans
- 2 t. sugar
- 6 c. water
- 2 medium onions (diced)
- one 16-oz. can tomatoes
- 3 medium potatoes (diced)
- 1 c. okra (sliced)
- 1 small can whole-kernel corn
- 1 small green pepper (chopped)

Bring chicken, salt, and peppercorns to boil in water. Reduce heat and simmer (covered) 1 hour (or until tender). Strain off broth and return to kettle. Remove meat from bones (discard skin) and cut into cubes. Add to broth together with all other ingredients and simmer (covered) until vegetables are tender. Adjust seasonings if necessary and serve with hot buttered cornbread.

Avocado Velvet Soup

- 3 T. margarine
- 1 large onion (chopped)
- 2 bunches watercress (washed, snipped)
- 4 c. chicken broth
- 4 large avocados (peeled, seeded)
- ½ c. nondairy topping
- salt and pepper
- paprika

Sauté onion in heated margarine about 2 minutes. Add watercress and cook an additional minute. Pour in 2 c. of the broth and allow to simmer 5 minutes. Meanwhile puree (with blender or fork) avocados and topping. Add heated broth and watercress, then blend. Return mixture to saucepan and add remaining broth. Heat without boiling. Add salt and pepper as desired. Pour into individual soup bowls, garnishing each (just before serving) with a last-minute spoon of additional nondairy topping, a sprinkle of uncooked watercress, and a sift of paprika for color. Nice? Ask any Californian!

Pea-Green Shrimp Soup

one 1-lb. pkg. split peas
broth (see directions)
1 c. milk
1/2 t. Tabasco sauce
1 T. margarine
1/4 c. onion (grated)
2 large tomatoes (peeled, diced)
1/2 c. grated cheese
one 6 1/2-oz. can shrimp (drained)

Cook peas according to directions on package but substituting ham broth for water (omit salt if broth is salted). When soup is very thick, measure out 2 c. Add milk and blend. Heat (do not boil) and add Tabasco and margarine. Fold in onion and tomatoes just before serving. Pour into large tureen as a "soup-supper" centerpiece. Sprinkle with grated cheese and float shrimp on top. Why not carry out the beauty of the pink-and-green soup? Try radish rosettes and crisp cucumber fingers with avocado dressing. In grand-slam ending, bring on the raspberry tarts or lime chiffon pie!

New England Clam Chowder

1/2 c. diced bacon
1/2 c. minced onion
one 10 1/2-oz. can potato soup
3/4 c. milk
two 8-oz. cans minced clams
1 T. lemon juice

Fry bacon and onion in not-too-hot skillet. Stir in soup and mix thoroughly, gradually adding milk. Add clams, including juice. Allow to simmer. Serve hot, sprinkled with coarsely ground (hand milled is best) black pepper and serve piping hot in "Grab-It" bowls. (Grab-It is the trade name for Corning dishes with single handles for easy handling.) Serves six.

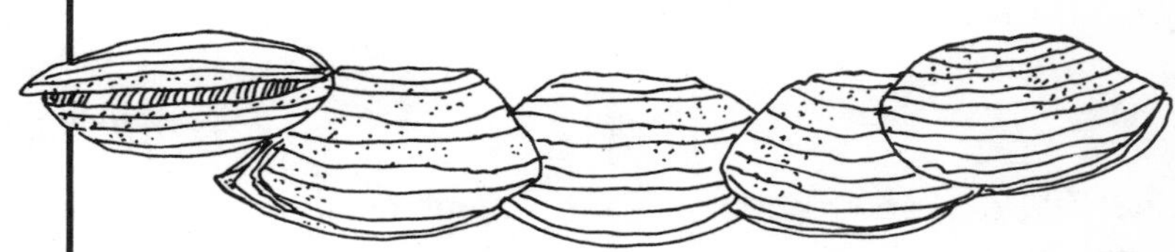

Choose up sides and serve clam chowder the way you like it. There's a battle raging, you know, over what constitutes "authentic chowder." Should the liquid be tomatoes, milk, or clam nectar? New Englanders vow that chowder is not chowder without salt pork, potatoes, onions, milk, and fresh clams. Manhattan dwellers get ready to aim and fire. Doesn't everybody know that their tomato-rich version is more flavorful and contains fewer calories? Wonderful thing about our country—its cooking is as diversified as its people! Our view? We're for the shortcuts!

We busy Americans consider canned soups an immediate blessing—adding a bit of this and a bit of that, according to the fancy. Create your own tradition!

Stormy Day Bean Soup

1 lb. dry navy beans
7 c. water
1 ham bone
2 c. cooked and cubed ham
1/2 c. minced onion
1/2 t. salt
1 bay leaf
1 t. sugar

Rinse beans, add to water, and boil gently two minutes. Remove from heat; cover and let stand for an hour. Add remaining ingredients. Heat to rolling boil (which cannot be stirred down). Reduce heat and simmer 1 1/2 hours (or until tender). Skim off foam (if any). Remove bay leaf and ham bone. Remove meat from bone and add to soup. Provides seven 1-c. servings. Pass the pepper mill often!

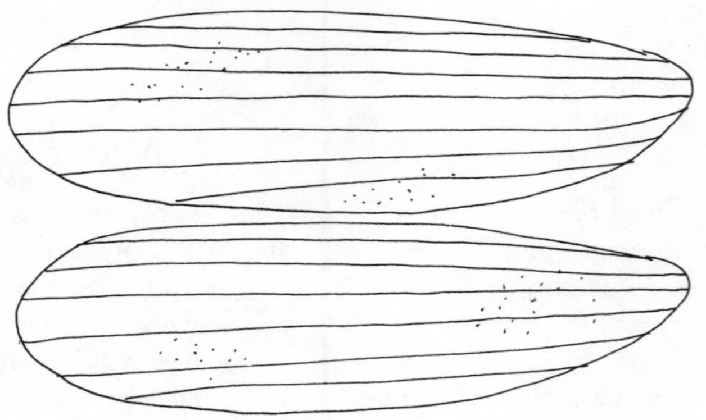

Appetizer Soup

one 10 1/2-oz. can cream of celery soup
1 soup can water
1/2 c. chopped, peeled, and diced cucumber sprinkled with celery salt
2 T. chopped green onion
2 T. chopped green pepper
1/2 c. sour cream

Combine all ingredients and chill. Serves 6 (1/2 c. each).

SANDWICHES

Sandwich and soup. Sandwich and milk shake (or French fries and cola). Sandwich and salad. You are looking at Lunchtime, USA! Sandwiches make a nice lunch. An expandable one, too—as light or filling as you choose. It is so easy to say, "Come on over for a sandwich!"

You and I recall the fun of childhood picnics—swinging a wicker basket packed with secret foods as we trudged across the daisy-filled meadows in search of the shadiest tree by the old swimmin' hole . . . the fun of looking forward to Mother's home-packed lunchbox when we tired of school cafeterias . . . or the easy "brown bag" lunches on workdays at the church, school, or community event.

But the sandwich has a history that dates back farther than our memories can reach. Food lore has it that an English earl discovered the convenience of the finger-food snack. But leave it to the ingenuity and imagination of us Americans to make the once-lowly sandwich a way of life. "Ham and egg!" "Tuna salad san!" "Big Mac, please!" The layered look is in. Fact is, these orders and all their cousins are a national (and often international) language everybody understands.

All sandwiches have three parts, of course. The bread. The spread. And the filling. But they need never be dull. Not when there's white, wheat, and rye bread; crusty rolls, seed-strewn buns; and all the fruit and nut breads from which to choose. And the spread (mayonnaise or margarine) comes richly flavored; or we spring a surprise with our mix. As for fillings, they are as numerous as the stars. Just try and count them! Hot or cold. Thick or thin. Crunchy or smooth, single layer, double-decker, or stacked precariously high and cut into wedges.

And sandwiches bring with them a bonus. You can freeze them ahead if you avoid mayonnaise and such juicy ingredients as coleslaw, lettuce, and tomatoes. Add those later. It is great to know that frozen sandwiches are safer when frozen in advance of taking out. It is also comforting to know that you have the foil-wrapped little helpers stashed away in the freezer in case you need a speedy snack or wish to stretch a meal in an emergency. Leave foil on if using the conventional oven or broiler to thaw or toast. Remove it if you use the microwave (then re-wrap to keep it steaming hot until serving time).

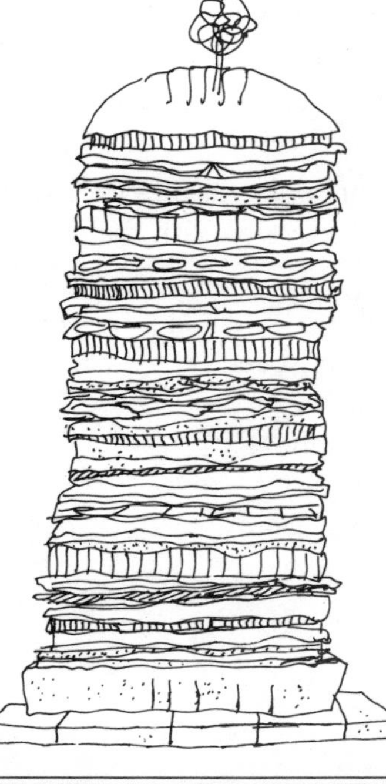

Wow! How a sandwich can prop up a light supper (made ahead and refrigerated or frozen and heated) on Sunday nights,

after-the-theatre snacks, or as a surprise for the Mothers' Chorus rehearsal your church plans with which the choir leader plans to wake up the congregation!

Or, maybe you'd like to have a sandwich supper just to get the "gang" together. Good, for sandwiches are universal favorites. Just spread out the makings and let each person create according to taste.

Boiled eggs, tuna fish, baked ham, luncheon meats, cheese, leftover roast or meatloaf (and a million other country cookin' meats) work well. Or, if you want to reach for the spectacular, spread your table with sliced avocado, asparagus tips, watercress, marinated cucumbers, and wafers of red onion. Then bring out the crab, shrimp, curried chicken, aspic, anchovy, caviar . . . and then some. Just add your own touch of elegance. But do remember that somebody is sure to ask: "Where's the peanut butter and jelly?" So, yes, add it to your list.

Questions on spreads? Here are a few suggestions:

Chili-Oregano Butter: 1/2 t. oregano and 1 T. chili sauce added to 1/2 c. butter. Great for beef sandwiches, hamburgers, and hot dogs.

Curry Butter: 1/2 t. curry added to 1/2 c. butter. Tasty on lamb or ham.

Horseradish Butter: 1 T. horseradish blended with 1/2 c. butter. Serve with tongue or roast beef.

Lemon-Herb Butter: 1 T. lemon juice, 1 t. parsley flakes, and 1/2 t. basil added to 1/2 c. butter. Excellent with seafood and beef.

Parsley Butter: 2 T. snipped parsley, 2 T. lemon juice blended into 1/2 c. butter. Perks up lamb and beef.

Take it from there. Do your spin-offs!

Main Dishes

The Unmatched Pleasures of Hearth and Home

Main dishes are the cook's best friend! They are fun to make, easy to serve, and so obliging. Patiently they stand and wait until they (and you) are ready for the spotlight. Make them ahead and refrigerate or freeze. When time counts, use our Quick-and-Easies. On occasion you may want to enjoy the remembered goodness of an all-day baking of Boston beans.

Whether you are planning the menu for a family meal or for entertaining, you will want to choose the main dish first. The rest of the meal will revolve around the meat or protein-rich dish (beef, pork, fish, poultry, shellfish, eggs, cheese, dried peas or beans, even—and children will love you!—peanut butter).

> *And they . . . breaking bread from house to house, did eat their meat with gladness and singleness of heart.*
>
> —Acts 2:46

Step 1 is to review your four basic food groups: *meat* (or substitute), *fruits* and *vegetables, breads* (cereals or pasta), and *milk products*. Remember that you can spread these over the three daily meals. Planning ahead for the day—or, better, the week—does not enslave you. It sets you free!

Step 2 is to think about contrasts. New concept? Then all the more fun! Balance leafy and starchy vegetables (or substitutes). Lima beans are starchy and would welcome a chilled cucumber salad by their side. Think of contrast in color, too. Whipped potatoes and turnips would look pale, but a green or yellow vegetable will add color. If you *must* serve two pale vegetables together, liven them up with a twist of orange and a few black olives. There is another contrast which will add zest. An all-soft meal (soups, souffles, and pasta casseroles) calls for something crunchy. Consider celery strips, radish rosettes, etc., or the addition of sliced almonds to the main dish. You will want to balance sweet and sour as well—and do

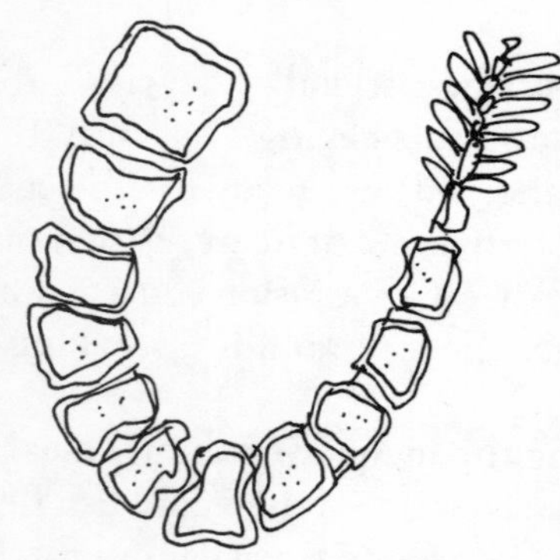

remember (no matter what the temperature) to include something hot and cold.

Step 3 concerns shopping. Use your head—not your legs. Buy staples in advance. Watch for specials, but beware of gimmicks. Check menus and recipes and make use of mixes as often as possible.

Step 4 reminds you to consider your diet (or that of others), then say as little as possible. Who is to know? Just do your own "spin-off?"

Sample Menu Which Follows all the Rules!

Shrimp, Tomato, and Snow Peas Casserole
Fresh Vegetable Relish Dish
Steamed Rice Sprinkled with Parsley
Chopped Spinach and Artichoke Salad
French Rolls
Fresh Fruit Compote on Cantaloupe Halves
Melba Toast   Cheddar Cheese Strips   Coffee

Here are just a few of a myriad of fine main-dish recipes. Try them for yourself, then do your own thing!

Sauerkraut (of German origin) has been a standby for the table from our country's humble beginnings. Cabbages grew happily almost anywhere, and the fermentation process made it possible for kraut to last all winter. Cabbage was shredded with sharp knives (until a wide, wooden board with a blade became available) and fermented in brine made with its own juice and salt. "Krauting" often brought a community together. Men "bladed" the cabbage heads into tubs. Women and children churned the cabbage (layered with handfuls of salt) using a "dasher" (a cross made of boards and attached to a broom handle) to push the shredded vegetable beneath the liquid. A filled churn was topped by a dinner plate, weighted with a rock, and set in a dark place for a week to "kraut." When it fermented, homemakers removed the kraut from the churn as needed, washed it, and heated it in a heavy skillet. Sometimes they added homemade sausages to make it a main dish. More often it was a vegetable to accompany pork chops, corned beef, beans, and peas. Children smuggled it from the churn by the handful and gobbled it down unwashed with nobody ever hearing of botulism or hypertension. It is recommended, however, that persons with elevated blood pressure rinse canned kraut well before using it in a recipe.

Company Kraut

- one 20-oz. can pineapple chunks
- 2 T. corn starch
- dash of cayenne
- 1 T. soy sauce
- 1 large dry onion (chopped)
- 2 green bell peppers (chopped)
- 1 pod sweet red pepper (chopped)
- smoked pork chops (or fresh chops rubbed with liquid smoke flavoring), 2 per person
- one 27-oz. can sauerkraut

Drain pineapple and make a sauce by adding the cornstarch, cayenne, and soy sauce. Bring to a boil. Turn off heat and add onion and peppers. Brown chops in heavy skillet. Layer kraut, pineapple, and chops in baking dish. Cover with sauce and place in 350° oven for half an hour. Beautiful with hot cheese bread, carrot and celery sticks, fruited rice (instant rice with chopped dried raisins, dates, or apricots), apple-nut salad, and chocolate-mint custard!

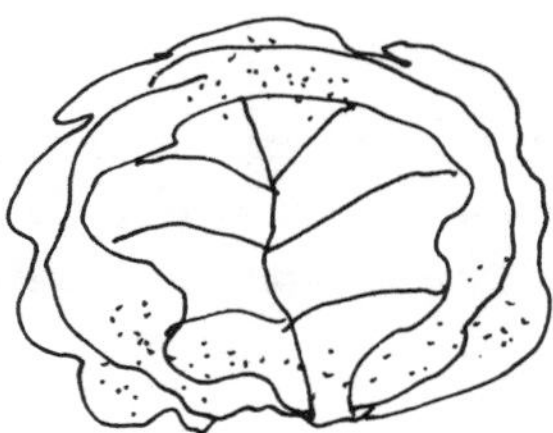

Good cooks, like good watches, are generally open-faced, pure gold, quietly busy, and full of good works.

Three-Bean Casserole

- 1 clove garlic (chopped)
- 1 large onion (chopped)
- one 27-oz. can pork and beans
- 1/2 c. catsup
- 1 T. molasses
- 1 t. dry mustard
- 1/4 t. white pepper
- 1 large green pepper (chopped)
- one 15-oz. can lima beans
- one 15-oz. can kidney beans
- 3 T. vinegar
- 1 T. brown sugar
- 1 t. salt
- dash of cayenne

Mix all ingredients and bake in bean pot or covered casserole. Bake at 350° for 30 minutes. Excellent with cold boiled ham, cabbage slaw, and lemon meringue pie!

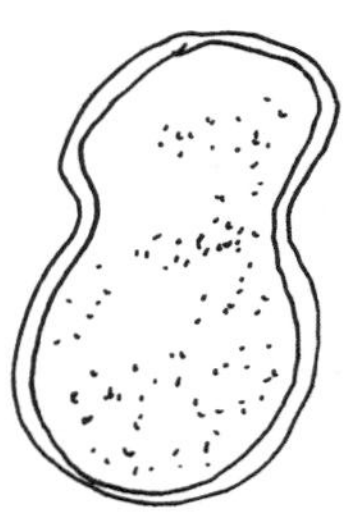
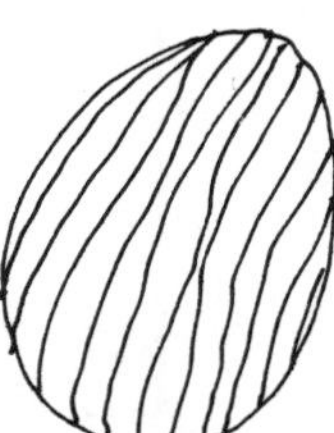
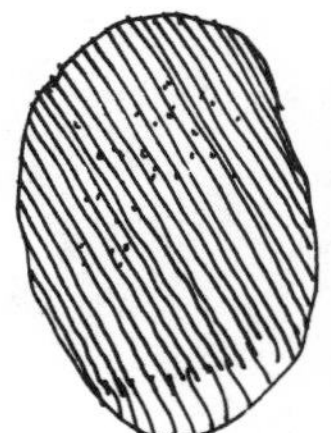

Pizza Puff

1 lb. sausage
8 slices white bread
1/3 c. tomato paste
1 1/2 t. crushed basil
8 oz. jack cheese (shredded)
3 eggs (beaten)
2 c. milk
1/2 t. salt

Break up sausage in skillet. Brown slowly about 20 minutes, stirring occasionally. Place 4 slices of bread in bottom of greased baking dish. Combine paste and basil. Spread over bread. Sprinkle half the cheese over bread and spoon sausage over cheese. Place remaining shredded cheese over sausage and top with remaining bread. Combine eggs, milk, and salt, then blend. Pour over casserole. Cover and refrigerate overnight. Bake uncovered at 350° for 45 minutes. And presto! A mock soufflé.

Here's a toast to the hosts who keep flavored butters on hand in the freezer to add that special touch to simple vegetables accompanying the meat dish—or as a surprising spread for hot breads. Simply blend a stick of butter or margarine with 3 T. fresh minced herbs, a squeeze of lemon or lime, and black pepper.

An example: 4 ounces butter mixed with 1 T. each tarragon, parsley, and chives; or why not try 3 T. basil, 1 small clove, minced garlic and 1 1/2 T. lemon juice? Shape into a roll and wrap in foil, and the flavor will last 2 months in the fridge, longer in the freezer.

Quick Chicken Tortillas

one 10 1/2-oz. can cream of chicken soup
1 large avocado
2 c. cooked and diced chicken (turkey will do)
one 7-oz. can mild green chilies (chopped)
10-12 tortillas
1 T. cooking oil
1/2 c. jack cheese (grated)
1/2 t. garlic salt
1/2 t. pepper
paprika

Heat soup (undiluted). Dice avocado and add to hot soup. Stir in chicken and green chilies. Set aside and fry tortillas in hot oil in heavy skillet. Spoon chicken mixture into tortillas, roll each, and place seam-side-down in ovenproof serving platter. Sprinkle with cheese which has been mixed with garlic salt, pepper, and paprika. Pop under the broiler until cheese melts. Serve from platter.

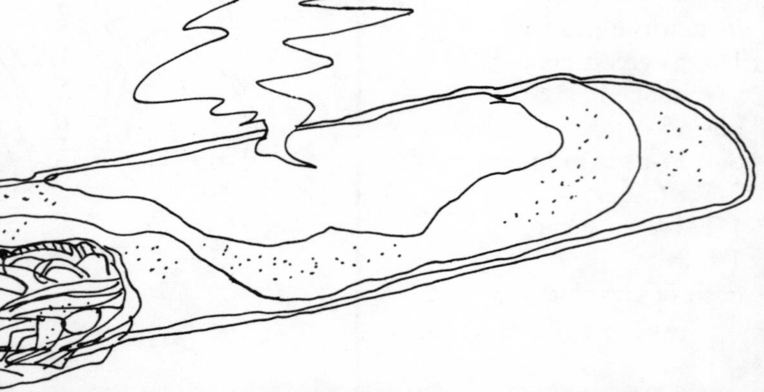

Speedy Tamale Pie

1½ lbs. lean ground beef
2 cloves garlic (minced)
1 large onion (chopped)
½ t. black pepper
two 8-oz. cans tomato sauce
2 eggs (beaten)
¾ c. white corn meal
1½ t. salt
1 c. milk
one 12-oz. can whole kernel corn
¼ t. Tabasco sauce
2 t. chili powder
1 T. sugar
1 doz. large black pitted olives

Brown slowly beef, garlic, onion, and black pepper. Stir in all remaining ingredients except olives. Pour into large baking dish and poke olives at random into mixture. Bake at 350° approximately 45 minutes. Cut into generous squares and serve hot. Serve with crispy celery and carrot sticks, congealed cucumbers, and onions in lime gelatin (prepared the night before). Bring in the peach melba!

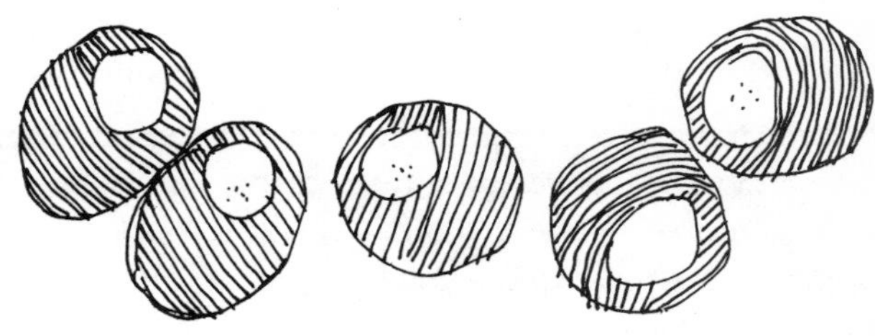

Gobble-Gobble Cobbler

1 T. flour
1 c. yellow cheese (grated)
1 c. almonds (sliced)
1 c. sliced celery
1 c. mayonnaise
1 t. sage
3 c. chopped, cooked turkey
1 T. lemon juice
½ c. sliced olives
salt and pepper to taste
1 can oven-ready biscuits
paprika

Sift flour over grated cheese. Mix. Mix together about ¾ c. of the cheese mixture, ½ c. almonds, and remaining ingredients except biscuits. Pour mixture into baking dish (approximately 11¾ x 7½″). Scatter biscuits at random over top and sprinkle with paprika. Top with remaining cheese and almonds and bake at 350° for 35 minutes, then gobble while hot!

Serve with cranberry relish (raw cranberries and 1 small orange sliced into strawberry gelatin dessert) and choice of chiffon pie.

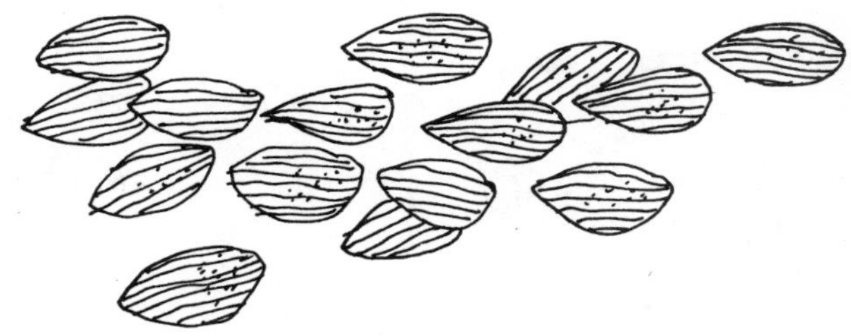

Tortilla Pie

1 doz. corn tortillas (uncooked)
two 15-oz. chili with beans
1 c. tomato catsup
1/4 t. cayenne
1 t. liquid smoke
1 c. grated cheddar cheese

Cut or tear (as they come from package—do not fry) tortillas into halves. Place a layer on bottom of baking dish, overlapping edges. Add a layer of chili, followed by another layer of tortillas. Repeat process until both ingredients are used. Mix catsup, cayenne, and smoke, then pour over casserole. Top with cheese. Bake immediately at 350° for 30 minutes or refrigerate overnight. Mixture may be frozen before baking or afterward without loss of flavor. Serve with guacamole, buttered ears of corn-on-the-cob, tossed salad, and watermelon wedges.

Another thought: Supper-in-a-hurry begins with broccoli florets. Sauté 2 or 3 cloves minced garlic in 4 T. olive oil. Add 4 c. florets and 1/2 c. chicken broth. Cover and let cook over low heat 3 minutes. Toss with hot pasta and lots of grated Parmesan. (NOTE: ***Do*** *include the garlic! It wards off colds and reduces hypertension. Grandmother said so!)*

Picnic-Style Main Dish

8 brown-and-serve French rolls
3/4 lb. each ground beef and bulk seasoned sausage
1 large onion (chopped)
1 clove garlic (minced)
1 large green pepper (seeded, diced)
2 eggs (beaten)
1/3 c. spicy prepared mustard
1 T. Worcestershire sauce
1 1/2 t. Italian herb seasoning
2 T. catsup
salt and pepper to taste
2 T. melted butter

Split rolls and remove centers (outside crusts should remain about 1/4" thick). Tear centers into crumbs, reserving 1 c. for filling. Crumble beef and sausage into heavy frying pan and cook over medium heat (stirring) until browned. Add onion, garlic, and pepper, and continue cooking until onion is clear. Drain off fat and stir in 1 c. crumbs, eggs, mustard, Worcestershire, Italian seasoning, catsup, salt, and pepper. Remove meat from heat. When cool enough to handle, pack filling into rolls. Brush tops with melted butter and bake at 400° for 15 minutes or until brown. Serve with green salad, barbecued beans, and Apple Dumplings.

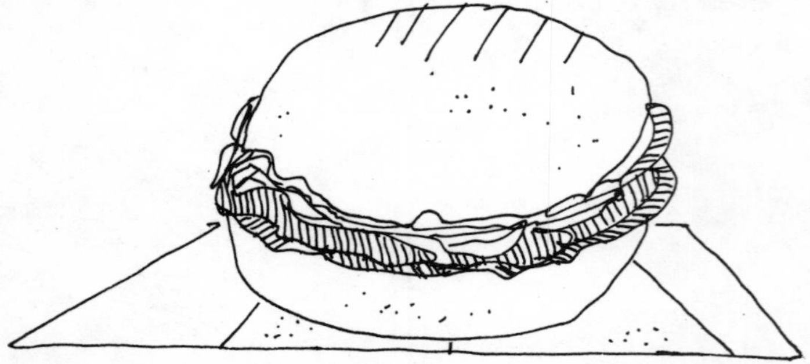

Mock Crab Foldovers

1 lb. turbot fish
milk to cover fish
1 boiled egg (chopped)
1 t. minced parsley
2 T. grated onion
4 T. cream of mushroom soup (do not dilute)
salt and pepper to taste
pastry

Cover turbot with milk and simmer until fish flakes. Drain and cool (discarding milk). Combine fish with all ingredients except pastry.

Cut pastry into 4″ squares. Spoon Mock Crab mixture onto center of each. Fold two opposite corners across filling and secure with toothpick. Place on cookie sheet and bake at 450° about 12 minutes. A definite do-ahead. Prepare Mock Crab and pastry in advance. Refrigerate separately or make into foldovers before refrigerating. May be refrigerated or frozen, baked or unbaked, for emergencies.

*(NOTE: **Do** eat lots of fish and poultry. It helps lower cholesterol. Your doctor says so!)*

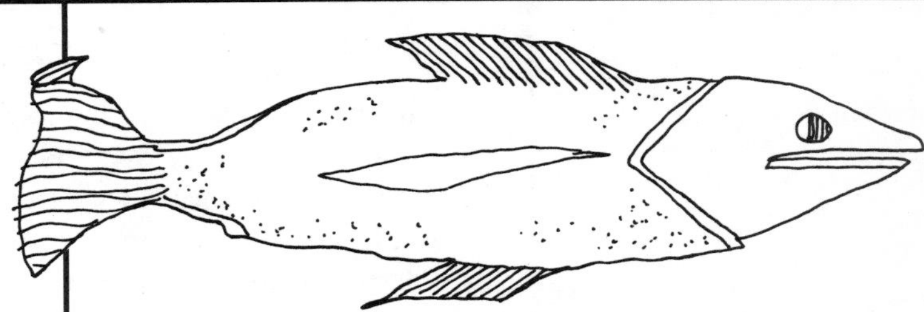

Salmon Bake

1 large green pepper (chopped)
4 green onions with tops (chopped)
1 large dry onion (chopped)
4 stalks celery (sliced)
3 T. margarine
2 c. cooked rice
one 16-oz. can salmon (drained)
6 boiled eggs (sliced)
one 10½-oz. can cream of mushroom soup
¾ c. milk
¼ t. paprika
½ c. cashew nuts

Cook pepper, onion, green onions, and celery in margarine until partially tender (about 5 minutes). Stir in rice and turn mixture into 2½-qt. casserole. Layer salmon (boned and flaked) over casserole. Place eggs over top. Combine soup with milk. Add paprika and heat (do not boil). Toss cashews on top and bake at 400° about 15 minutes. Serve bubbling hot to six hungry persons!

Fruited Tuna Dish-Up

two 6½-oz. cans tuna
2 T. dry onion (chopped)
1 c. celery (sliced)
1 large green pepper (sliced)
1 T. curry powder
¼ t. ginger
1 t. salt
one 14-oz. can pineapple chunks
1 can cream of mushroom soup
1 T. lemon juice
cooked rice

Drain oil from tuna and retain in saucepan. Add onion, celery, and green pepper. Sauté. Stir in curry powder, ginger, and salt. Drain syrup from pineapple and measure 1 c. Add syrup to soup and stir until smooth. Bring to a boil (stirring) and add lemon juice, pineapple, and tuna. Dish over hot rice and serve with orange gelatin salad, bread sticks, and Tomato Soup Cake.

Ham Elégante

12 thick slices ham (leftover or canned)

Glaze:
½ c. catsup
juice and rind (grated of one orange
½ c. brown sugar
1 T. prepared mustard
⅓ c. pineapple juice
whole cloves

Place ham on oven-proof platter (overlapping edges). Prepare glaze and spoon over ham, making sure all slices are covered. Stick a whole clove in middle of each slice and pop under broiler. Broil about 10 minutes (checking to make sure ham does not burn). Serve with Minute Cherry Sauce (below).

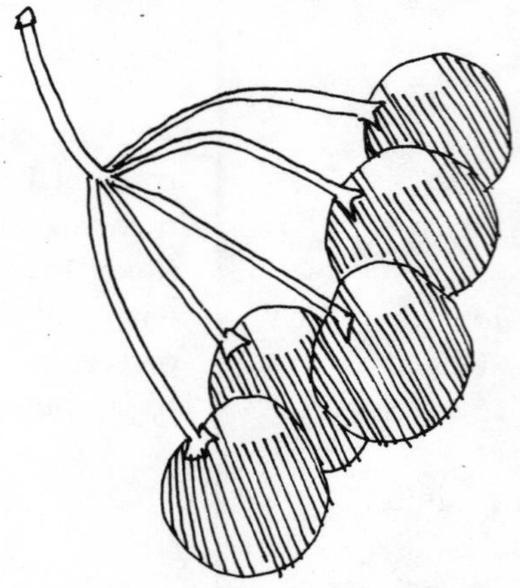

Minute Cherry Sauce

1 can cherry-pie filling
½ c. white raisins (plumped 5 minutes in hot water)
1 T. brandy flavoring

Heat filling but do not boil. Add drained raisins and flavoring. Spoon enough sauce over ham to make it elegant. Serve remainder in individual side dishes. Bring on the yams and sautéed bananas!

California Make-Ahead Lasagna

½ lb. large noodles
1 lb. lean ground meat
two 8-oz. cans tomato sauce
1 c. cottage cheese
one 8-oz. pkg. cream cheese
one 8 oz. carton sour cream
⅓ c. green onions and blades (minced)
1 T. green pepper (chopped)
1 t. oregano
1 T. margarine
1 c. jack cheese (grated)

Cook noodles according to directions on package. Drain. Brown meat, drain, and add tomato sauce. Combine cottage cheese, cream cheese, sour cream, onions, green pepper, and oregano. Spread half the noodles in 2-qt. greased baking dish. Cover with cottage cheese mixture. Add remaining noodles. Dot with margarine. Add meat sauce and top with grated cheese. Refrigerate 1 hour or overnight. Advance preparation is the shortcut trick that makes a company-good meal possible in 20 minutes! Oven should be 350°.

Quick-Chick Divan

2 c. instant rice
2 c. boiling water
two 10-oz. pkgs. frozen broccoli (chopped)
1 c. mayonnaise
¾ c. plain cheese spread (Cheese Whiz, etc.)
2 c. cold chicken (chopped)
1 T. lemon juice
1 can cream of celery soup
1 can cream of chicken soup
½ c. almonds (chopped)

Cook instant rice in 2 c. boiling water (no salt or fat). Turn off as directed on package and set aside. Cook broccoli according to instructions. Fold in mayonnaise and set aside. Stir cheese spread into hot rice and place one layer on bottom of greased casserole; spread with 1 c. chicken. Add lemon juice to celery soup. Heat and pour over chicken. Add broccoli mixture. Add remaining chicken and rest of rice. Heat chicken soup and pour over entire casserole. Sprinkle with almonds. May be frozen at this point. Bake only long enough to heat to bubbly stage, and serve hot with hard rolls, Cheese Stuffed Onions, carrot and black raisin salad, and brandied peaches (peach halves sprinkled with sugar and brandy or brandy flavoring and broiled about 5 minutes).

Easter Eggs

6 boiled eggs (shelled)
1/4 c. milk
1 t. salt
1 T. catsup
1 lb. seasoned sausage (bulk)
1 c. cornflakes (crushed)
1/2 t. coarse black pepper
additional catsup

Mix salt and pepper into sausage and divide mixture into 6 equal parts. Flatten mounds and place 1 egg in each, gently squeezing meat to cover. Pour milk into bowl. Dip each egg in milk and roll in cornflakes. Place wrapped eggs in baking dish—not allowing them to touch—and bake at 400° for 30 minutes. Serve hot. Pass additional catsup sprinkled with snipped onion blades.

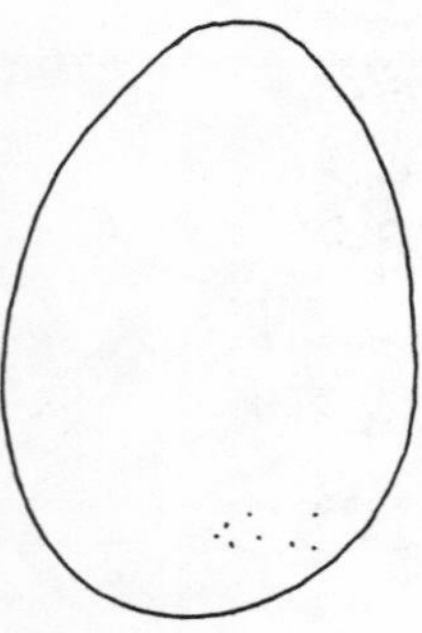

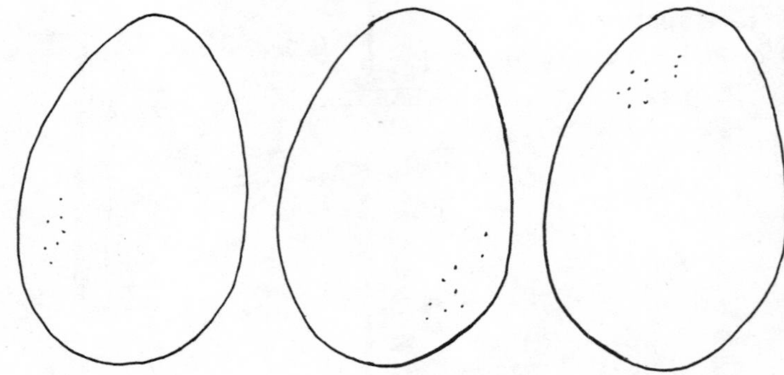

Scalloped Potatoes-on-the-Run

1 can cheddar cheese soup
dash of pepper
one 2 1/2-oz. jar mushroom pieces
1/2 c. milk
4 c. thinly sliced potatoes
1/2 c. grated onion

Blend soup, milk, pepper, and liquid from mushrooms. In a well-greased 1 1/2-qt. casserole arrange alternate layers of potatoes, soup, onion, and mushroom in casserole. Now dot top with butter and sprinkle with paprika. Bake *covered* at 375° for 30 minutes. Uncover and bake an additional 15 minutes. Goes well with any meat dish, may serve as main dish, or is a man-pleaser served with cold ham salad!

Excellent with fresh fish. Try this new approach: "Bread" fish fillets with sesame seeds and oatmeal. For a no-guilt sauce, mix tomato juice with a touch of lemon juice and parsley. Add a pinch of artificial sweetener.

Aloha Sweet-Sour Chicken

1/2 c. flour
1 t. salt
1/4 t. pepper
two 2-lb. frying chickens
1/3 c. salad oil
3 T. brown sugar
1 T. Worcestershire sauce
1 T. soy sauce
1/2 c. vinegar
1/3 c. sweet cucumber relish
1 T. catsup
1 c. water chestnuts (sliced)

Combine flour, salt, and pepper. For easier coating, place mixture in brown bag and drop cut-up chicken inside. Shake well and brown in hot oil, using heavy skillet. Lay chicken in 13″ x 9″ x 2″ baking dish and cover with sauce made by combining remaining ingredients except chestnuts. Drop chestnuts at random and bake *covered* at 350° for 1 1/2 hours. Baste and continue baking uncovered 15 minutes. Spoon sauce from bottom over chicken before serving. Recipe doubles nicely. Freeze ahead for a quick Hawaiian chicken dinner.

Meatball Stew

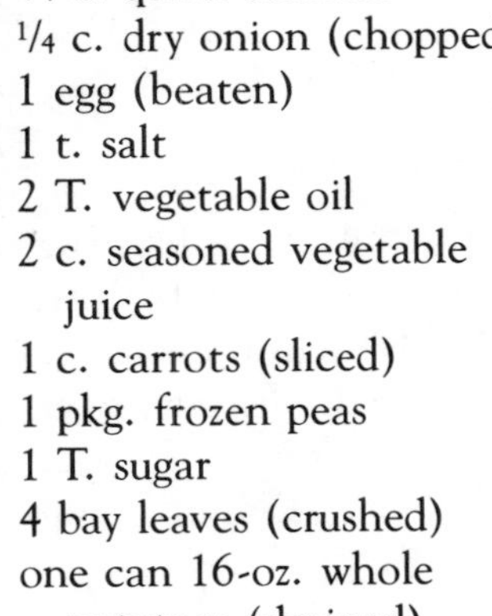

1 lb. lean ground meat
1/4 c. quick oatmeal
1/4 c. dry onion (chopped)
1 egg (beaten)
1 t. salt
2 T. vegetable oil
2 c. seasoned vegetable juice
1 c. carrots (sliced)
1 pkg. frozen peas
1 T. sugar
4 bay leaves (crushed)
one can 16-oz. whole potatoes (drained)
2 T. flour
1/2 t. nutmeg

Mix meat, oatmeal, onion, egg, and salt. Shape into 12-16 meatballs. Brown in oil (pouring off fat). Add 1 1/2 c. vegetable juice, carrots, peas, sugar, and bay leaves. Cover and cook slowly 15 minutes. Add potatoes and cook 5 minutes more. Blend remaining juice with flour and nutmeg and add gradually, stirring constantly. Cook until thickened. Warms up well and keeps the secret!

Instant Souped-Up Casseroles

one 10-oz. can cream of celery soup
1½ c. turkey broth (see "Soups")
1½ c. instant rice (uncooked)
one 7-oz. can tuna (drained)
1 T. grated cheddar cheese
grated parsley

Prepare soup according to directions on package, substituting broth for water. When soup reaches a boil, stir in rice. Turn off heat, cover, and allow to stand 10 minutes. Flake tuna and stir into rice. Sprinkle cheese on top. Cover for 1 minute, garnish with parsley, and serve without baking! (Hint: Prepare in serving dish.)

Variations are endless! Try cream of asparagus soup with chopped Spam. Top with buttered croutons. Another day, try spring cream of vegetable soup and Vienna sausages, topped with grated jack cheese, on your family. Then there is creamed onion soup with minced clams. Top with Parmesan cheese and chopped chives, or cream of tomato soup with shrimp (top with whipped cream *just* before serving) or cream of chicken soup, or leftover turkey with a spoon of current jelly on top—you get the idea. Make up your individual spin-offs!

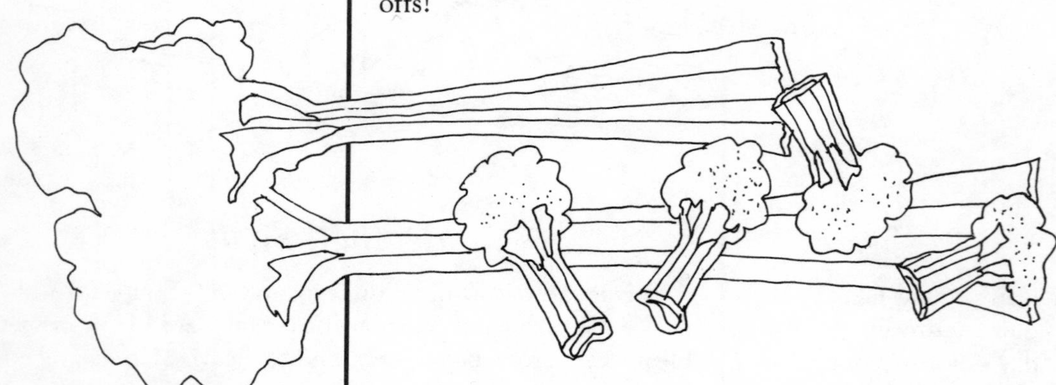

Peppery-Fondue Casserole

½ c. margarine
12 slices white bread (trimmed)
one 12-oz. can whole kernel corn (drained)
one 7-oz. can green chilies (seeded, cut in strips)
2 c. jack cheese (grated)
4 eggs (beaten)
3 c. milk
1 t. salt

Butter bread and cut slices in halves. Arrange half the bread in greased 3-qt. baking dish. Cover with half the corn topped with half the chilies. Sprinkle with half the cheese. Repeat layers. Combine eggs with milk and salt. Pour over casserole. Cover and refrigerate 4 hours or longer. Bake at 350° for 45 minutes until brown and poufed. Delicious and loves to be eaten hot!

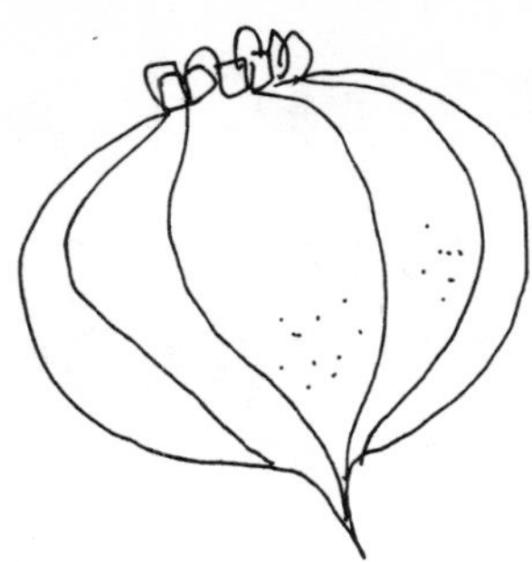

Cheese-Stuffed Onions

8 medium onions (peeled)
3/4 c. cottage cheese
1 T. pimiento (chopped)
1 T. green pepper (chopped)
1/2 c. cooked ham (cut in thin strips)
1/2 t. garlic salt
dash of pepper
1/2 c. cracker crumbs
paprika
1 can mushroom soup (undiluted)

Cook whole onions in boiling water until tender (no more than 20 minutes). Drain and chill. Carefully remove centers (leaving a 2-layer shell). Dice centers and combine with cottage cheese, pimiento and green peppers, ham strips, garlic salt, and black pepper. Stuff onion shells and place in greased baking dish. Sprinkle with cracker crumbs and add a dash of paprika. Surround onions with soup (do not cover tops) and bake at 350° for 15 minutes in covered dish. Uncover and allow onions to brown.

*Are you a sole-purpose cook or a **soul**-purpose cook? The taste may tattle.*

Butter Beans Au Gratin

two 10-oz. pkgs. frozen butter beans
3 T. flour
2 c. cottage cheese
1/2 t. salt
1/4 t. white pepper
1/2 t. Worcestershire sauce
2 t. sugar
1/4 c. dry onion (grated)
1/2 c. jack cheese (grated)
1 T. butter or margarine

Cook beans as directed. Drain. Mix and stir in flour and 1 c. cottage cheese. Add salt, pepper, Worcestershire, sugar, and onion; mix well. Fold in remaining cottage cheese. Sprinkle cheese on top, dot with butter, and bake uncovered at 350° for 30 minutes or until golden good!

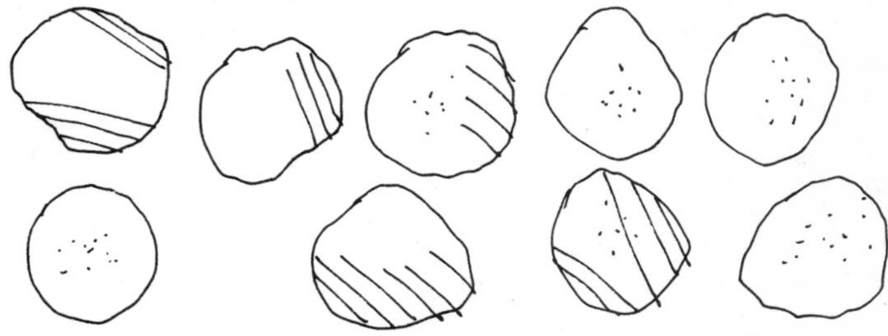

WHEN THE MAN OF THE HOUSE GOES ON KITCHEN PATROL

Easy Goulash

1 lb. lean ground meat
salt and pepper
1 can spaghetti (Franco-American, etc.)
1 medium onion (chopped)
1 can red kidney beans
1 t. Worcestershire sauce

Salt and pepper meat. Brown in hot skillet and drain off fat. Add spaghetti, onions, beans, and Worcestershire. Heat through and serve hot. "Come and get it!"

Soupy-Jo's

1 lb. ground lean meat
1 large onion (chopped)
1/2 t. black pepper
1 can vegetable soup (undiluted)
4-6 hamburger bun halves (toasted)
1 c. yellow cheese (grated)

Brown meat, onion, and pepper, in heavy skillet. Drain. Add soup and heat. Serve piping hot over buns topped with cheese. *Encore!*

Minute Rarebit
(Welsh Rabbit)

1 can cream of tomato soup
1 c. milk
1 T. cornstarch
1/2 t. black pepper
1 T. sugar
1 t. Worcestershire sauce
4-6 eggs
English muffins
6 slices American cheese

Combine soup with milk. Blend. Mix cornstarch, pepper, sugar, and Worcestershire sauce. Moisten with some of the soup mixture and add to soup. Bring to a boil (stirring). Break eggs into the soup, being careful not to break yolks, cover, and reduce heat. Allow eggs to "set" to desired consistency. Place each egg on a toasted and buttered English muffin. Lay a top of cheese on each and spoon hot soup mixture over.

Tacos

$1^1/_2$ lbs. lean ground meat
salt and pepper
1 can refried beans
1 pkg. prepared taco shells
2 tomatoes (peeled and sliced)
1 small carton sour cream
shredded lettuce
1 large onion (diced)
1 c. sharp yellow cheese (shredded)

Brown meat, adding salt and pepper to taste. Add beans. Keep warm while heating taco shells in oven. Place about 1 T. meat-and-bean mixture inside each shell. Add a slice of tomato and a bit of sour cream. Add lettuce and onion to fill shell, being careful not to break shells. Sprinkle with shredded cheese and serve hot, toasty, and dripping!

The entire family can have fun with tacos. Let some members shred and some stir. Form an assembly line when ready to stuff the shells. Listen to the laughter (and complaints of shortages!).

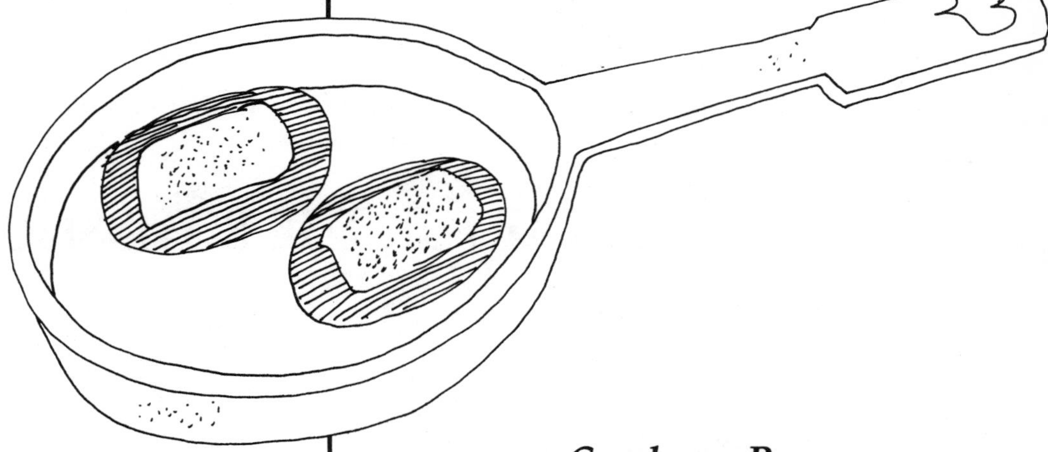

Cranberry Burgers

$1^1/_2$–2 lbs. ground meat
1 T. prepared mustard
salt and pepper to taste
2 T. catsup
jellied cranberry sauce
hamburger buns

Combine first four ingredients. Shape into very thin patties. Place 1 t. jellied cranberry sauce on one patty and top with a second round of meat. Brown quickly in heavy skillet. Serve on toasted buns with an additional spoonful of sauce on top of each patty.

Burgers-on-a-Stick

Cranberry Burger ground meat mixture
onion slices
cherry tomatoes

Shape meat mixture from previous recipe into balls and thread onto skewers with alternate onion slices and cherry tomatoes. Broil about 5 minutes on each side. Everybody's favorite!

GREAT FOR THE GRILL

Beef: Steaks of all kinds—ground for hamburgers, cubed for kabobs, or man-size steaks.

Pork and ham: Chops, tenderloin, Canadian bacon, canned ham, fully cooked ham slice, spareribs, or back ribs.

Lamb: Chops (cubed for kabobs or else ground), ribs.

Miscellaneous meats: Frankfurters and other sausages, luncheon meats, etc.

Poultry: Chicken (halves, quarters, pieces), small turkey pieces, Cornish hen halves.

Fish and seafood: Whole, fillets, or steaks; lobster; lobster tails; shrimp, scallops, and oysters.

(Pass the hot rolls, corn-on-the-cob, and all kinds of sauces!)

GREAT FOR THE ROTISSERIE

Beef: Rib roasts; rolled rump roast; tip roast cubed for kabobs.

Pork and ham: Boneless fresh pork roasts, smoked boneless ham, spareribs, Canadian bacon.

Veal: Boned and rolled roasts (shoulder, sirloin, leg).

Lamb: Boned and rolled roasts, rib roast.

Miscellaneous meats: Bologna (whole or sliced) and other sausages.

Poultry: Chicken, small turkey, Cornish hens.

(Bring on the baked potatoes, green salad, and condiments!)

NOTE: Grilling is the quickest way to cook over charcoal or wood fire. Almost any cut of meat is suitable for broiling, panbroiling, or panfrying. Rotisseries are ideal when the main course of your outdoor meal is to be roasted. Either method will spice the air with nostalgia!

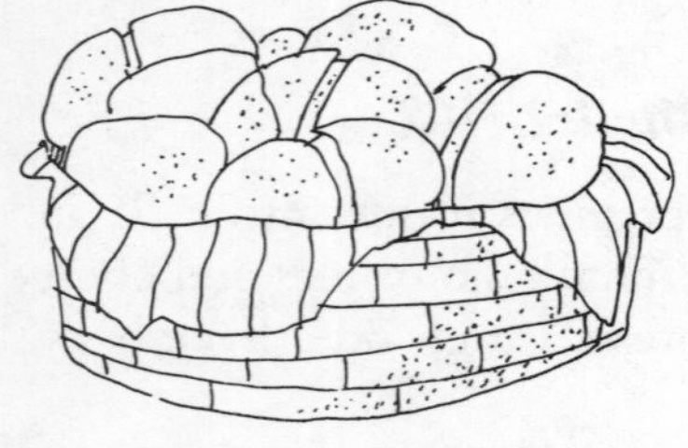

EATING "OUT"—OUTSIDE, THAT IS!

Perhaps it's a throwback to our ancestors—those who enlarged the New World. The route was new, the territory unknown and untamed. The mythical stories soon became a vivid reality of breathtaking sunsets, wild adventures, and deepening friendships with each gathering around a meal prepared over an open fire.

There's still something that stirs the blood about a meal prepared over glowing coals of a barbecue fire. It doesn't matter whether food is cooked on an inexpensive grill or a complicated rotisserie—it's a feast for happy diners when handled simply. (And do plan group singing, hopefully to the accompaniment of a stringed instrument, as meat cooks over fire that sends up smoke signals of goodness-to-come!)

VEGETABLES

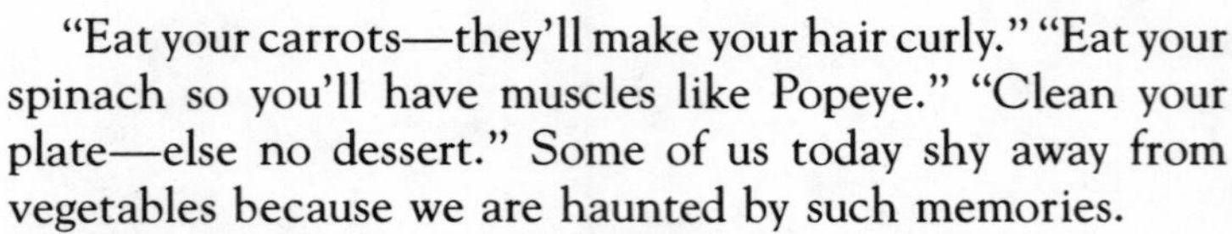

"Eat your carrots—they'll make your hair curly." "Eat your spinach so you'll have muscles like Popeye." "Clean your plate—else no dessert." Some of us today shy away from vegetables because we are haunted by such memories.

But now we can have snappy green beans with bacon bits, candied carrots, and all your other favorite vegetables throughout the year instead of waiting for gardens to "come in" (and then growing tired of the monotony). There are fresh vegetables, canned vegetables, and frozen vegetables. And in that corner (once hidden beneath a slice of bread!) which the vegetables occupied on the dinner plate you will find such delicacies that you rush to them as you once rushed for dessert.

It's all in the preparation! Just as one glorifies ice cream with toppings, a creative "kitchen engineer" can top off the vegetables by using the same method. An alternative is creaming, combining, or "saucing."

QUICK FIX for those who "hate vegetables": Sprinkle with chopped walnuts, pecans, or almonds; or go exotic by using cashews or macadamias (and most children adore peanuts). For a change, grate cheese (any kind or try combining them) over the top of steaming vegetables. Toss crisp croutons on top. And here's a secret ingredient that every vegetable snuggles up to: *sugar*! Sprinkle a bit of brown sugar on top of such vegetables as winter squash, yams, and carrots (if you have no time to candy or caramelize); but, in addition, add just a whisper of sugar to *any* kind of vegetable during the cooking.

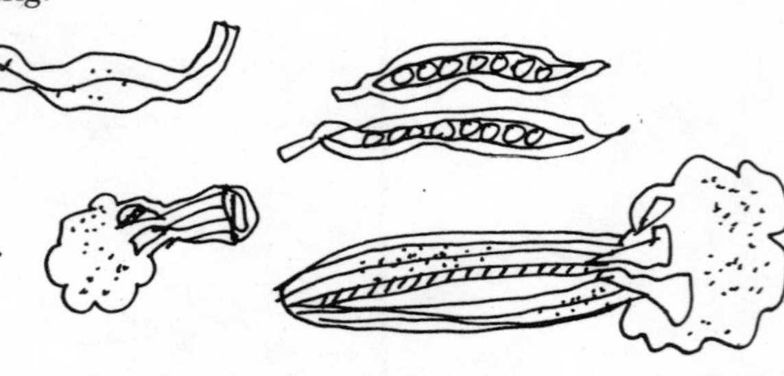

To cream, use your favorite cream sauce; or why not take advantage of the canned soups available? And bear in mind that creaming can play two roles: It can change the mundane to the spectacular, and it can stretch a dish when an extra guest drops in.

And, oh, those combos! They are meal-savers:

- Corn and green peas
- Cauliflower and green peas
- Little pearl onions and green peas
- Mushroom and green peas
- Carrots and green peas
- Acorn squash rings and green peas

See what you can do with peas? But man does not live by peas alone (unless brought up during the depression years down South!). So launch out and see what you can do with brussels sprouts and carrot slices (call them "coins" to spark children's appetites!); okra and tomatoes; green limas in acorn squash halves; and simply combining red and green cabbage (cooked separately before putting together).

The ideas for sauces are endless. Try sunshine sauce for asparagus and artichokes, by adding lemon juice, finely chopped onion, and sweet relish to mayonnaise. Or what about mustard sauce for any members of the bean family? Make by blending 1/2 c. salad dressing with 1 t. prepared mustard and 1 T. cream; season with a sift of garlic. Sprinkle top with paprika for color. Experiment with catsup mixtures (an all-American favorite) or choose from the countless bottled sauces available.

Other ways of making sure we get our daily vitamins is to use vegetables in omelets, stews, and casseroles. And if you want something truly different to top the casseroles, try cereal topping. It's so easy to stir together 1/2 c. crushed cornflakes, 1 T. margarine (melted), and a dash of salt. Good for the fresh casserole and a great disguise for leftovers. Yields 1/2 c. For variations, stir in 1/8 t. marjoram to topping, or 1/4 t. oregano. Another way to enhance the mixture is by adding 1/4 t. sage and 1 t. mustard.

Vegetables need no longer be dreary. They can stop the show with applause!

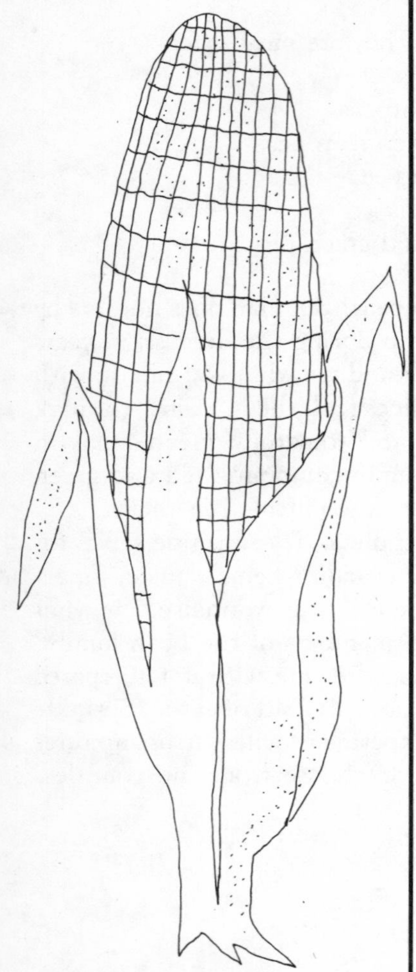

And then there is corn! Oh, those golden ears of corn-on-the cob, drowning in butter . . . those side dishes of creamed corn peppered with hot green chilies and garnished with bright strands of pimiento . . . and whole-kernel corn prepared to your liking. Rich in carbohydrates, it serves as a nice departure from potatoes and pastas.

But there is more. We want to take a good look at cornmeal. Primarily peasant food and the gruels and porridges that filled European stomachs, cornmeal now refuses to be snubbed. Always a staple in the Colonies and following the trail of the pioneers into the South, cornmeal now stars in the menus of some of the most highly regarded restaurants in the country, from New York to San Francisco. So, while fresh corn continues to be the epitome of late-summer eating in, eating out, or entertaining, it is fashionable now to include grits, hush puppies, cornbread sticks, and something called *polenta* (a classy name for cornmeal mush!). The story does not end there, either. Using cornmeal, Americans have developed elegant, soufflé-like spoonbreads and savory Indian puddings (so called not because it was a native early-American dish but because it used "Indian" meal), spiced with ginger and molasses.

If you hail from the Southern states and grew up on black-eyed peas, okra, and hot cornbread, you have an advantage. Now you (and I!) can order *polenta* (and some of its relatives) and be considered "in the know." We will forgive those who think it is a hot new item!

Another memory for some people goes back to the days when farmers' wives used eggs as their medium of exchange at the country store. What did the hens eat? Money was in short supply, so they dined on:

Egg-Producing Mash

300 lbs. yellow cornmeal
100 lbs. each—middlings, oats, and whole bran
1 pt. to each lb. cod liver oil
8 lbs. iodized salt
50 lbs. each—alfalfa meal, fish meal, meat scraps, and dried buttermilk
20 lbs. each—oyster shell and bone meal

Herbs and Spices

Grandmother's Pinch-and-a-Dab Seasoning Secrets

Every noble life leaves the fiber of it interwoven forever in the work of the world.

—Ruskin

And so it is with herbs in food. Herbs can elevate the most ordinary recipe to high places, leaving fond memories stamped indelibly on the tongue of the diner—but discreetly so, if the chef is wise. Herbs, like the color red, go a long way. Begin with less than you know you need, especially with dried herbs. Taste. Too delicate? You can add more with just a shake of the container. Even then, shake cautiously.

Herbs, coming from bark, root, fruits, or berries of plants (first wild, then domesticated, with many imported), have been around for a long time. Leaves and stems of both annual and perennial shrubs are used also.

Of all the herbs, saffron appears to be finding more favor among creative chefs these days. But it is not new. Always prominent in Middle Eastern, Asian, and European cooking, saffron (an expensive, exotic spice dating back to ancient times) is sprouting up on trendy dishes all over the America.

What does it do? The delicately flavored spice is as useful for its brilliant yellow color as for its subtle flavor. And don't let the price scare you. It's expensive by the ounce, but most recipes require only a few threads. Saffron turns corn to instant gold and lifts the pale mushroom from the doldrums with a sunny blush. Until recently one found the colorful, aromatic herb mostly in Scandinavian breads and teas. But now it is coloring and flavoring rice and white potato dishes as well as soups, pastas, butter sauces, and even desserts.

Saffron's home is Spain (70% of our source). Known as "red gold," the red threads (stamens) are removed by hand from the saffron rose (a purple night-blooming rose) and then roasted yellow. You can still buy the threads, but it also comes in powder ready for Mexican dishes, black-eyed peas, and so much else.

HERBS AND SPICES AND SOME SUGGESTED USES

	Allspice	*Basil*	*Chili Powder*
Soups, Stews, and Sauces	Potato soup Oyster stew Barbecue sauce Brown sauce Tomato sauces	Manhattan clam chowder Tomato soup Vegetable soup Beef stew	Pea soup Beef stew Chili con carne Cheese sauce Gravy
Fish, Poultry, and Game	Poached fish Chicken fricassee	Crabmeat Fish Shrimp Tuna Fried chicken	Shrimp Barbecued chicken Fried chicken
Meats and Main Dishes	Ham Meatballs Meat loaf Pot roasts	Beef Lamb Pork Pizza Spaghetti	Hamburgers Meat loaf
Vegetables	Eggplant Parsnips Spinach Squash Turnips	Asparagus Green beans Squash Tomatoes Wax beans	Cauliflower Corn Lima beans Onions Peas
Salads and Salad Dressings	Cabbage Cottage cheese Fruit	Tomato aspic Cucumber Seafood Tomato French dressing Russian dressing	Cottage cheese Potato French dressing Guacamole
Desserts	Chiffon pie Fruitcake Mince pie Pumpkin pie Steamed pudding Tapioca pudding	Fruit compotes	
Miscellaneous	Egg dishes Coffee cakes Sweet rolls Cranberry sauce	Creamed eggs Omelets Soufflés Seafood cocktails	Cheese fondue Scrambled eggs Welsh rabbit Biscuits French bread

	Cinnamon	*Cloves*	*Ginger*
Soups Stews, and Sauces	Fruit soup Beef stew	Bean soup Onion soup Pea soup Tomato sauces	Bean soup Onion soup Potato soup Cocktail sauces
Fish, Poultry, and Game	Sweet-sour shrimp Stewed chicken	Baked fish Chicken à la king Roast chicken	Fish Roast chicken Roast Cornish hens Roast duckling
Meats and Main Dishes	Ham Pork chops Sauerbraten	Corned Beef Ham Tongue Baked beans	Beef roasts Beef steaks Baked beans
Vegetables	Carrots Onions Spinach Squash Sweet potatoes	Beets Carrots Onions Squash Sweet potatoes	Beets Carrots Squash Sweet potatoes
Salads and Salad Dressings	Fruit	Spiced fruit Fruit salad dressings	French dressing Fruit salad dressings
Desserts	Apple desserts Chocolate pudding Fruit compotes Rice pudding	Applesauce Chocolate cake Chocolate sauce Gingerbread Pears	Broiled grapefruit Pears Steamed pudding Stewed dried fruit
Miscellaneous	Biscuits Nut bread Sweet rolls Tea, coffee Chocolate	Coffee cakes Nut bread Sweet rolls Fruit punch	Macaroni and cheese Rice dishes Cookies Nut bread

	Mace	*Marjoram*	*Nutmeg*
Soups, Stews, and Sauces	Vegetable soup Oyster stew Veal stew	Chicken soup Onion soup Potato soup Brown sauce Gravy	Oyster stew
Fish, Poultry, and Game	Baked fish Shrimp creole Chicken fricassee	Salmon loaf Shellfish Chicken Turkey Venison	Fish Fried chicken
Meats and Main Dishes	Meatballs Meat loaf Veal	Beef Hamburgers Lamb Pork Veal	Meatballs Meat loaf Pot roast
Vegetables	Broccoli Brussels sprouts Cabbage Succotash	Celery Eggplant Greens Potatoes Zucchini	Beans Carrots Cauliflower Corn Onions
Salads and Salad Dressings	Fruit	Chicken Eggs Greens Seafood	
Desserts			Apple pie Custards Pumpkin pie Vanilla ice cream
Miscellaneous	Quiche Lorraine Welsh rabbit Banana bread Doughnuts	Omelets Scrambled eggs Soufflés Fruit juice	Coffee cakes Nut bread Sweet rolls

	Oregano	*Sage*	*Thyme*
Soups, Stews, and Sauces	Beef soup Bouillon Stews Butter sauces Mushroom sauce	Chicken soup Consommé Tomato soup Stews Cheese sauces	Borscht Clam chowder Stews Bordelaise sauce
Fish, Poultry, and Game	Broiled fish Shellfish Chicken Pheasant	Fish Chicken Duckling Turkey Poultry stuffing	Tuna Fried chicken Roast chicken Poultry stuffing
Meats and Main Dishes	Hamburgers Liver Swiss steak Veal Pizza Spaghetti	Cold roast beef Lamb Pork Veal	Roasts
Vegetables	Broccoli Cabbage Mushrooms Onions Tomatoes	Brussels sprouts Eggplant Lima beans Squash Tomatoes	Artichokes Carrots Green beans Mushrooms Peas Potatoes
Salads and Salad Dressings	Egg Seafood Vegetables	Chicken French dressing	Chicken Cottage cheese Greens Tomatoes Tomato aspic
Desserts			Custards
Miscellaneous	Boiled eggs Egg sandwich spread Guacamole dip Cheese spreads	Cheese fondue Omelets Biscuits Corn bread Hot milk Tea	Omelets Scrambled eggs Soufflés Biscuits Corn bread

Do you like your herbs fresh—*really* fresh? Then grow your own. The experience will enrich your life as much as the fresh flavor enriches your recipes. And what a conversation piece: "Come see my garden"!

Pots of herbs occupying just a few square feet of space in the shade of your house, patio, outside balcony, or deck bring year-round freshness right to your tables. Better yet, try your windowsill!

Here are a few prime herbs for lovers of French, Mexican, and Oriental food (assuming that you know how to tend members of the onion family—chives, garlic, etc.—as well as watercress):

Basil: Seeds sprout quickly in warmth. Transplant at 2-leaf stage singly into 4″ pots (or one flat pan). Use rich, loose mix, and give plants a warm, bright place for sunning.

Chervil: Sow seeds thinly over rich soil mix in 8″ or 9″ pot. Thin when plants make true leaves (thinnings are good to eat, too!). Allow 4 or 5 plants to grow. If you really like chervil, transplant a month later to prolong season.

Coriander: Sow the big seeds thinly, and thin the plants as you do for chervil. Coriander (also called cilantro and Chinese parsley) matures fast and is quickly spent, so replant at monthly intervals. (TIP: If you are unable to find coriander seed in packets, use the seed from your spice shelf—easier to find and cheaper than packets anyway.)

Tarragon: The seed is useless, so dig a plant from your garden or beg one from a friend. Shake soil from roots, trim tops, shorten rhizomes (peculiar root system) to fit in 6″ to 8″ pot. Plant in rich mix and watch it grow!

Chives: Chives, bless them, grow outside in mild-winter regions. Where cold freezes them to the ground, dig clumps and plant in 4″ to 6″ pots. No outside garden? You will find potted clumps in grocery stores. They are easy to grow from seed, too, so you can share unique gifts with guests.

Dill: Sow like chervil. Dill is happiest in a sunny but cool place. Make frequent sowings if you really like dill. It sprouts and grows easily.

Summer savory: Sow seeds like chervil. Plants grow quickly. Pinch out tops to make plants bush (and, of course, make use of the tips). The flavor resembles oregano. Wonderful in fresh green beans.

Breads

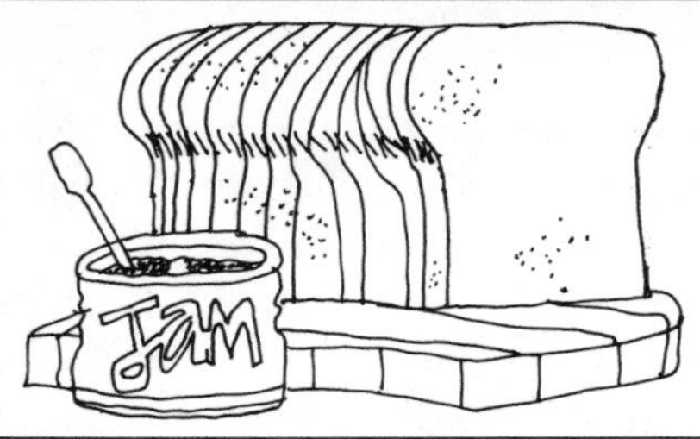

Lovin' from the Oven

Bread is the staff of life. Is anything more sustaining? Did anything in the world smell quite as tantalizing to childhood nostrils as a brown-crusted loaf of just-baked bread? And does anything bring more sense of achievement than pulling yeasty loaves you've just made from the oven? Is there a sight more beautiful than lined-up loaves of crusty bread? And, oh, the incomparable goodness of the oven-fresh "heel" that Grandmother let us butter and sample!

Homemade breads are back "in" these days. It is possible to do more than remember. We can rediscover the pleasures of baking—and even improve the methods—if we use mixes and shortcuts available now. There are new, improved techniques and ingredients that streamline the project yet retain that grandmother-goodness. Be cautious, however, about the liberties you take. Be prudent in regard to the basic ingredients: *1) add nothing to speed up the action of the yeast; 2) do not increase the flour, sugar, or salt called for (it toughens the dough)*; and *3) remember that all ingredients should be room temperature for "Grandma-good" results!*

Give us day by day our daily bread.
Luke 11:3

Basically, breads fall into two main categories: accompaniments to the meal and main dishes (with the addition of other ingredients). Each category has its variables. There are yeast breads and so-called "quick breads" using soda or baking powder as a leavening agent. There are corn breads, muffins of all kinds, waffles and loaf breads, to name a few. And, with a bit of planning, some of them become desserts!

And remember that with these quick yeast bread recipes you can be creative. Put your spin-off know-how to use. You can turn your favorite basic recipes into almost anything with the use of toppings and shapings. For example, a basic yeast bread becomes the makings of cinnamon rolls when flattened and sprinkled with a mixture of sugar, butter, and spice, then

rolled up jelly-roll fashion, and sliced, and baked. Make braids by dividing recipe into three equal parts. Roll into strands and braid. Top with poppy seed mixed with 2 T. honey . . . sprinkle with cinnamon, brown sugar, and chopped raisins . . . decorate with chopped fruit mix . . . or make into garlic bread by topping with 1 T. garlic cheese . . . now, try others.

Try your hand at baking breads. You'll never regret it, and others will never forget it! And it no longer takes all day.

The Judeo-Christian's first cookbook was the Holy Bible. "In the beginning" was the Garden. Later the Mosaic Law differentiated between the clean and unclean foods. Then there were the leavened and the unleavened breads . . . the herbs . . . and so much more to point (literally and figuratively) to the importance of "breaking bread" together.

Thirty-Minute Cloverleaf Rolls
(that used to take all day)

- 1 pkg. dry yeast
- 1¼ c. warm water
- ½ c. sugar
- ¼ t. salt
- 2 eggs (unbeaten)
- 3 c. flour
- ¼ t. cinnamon (optional)
- 2 T. cooking oil

Dissolve yeast in water in large bowl. Sift in sugar and salt. Beat in eggs one at a time. Add flour gradually (sifted with the cinnamon, if desired). Beat with mixer or vigorously by hand with wooden spoon. Add cooking oil and mix well. Butter hands and shape dough into marble-size balls. Place in muffin tins (three to each cup) and press down gently. Let rise in warm place for 30 minutes. Bake at 400° for 15-20 minutes until brown.

Mashed Potato Rolls

- 1 yeast cake
- 1 c. milk (scalded)
- 2 eggs
- 1/2 c. sugar
- 1 t. salt (unless potatoes are salted)
- 2/3 c. margarine (melted)
- 1 c. cold mashed potatoes (leftover or instant)
- 5 c. flour

Add yeast to milk (scalded and cooled slightly). Beat in eggs. Add sugar (and salt if used) and melted margarine. Add potatoes and mix. Sift in 4 1/2 c. flour, reserving 1/2 c. for kneading. Knead lightly only until mixed, using the 1/2 c. of reserved flour to dust hands and kneading surface and reduce stickiness of dough. Shape into a ball and let rise in large bowl in warm place 2 hours. Shape into rolls and bake at 400° for 15 minutes.

Make-and-Store Snowflakes

- 1 pkg. yeast
- 5 T. warm water
- 3/4 c. margarine
- 5 c. flour (sifted)
- 5 t. baking powder
- 3 T. sugar
- 2 t. salt
- 1 t. soda
- 2 c. buttermilk

Dissolve yeast in water. Set aside while blending margarine with all dry ingredients sifted together. Add buttermilk to yeast mixture. Pour into dry mixture slowly, mixing to make a stiff dough. Cover and store in refrigerator. Pinch off dough as needed to make into flake-biscuits. Shape into balls, flatten, and lay on greased baking sheet. Place in *cold* oven! Set temperature at 450° and bake until biscuits are high and golden (about 15 minutes). As oven heats, biscuits will rise and shine! Refrigerated dough keeps 2 weeks.

A quick way to make a quick meal (and a quick hit!) is to make use of pop-in-the-oven biscuits for ***any meal****. Close your eyes and visualize: Golden, high-rise biscuits with Southern fried chicken . . . piping hot, buttered biscuits with Virginia baked ham . . . with scrambled eggs and steaming coffee as an eye-opening breakfast . . . drop biscuits, cut-out biscuits, (you name it) with salads . . .*

And the good news is that you need not think of biscuit dough as "bread alone." Add a bit of sugar and pat it into mounds for fruit shortcakes. Roll it thin for chicken, turkey, meat, or tuna pies. Or cut it into strips and make a batch of delectable chicken and dumplings. Things go better with biscuits!

Cornbread Sticks

- 2/3 c. white corn meal (may use yellow)
- 1/2 t. salt
- 2 t. baking powder
- 1/3 c. flour
- 1/4 t. soda
- 1 T. sugar
- 1/2 c. milk
- 1 egg (beaten)
- 2 T. margarine (melted)

Sift together dry ingredients. Add milk gradually and beat in egg. Mix. Oil cornbread stick pans and heat oven to 450°. Just before setting pans in oven, add margarine to mixture. Mix well. Bake 10-15 minutes to a light brown, being careful not to overbake.

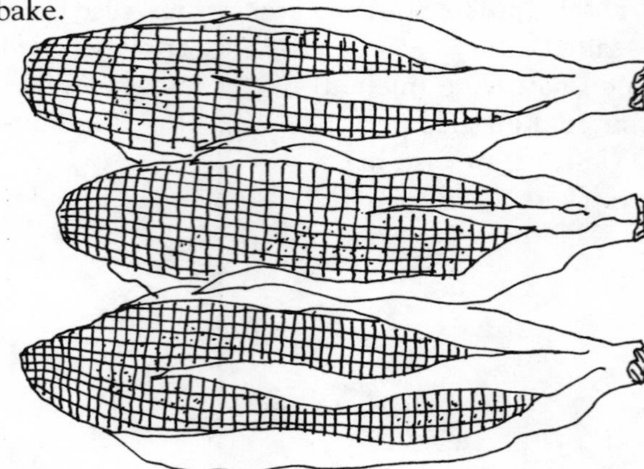

Marjorie's blackberry jelly! Aunt Lulu's apricot conserve! Remember those shelves crowded with shining glasses and jars of preserved fruit? You can do it in a jiffy now with all the pectin, fresh fruit, and canned juices available. And there's a sense of satisfaction that comes with being able to say (without saying so!): "You are important to me, so I made this for you!" Try our Lime-Peach Conserve.

Lime-Peach Conserve

- 4 c. peeled and chopped fresh peaches
- 1 t. grated lime peel
- 1/4 c. fresh lime juice
- 1 pkg. (1 3/4 oz.) powdered fruit pectin
- 5 c. sugar
- 1/2 c. golden raisins
- 1/2 c. slivered almonds

Combine peaches, peel, lime juice, and pectin in large pan. Bring to rolling boil (one which cannot be stirred down), stirring constantly. Add sugar and bring to boil again. Boil hard 1 minute (stirring constantly). Stir in raisins and almonds after removing from heat. Skim and ladle into clean glass containers. May be refrigerated, frozen, or sealed with melted paraffin for later use.

Beaten Buttermilk Biscuits

2 c. sifted flour
2 *heaping* t. baking powder
1/2 t. salt
2/3 c. buttermilk
1/2 c. cooking oil

Sift flour, baking powder, and salt together (notice there is *no* soda!). Make a well and add buttermilk. Beat vigorously with spoon. Turn onto lightly floured board and roll out with floured rolling pin (no need to knead!). Use small cookie cutter for cutting.

Heat cooking oil. Dip biscuits individually on top and bottom sides (working quickly). Place on ungreased cookie sheet with space between for brown and crusty look (or touching if brown tops and light sides are desired). With these unusual biscuits, you will want to serve butter and:

Fig-Berry Jam

3 c. mashed fresh figs
3 c. sugar
1 large (or 2 small) packages strawberry gelatin dessert

Peel and mash fresh figs. Add sugar and strawberry gelatin dessert (unnecessary to heat). Allow to stand 30 minutes and then bring to rolling boil. Pour into jars and seal, or allow to cool and refrigerate. It's special!

Deliciously Quick Honey Buns

2 c. buttermilk biscuit mix
1/2 c. water
1/2 c. black walnuts (or other nuts), chopped
1/2 c. raisins (snipped)
3 T. honey
1/3 c. margarine (melted)
3 T. sugar
1/2 t. cinnamon

Add water to mix. Beat. Turn onto floured board and roll to rectangle about 12″ x 9″. Cut into 3″ squares. Mix together walnuts, raisins, and honey. Place 1 T. of mixture over each square and fold together four corners of each. Gently form each into a ball. Dip into melted margarine and place on ungreased cookie sheet, not allowing buns to touch. Bake at 400° for 12-15 minutes or until light brown. While buns bake, mix sugar with cinnamon. Remove buns from oven, brush with leftover margarine, and roll individually in sugar and cinnamon mixture. Real pleasers, especially fresh from the oven. Makes 1 dozen. Feeds far fewer!

What a boon for the busy hostess! Those frozen and foil-wrapped loaves of nut bread, fruit bread, or both.

Peanut-Butter-and-Carrot Loaf

1 c. brown sugar (packed)
1/2 c. chunky peanut butter
1/4 c. salad oil
1 t. vanilla
2 eggs (beaten)
2 c. carrots (shredded)
3/4 c. flour
1 t. baking soda
1 t. baking powder
1/4 t. each allspice and nutmeg
1/2 t. salt
1/2 c. milk
1/2 c. raisins
1/2 c. nuts (chopped)

Beat with mixer (or vigorously by hand) sugar, peanut butter, oil, vanilla, and eggs. Fold in carrots. Sift together dry ingredients and add them alternately with milk. Add raisins and nuts. Pour into greased loaf pan and bake at 350° for 1 hour. Double-good!

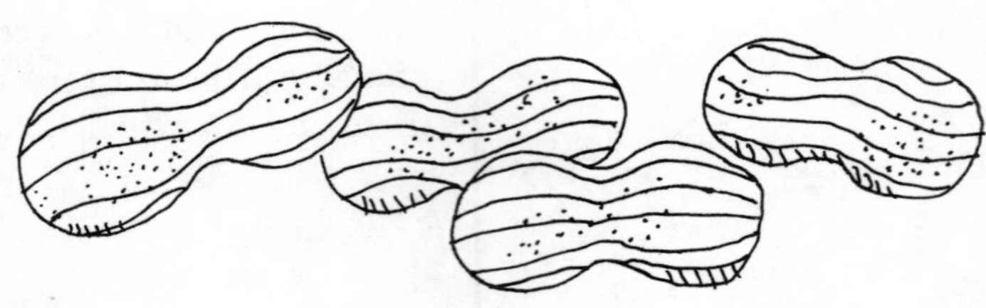

All-Kinds-of-Muffins Recipe

1 egg
1/2 c. milk
1/4 c. salad oil
2 c. all-purpose flour or 1 c. wheat flour (reducing baking powder to 3/4 t.)
1/2 c. sugar
2 t. baking powder
1/2 t. salt

Blend all ingredients and bake in greased muffin cups (or muffin tins lined with waxed-paper cups). Bake 25 minutes at 400°. Makes a dozen.

To vary make:

Apple muffins by stirring in 1 c. grated apple with oil; 1/2 t. cinnamon with flour. Top with nut-crunch (1/3 c. each brown sugar and chopped nuts and 1/2 t. cinnamon). Spread on muffins *before* baking.

Blueberry muffins by folding in 1 c. fresh blueberries.

Cranberry-orange muffins by folding in 1 T. grated orange peel and 1 c. cranberries into batter.

Surprise muffins by filling tins half-full, then dropping in 1 t. jelly in center of each. Add batter to fill to 2/3. Serve *very* hot.

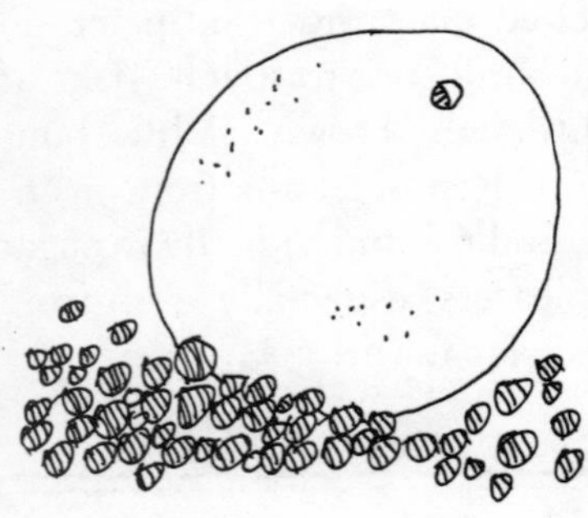

Wonderful thing about muffins—you can mix them from scratch in 2 minutes. Just dump ingredients in together and stir. Muffins cooperate! The bride, the seasoned cook, or the little girl who wants to lend a hand can pop them into the oven and ***know*** *that what pops out will be delectable—hot or day-old (split, buttered, and warmed under the broiler).*

And now our favorite because they are delicious, deliciously simple, and keep unbaked (refrigerated) six weeks—still delicious!

"Shaker" Bran Muffins

2 c. boiling water
6 c. whole-bran cereal
3 c. sugar
1 c. margarine
3 c. raisins
1 qt. buttermilk
4 eggs
5 c. sifted flour
1 t. salt
5 t. soda

Pour water over 2 c. cereal and set aside. Beat sugar, margarine, raisins, buttermilk, and eggs together. Fold dry ingredients and remaining 4 c. cereal into mixture. Add softened cereal. Mix only until dry ingredients are moistened. Cover and refrigerate. When ready to use, *do not stir*. Simply spoon into greased muffin tins or paper cups and bake at 400° for 20 minutes. We confess that nobody knows for sure how many muffins this wonderful old recipe makes. Nobody counts. Besides, many disappear as they come from the oven!

Cakes

Blue-Ribbon Memories

"LET THEM EAT CAKE!" Marie Antoinette said of the starving French peasants when they begged for bread. The flip remark went down in infamy but may well have led to what has become an American tradition. Given a choice, who would choose a slice of bread over a wedge of Aunt Het's chocolate layer cake, slathered with rich frosting? Coffee and cake . . . cake and ice cream . . . and what's a birthday without a candle-lighted cake? Cake is filling—and down-right comforting somehow. Maybe that's because, stored with our recipes, we hold tender memories of blue-ribbon cakes cooling on the windowsill in preparation for the morrow's country fair . . .

The crown of the kitchen is goodness;
The beauty of the kitchen is order;
The glory of the kitchen is contentment:
All reflected in the perfect cake!

Plain or fancy, light or dark, silver, gold, or ribbon cakes, made in layers or loaves—you can master them all through the mastery of a few basic recipes. Each basic recipe (angel food, sponge, pound, etc.) has a method all its own. Learn its peculiarities and then you will find yourself able to do dozens of spin-offs from each. *Do* choose simple recipes whenever possible. *Do* follow them closely. And *do* make use of the mixes available on today's grocery shelves. That is how the good become the best!

FAVORITE CAKES AND SPIN-OFFS

Hot Milk Sponge Cake

1 c. sifted cake flour
1 t. baking powder
3 eggs
1 c. sugar
2 t. lemon juice
6 T. hot milk

Sift together previously sifted flour and baking powder. Beat eggs until almost white and begin adding sugar gradually, beating constantly. Add lemon juice. Fold in flour mixture slowly. Blend. Add hot milk, mixing quickly until batter is smooth. Turn into ungreased tube pan. Bake at 350° for 35 minutes. Remove from oven and invert pan until cold. "Frost" according to directions below or make into a Lemon Blossom Cake or a Banana Split Cake.

To make a *Frost Pattern Cake*, place a lacy doily on top of the cooled sponge cake. Sift with powdered sugar and remove doily. Interesting to look at and kind to those counting calories.

To make a *Lemon Blossom Cake*, split cake in the middle, crosswise. Lift top layer off carefully and set aside. Spread with lemon-custard filling and replace top (filling should be about 3/4″ deep and show from sides). Spread top with remaining filling. Cover entire cake with whipped nondairy topping and decorate with candied lemon slices.

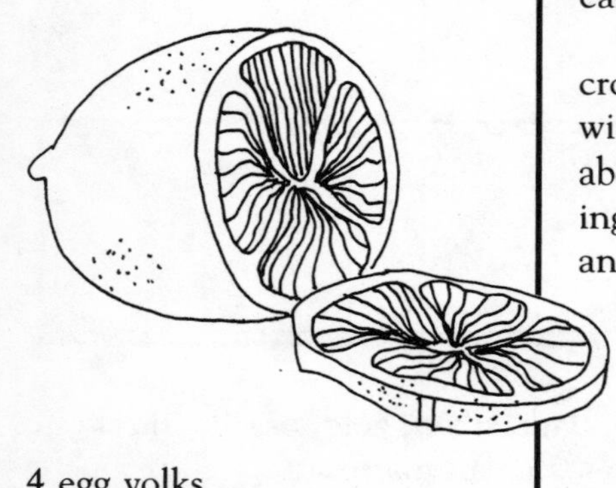

Lemon Custard Filling

4 egg yolks
2 c. milk
1/2 c. sugar
1/3 c. cornstarch
3 T. fresh lemon juice
1 T. grated lemon rind

Beat yolks well. Add milk and blend. Sift in cornstarch and sugar mixed together. Add lemon juice and rind. Cook over low heat, stirring constantly, until mixture is thick (about 10 minutes). Cover and chill before using.

To make a *Banana Split Cake*, follow directions above, substituting one 8-oz. vanilla instant pudding for boiled filling. Make pudding according to directions. Spread half of it on bottom layer of cake and add a layer of sliced bananas. Sprinkle with lemon juice and replace top layer. Cover with remaining pudding. Top with bananas and lemon juice. Cover entire cake with whipped nondairy topping and sprinkle with chopped walnuts. Serve in wedges drizzled with chocolate syrup. Rich—but worth it!

I-Did-It-Myself Angel Food Cake

- 1¼ c. powdered sugar
- 1 c. cake flour
- 12 egg whites (from large eggs)
- 1½ t. cream of tartar
- 1½ t. vanilla
- ½ t. salt
- ¼ t. almond flavoring
- 1 c. granulated sugar

Sift together powdered sugar and flour and set aside. Beat with electric mixer (or with rotary beater) at high speed the egg whites, cream of tartar, salt, vanilla and almond flavorings. Sprinkle in granulated sugar, a small amount at a time, beating until sugar is dissolved. When mixture stands in stiff peaks, fold in flour mixture by hand, (preferably using rubber spatula). Be gentle, but be sure that all flour disappears. Pour into ungreased 10″ tube pan and cut through mixture with spatula. Bake 35 minutes in 375° oven. Test for doneness: 1) Cake should spring back if touched, and 2) cracks on top should appear dry. Cool with pan inverted on wire rack. Loosen with spatula before removing from pan.

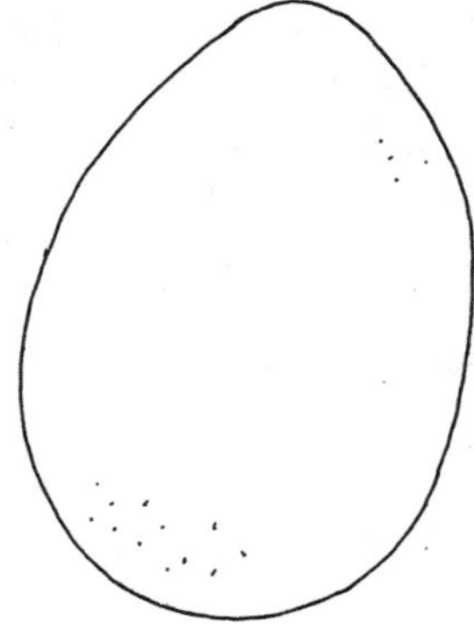

Using this recipe, your favorite angel food mix, or a bakery cake, now is the time to be creative. How about one of the following?

Lady Baltimore Cake

- 2 pkgs. fluffy white frosting mix
- ¼ c. candied cherries (chopped)
- ½ c. dried figs (chopped)
- ⅓ c. raisins (chopped)
- ¼ c. unsalted nuts (chopped)

Prepare 2 packages commercial fluffy white frosting mix according to directions and stir in about half of the fruit-nut mixture. Frost top and sides of angel food cake and toss remaining fruit-nut mixture on surface for garnish.

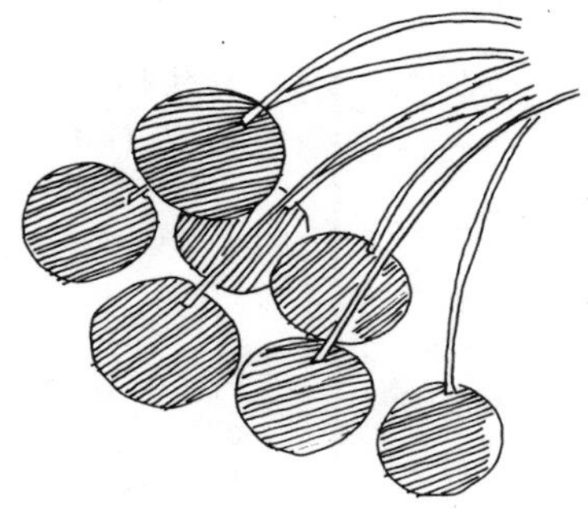

A good dinner sharpens the wit while it softens the heart. —*Doran*
(And we would add that it sweetens the disposition as well.)

Easy Mocha Cake

3 T. instant coffee
1 9-oz. carton nondairy topping
hot water

Using basic angel food recipe or a mix, fold in 2 T. instant coffee granules before baking. When cake is cool, swirl top and sides with one 9-oz. carton of nondairy topping to which has been added 1 T. instant coffee dissolved in several drops of hot water and cooled.

Peppermint Cream Cake

nondairy topping
4 sticks peppermint candy (crushed fine)

Using basic angel food recipe, mix, or bakery cake, swirl cooled cake with nondairy topping. Decorate with peppermint candy. Allow cake to stand several hours so that peppermint color will dissolve somewhat. Children love this!

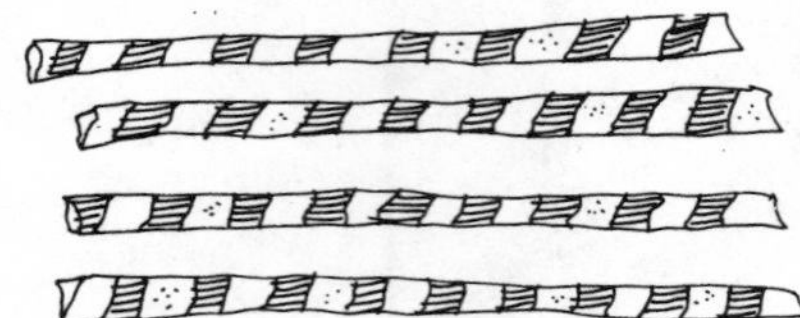

Strawberry Angel Food Prizewinner

Prepare your favorite angel food cake, use a mix, or purchase a large bakery cake. Slice carefully crosswise. Lift the top layer and spread the bottom layer with about half of the strawberry filling given below. Replace the top layer and cover with remainder of the filling. Refrigerate until ready to serve.

Just before serving, frost entire cake with nondairy topping and garnish with a few whole strawberries. Serves 8-12, depending on size of serving. The remainder keeps well (if not discovered by refrigerator raiders!).

Filling

1 qt. strawberries
1/2 c. water
1 1/4 c. sugar
3 T. cornstarch
1 T. butter or margarine
few drops of red food color
1/4 c. fresh lemon juice

Crush 1 c. of the strawberries and combine with water. Sift sugar and cornstarch into the liquid and mix well. Cook until thick. Remove from heat (do not overcook!). Add butter, color, and lemon juice. Too beautiful to eat—and too good not to!

Variety is the very spice of life that gives it all its flavor.

Angel Food Pudding

1 15-oz. package vanilla flavor instant pudding
1½ c. cold milk
1 3-oz. package cream cheese
one 15½-oz. can crushed pineapple
1 9-oz. carton nondairy topping
Maraschino cherries

Half an angel food cake left over? That's exactly right for this delightful dessert.

Whip together pudding and milk until thickened. Add softened cheese and mix well. Drain pineapple and add to pudding, blending until smooth. Pour over cubed angel food cake and fold in about ⅔ of the nondairy topping. Use remainder to spread over the top. Allow to mellow several hours in the refrigerator (preferably overnight). Spoon into parfait glasses and top each with a bright red cherry.

Basic Butter-'n-Egg Cake

2¼ c. cake flour
1½ c. sugar
¾ c. margarine
¾ c. evaporated milk
3 eggs
2½ t. baking powder
½ t. salt
1 t. vanilla
½ t. lemon extract

Easy-method mix: Measure all ingredients into mixing bowl and set mixer at low speed. Beat until mixed thoroughly, scraping sides of bowl. Set speed at medium and beat for five minutes more. Pour into greased and floured cake tins. Cut through with spatula. Bake at 375° for 25 minutes. Test with toothpick for doneness.

Frost with recipe of your choice or try one of these tricks:

Orange-Peak Frosting

2 egg whites
½ t. vanilla flavoring
pinch of salt
several drops orange food color
one 12-oz. jar orange marmalade
chocolate swirls

Beat egg whites at high speed until frothy. Add vanilla, salt, and food coloring. When mixture stands in froth, pour in hot marmalade, beating all the while. Continue until frosting stands in high, orange peaks. Swirl on cake and top with chocolate curls.

Butter-Pecan Frosting

one 9-oz. carton nondairy topping
one 15-oz. package butter-pecan flavor instant pudding
chopped nuts

Bake Basic Butter-'n-Egg Cake, use your favorite mix, or purchase a large pound cake.

Beat topping and pudding together until frosting takes shape. Frost cake and refrigerate until serving time. Serve in wedges sprinkled with chopped nuts.

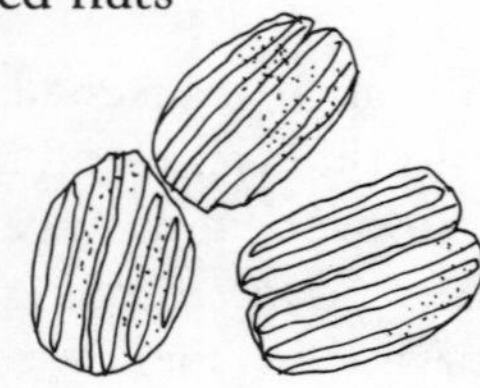

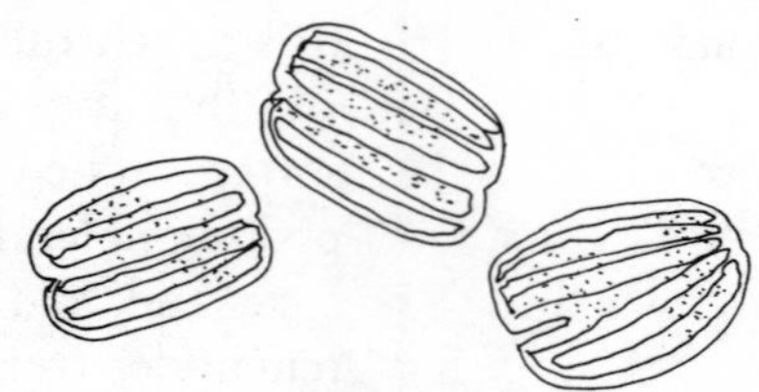

One-Minute Caramel Frosting

1/4 c. margarine (melted)
1/2 c. brown sugar (packed)
3 T. cream
1/3 c. chopped nuts
3/4 c. sweetened coconut
1 t. vanilla

For frosting Basic Butter-'n-Egg Cake, your mix, or a bakery cake, just blend these ingredients and spread on cake.

An artist can sketch a forest so real that one can imagine the trees lean slightly with the breeze. He can reproduce a sunny meadow so authentically that the viewer walks on tiptoe to avoid the daisies. But has ever a painter caught the glow on the face of the cook whose child just said, "Great cake, Mom!"?

Rainbow-in-a-Cloud Cake

1 t. fresh lime juice
1/2 t. grated lime rind
1-2 drops green food coloring
1/2 t. strawberry extract
1-2 drops red food coloring
1/2 t. orange extract
1/2 t. grated orange rind
1-2 drops orange food coloring

Follow instructions for Basic Butter-'n-Egg Cake. Divide batter into three equal parts. To first batter add lime juice, lime rind, and 1 or 2 drops of green food coloring (experiment, as batter should be only tinted). To the second batter add strawberry extract and 1 or 2 drops of red coloring. To the third batter add orange extract, grated orange rind, and 1 or 2 drops of orange coloring.

Alternately spoon colored batters into baking pan. Cut through batter with rubber spatula, but do not mix! Bake as directed and frost with Black Cloud Frosting:

Black Cloud Frosting

one 6-oz. package semisweet chocolate chips
one 9-oz. carton nondairy topping
1/4 c. powdered sugar
1/8 t. salt
1 t. vanilla flavoring
1/2 t. peppermint flavoring

Melt chocolate over hot water (not boiling). Set aside to cool. Beat together next three ingredients until mixture stands in stiff peaks. Fold in cooled chocolate. Add flavorings. Mix well and frost cake, decorating sides and top with scallops made with prongs of table fork.

What sweeter music to the ears of the cook than: "Will you share this recipe with me?"

Golden Carrot Cake

2 c. flour, sifted
2 t. baking soda
2 t. cinnamon
1/2 t. salt
3 eggs
1/4 c. vegetable oil
1/2 c. buttermilk
2 c. sugar
2 t. vanilla
one 3-oz. crushed pineapple
2 c. grated carrots
1 c. chopped walnuts
3 1/2-oz. can coconut
1 cup golden raisins

Sift dry ingredients together. Beat eggs and then add oil, buttermilk, sugar, and vanilla. Add to dry ingredients and mix well. Mix in drained pineapple, carrots, nuts, coconut, and raisins. Pour into lightly greased and floured 13″ x 9″ x 2 1/2″ pan. Bake at 350° for 55 minutes. Remove from oven and pour Buttermilk Frosting over top immediately. Cool. Yields 18 half-inch slices.

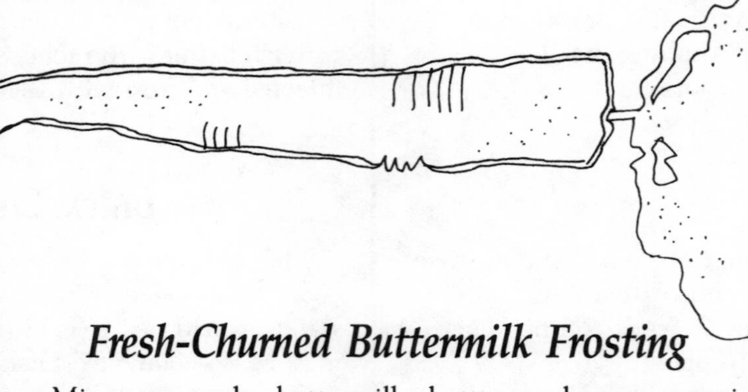

Fresh-Churned Buttermilk Frosting

1 c. sugar
1/2 t. baking soda
1/2 c. buttermilk
1 cube butter
1 T. white corn syrup
1 t. vanilla

Mix sugar, soda, buttermilk, butter, and corn syrup in saucepan. Boil 5 minutes. Remove from heat. Add vanilla and pour over hot cake.

Husband's Delight Cake

1½ c. sugar
4 T. cocoa
2½ c. water
2 c. dark raisins
⅔ c. margarine
3½ c. flour
2 t. baking powder
1 t. soda
2 t. cinnamon
½ t. cloves
½ t. nutmeg
1 t. vanilla
½ c. chopped nuts

Boil together sugar, cocoa, water, raisins, and margarine 4 minutes. Cool. Sift together flour, baking powder, soda, cinnamon, cloves, and nutmeg. Add flour mixture to raisin mixture and blend well. Add vanilla. Stir in nuts. Bake 35 minutes in greased and floured 13″ x 9″ x 2″ pan (35 minutes at 350° in metal pan or 325° in glass pan). Cool on rack. Yields nine 3″ x 4″ servings.

Grandma's Barn-Raisin' Cake

3 c. raisins
2 c. water
½ c. shortening
1½ c. sugar
3 eggs
3 c. flour
2 t. soda
1 t. nutmeg
1 t. cinnamon
1 c. raisin juice
1 c. chopped nuts

Simmer raisins 10 minutes in 2 c. water. Strain. Reserve juice and allow it to cool. Cream shortening and sugar. Add eggs and blend well. Add dry ingredients alternately with 1 c. raisin juice, blending after each addition. Fold in nuts and well-drained raisins. Bake in greased and floured 9″ x 13″ x 2″ pan at 375° one hour. Serve hot or cold. Yields twelve 3″ x 4″ slices.

Recipe may be doubled or tripled for hungry workers (or party). *Always* serve with steaming coffee! (Use freshly ground beans if possible.)

In early-day America folks from all over the countryside were excited when a neighbor's floors were laid. Rough boards were in need of planing down. And everybody knew that the best way to remove the splinters was by dancing them away. So the gingham-clad ladies do-si-doed with their best beaux to the wail of a fiddle from dusk to dawn. This was usually an autumn activity—just right for Harvest Moon Cake (made with sun-dried raisins and iced with a rich burnt-sugar concoction). As effective as molasses for "thickening the blood" for approaching winter, the cake was sometimes called Better 'n Molasses.

Harvest Moon Cake

1 c. flour
2 t. soda
1/2 t. cinnamon
1 c. sugar
1/2 t. salt
1 egg
1 c. persimmon pulp
1/3 c. vegetable oil
1 c. light raisins
1/3 c. chopped nuts
1 t. vanilla

Sift together flour, soda, cinnamon, sugar, and salt. Set aside. Combine egg and persimmon pulp with oil and mix slightly. Add dry ingredients, raisins, nuts, and vanilla. Blend batter. Bake in two greased and floured round pans (18″ wide, 1 1/2″ deep, easy-out pans) in 325° oven for 50 minutes. Cool and use butterscotch filling between layers. Yields eight generous wedges.

Butterscotch Filling

1 3-oz. package instant butterscotch pudding
1 c. sour cream

Blend butterscotch pudding mix with sour cream (or imitation). Double the recipe for "sky-high" cake (to match mood of merrymakers!)

Fun after a hayride or sleigh ride!

Raisin Pound Cake

- 4 eggs, unbeaten
- 1/2 c. vegetable oil
- 1 c. water
- one 3-oz. package lemon pudding mix
- one 17 1/2-oz. package white cake mix
- 1 c. raisins

Combine eggs, oil, water, and pudding mix; blend slowly. Add cake mix and continue to mix thoroughly. Stir in raisins. Pour into a 10″ tube cake pan and bake in preheated 325° oven 30 to 45 minutes (or until center tests done). Invert and cool in pan. Sprinkle with powdered sugar when cool. Yields 12-14 generous slices.

The English pound was the old commercial weight used to measure gold and silver at fairs, and also standard weight for bread. From that background, "pounding" came into use in America's early history. The preacher, who often was unpaid and always underpaid, received his reward when good folks of the congregation surprised him with pounds of this and that to feed his family. The practice led cooks to the making of pound cakes (everything measured in pounds and super-delicious!). Now we can enjoy the same mellow-sweet goodness without a scale.

Brandied Raisin Applesauce Cake

- 2 c. raisins
- brandy or water
- 3 c. sifted flour
- 3 T. ground chocolate
- 2 t. baking soda
- 1/2 t. salt
- 1 t. each allspice, cloves, nutmeg, and cinnamon
- 3/4 c. margarine (1 1/2 sticks)
- 1 c. white sugar
- 1 c. brown sugar (packed)
- 2 eggs
- 1 t. vanilla
- 2 c. chopped nuts
- one 25-oz. jar applesauce

Soak raisins overnight in brandy or water.

Sift together, three times, flour, chocolate, baking soda, salt, and spices. Set mixture aside. Cream margarine and add sugars, eggs, and vanilla. Mix well. Add nuts, raisins (drain off brandy or water), and applesauce alternately with flour mixture. Pour batter into greased and floured tube or 13″ x 9″ x 2″ baking pan. Bake in preheated 350° oven 60 to 90 minutes (or until toothpick comes out clean). Age for several days, spooning a few drops of raisin liquid on top. Very good with whipped cream topped with a sift of grated whole nutmeg.

The story is told of a circuit rider's appreciative remark when served the brandied cake: "Well, Ma'am, that was right nice—especially the *spirit* in which it was prepared."

Pennsylvania Dutch Crumb Cake

2 c. all-purpose flour
1 c. sugar
1/2 t. each salt, cinnamon, and nutmeg
1/2 t. ground cloves
1/2 c. (1 stick) butter
1 T. lemon juice
1 c. evaporated milk
1 t. baking soda
1 egg (beaten)
2 T. molasses
1/2 c. currents

Into mixing bowl sift together flour, sugar, salt, and spices. Cut in butter with pastry blender or two knives until mixture resembles cornmeal. Set aside 1 cup of the mixture for topping. Combine lemon juice and milk; add soda and dissolve. Add to flour mixture along with egg, molasses, and currents. Stir until dry ingredients are moistened. (Batter will be lumpy.) Turn into buttered 11″ x 7″ x 1 1/2″ pan. Sprinkle reserved cup of mixture on top and bake 35 to 45 minutes in oven preheated to 350°. Cool in pan on wire rack. Serve piping hot or cold with thick cream.

Mile-High Yellow Butter Cake

3/4 c. butter (1 1/2 sticks)
1 3/4 c. sugar
3 eggs
1 t. vanilla
3 c. sifted cake flour
1 T. baking powder
1 t. salt
1 1/2 c. milk

Instant mixes are to the cook what the computer is to the stock market. But suppose something inside yearns for "a slice of home." We had you in mind when we included this recipe. It has the goodness you remember, reminiscent of the wedge that Mother had waiting when you returned from searching the hills for wood violets. The shortcut recipe saves time but retains yesterday's appeal.

Generously butter bottoms of three round cake tins and dust with flour. In mixing bowl cream butter; gradually add sugar and beat until light and fluffy. Beat in eggs, one at a time. Add vanilla. Sift together flour, baking powder, and salt; add to creamed mixture alternately with milk, beginning and ending with dry ingredients. Divide evenly into pans. Bake 25 to 30 minutes. Cool in pans on wire racks 5 minutes. Turn onto racks and cool completely. Frost with:

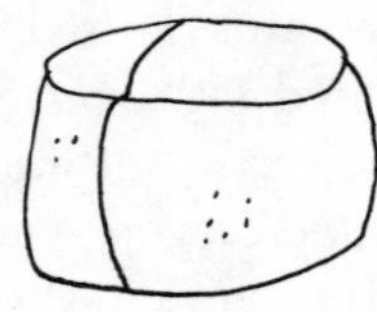

A Quickie Butter-Marshmallow Creme Frosting

3/4 c. (1 1/2 sticks) *hard, firm* butter
3 c. (1 1/2 7-oz. jars) marshmallow creme
1 t. vanilla

In small mixing bowl cream butter until light and fluffy. Continue to beat (medium speed if using a mixer) while adding marshmallow creme, 1 T. at a time. Add vanilla. Sufficient frosting to fill your three-layer cake (as good as you remembered!).

Pear Ginger Cake

1/2 c. (1/2 stick) butter
1/3 c. sugar
1 egg
1/2 c. molasses
1/2 c. water
1/2 c. nonfat dry milk
1 c. sifted all-purpose flour
1 t. baking soda
1/2 t. baking powder
1/2 t. ginger
1/2 t. each cinnamon, salt, ground cloves
2 c. thinly sliced fresh pears

Topping:

2 T. butter, cut in pieces
1/2 c. light-brown sugar (packed)
1/4 t. ginger
sift of cinnamon (1/8 t.)
whipped cream

Beat butter, sugar, and egg until light. Combine molasses, water, and dry milk. Sift together dry ingredients and add to butter mixture alternately with molasses mixture. Spread over thinly sliced fresh pears arranged in greased 9″-square baking pan. Top with butter and sprinkle with brown sugar, ginger, and cinnamon (sift, like a pinch, means about 1/8 t.). Bake 40 to 50 minutes at 350°. Invert on serving dish and serve with generous swirls of whipped cream.

To use canned pears, drain 1-lb. can of pear halves. Split each half lengthwise and arrange on butter mixture.

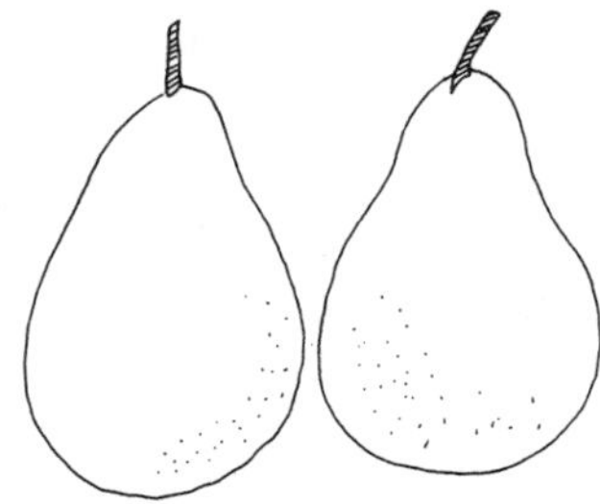

Remember the comfort of a moment alone with Grandmother before sheepishly handing the not-so-great report card to Mother and Dad? The smell of her apron? Her quiet voice? And wasn't that slice of matchless cake the world's best soothing syrup?

I used to hear the kettle sing
As if it heard the prayer
That grandma said at start of day
While rocking in her chair:
"Lord, You have given me this day
And planned the tasks for me,
Just simple things these hands can do
To serve my family.
I thank You for these kitchen walls
And window with a view
Where I can watch loved ones come home
When their day's work is through.
Teach me nobility that lies
In loaves of fresh-baked bread,
So my heart finds fulfillment when
Each hungry spirit's fed;
And let me know when this day ends
That I have done my best
With tender cakes and tender thoughts,
Love earned me a rest.

HERE, THERE, AND EVERYWHERE NOVELTY CAKES

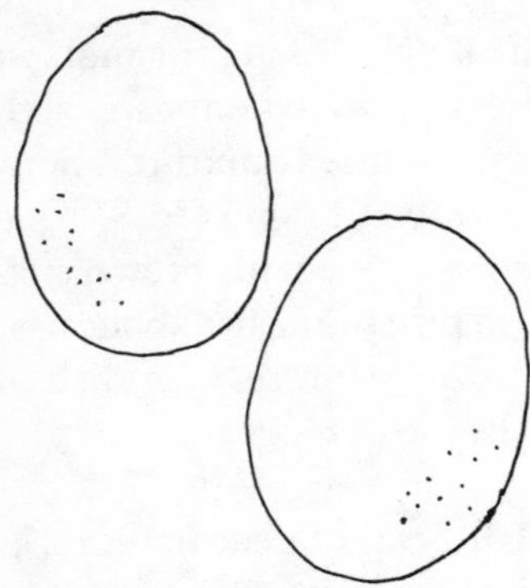

Cake baking is an art as well as a pleasure. And it can become a novelty when you stick with the tried-and-true while bravely tackling the new. So put on your prettiest apron and bake a brand-new, magnificent, absolutely *splendiferous* cake today. It is more fun if the cake is for a special person or a special occasion. Is someone at the office having a birthday? Is there a neighbor-child, niece, or nephew recovering from measles? What about Grandmother, Aunt Josie, or your mother? If one of them taught you to cream, whip, and fold in, she deserves to see that you will be the next family legend. Be confident that your cake will be as fluffy-moist as hers. Both of you will be proud!

Avocado Cake

- 2 c. sugar
- 3/4 c. margarine
- 3 eggs (beaten)
- 2 ripe avocados (mashed)
- 2 2/3 c. flour sifted with 1/2 t. salt
- 3/4 t. each cinnamon, allspice, nutmeg
- 3/4 c. buttermilk
- 1 1/2 t. soda (dissolved in buttermilk)
- 3/4 c. white raisins
- 1/2 c. dates (chopped)
- 3/4 c. walnuts (chopped)
- 1/2 c. almond slivers

Cream together sugar and margarine. Add eggs, then avocados, mixing thoroughly. Sift together flour mixture and spices. Add to creamed mixture alternately with buttermilk mixture. Stir in raisins, dates, and nuts. Pour mixture into greased and lightly floured angel food tin and bake at 350° for 1 hour or until a toothpick comes out clean when inserted. Freezes well and makes a nice departure from the traditional fruitcake.

"It has been my experience," said my grandmother, "to be suspicious of any cake whose recipe the cook refused to share."

Tomato Soup Cake with Raw-Apple Icing

½ c. margarine
1 c. sugar
2 c. flour
1 t. soda
2 t. baking powder
1 t. cinnamon
½ t. cloves
1 t. nutmeg
¼ t. salt
10-oz. can tomato soup plus 2 T. milk
½ c. chopped nuts
1 c. raisins

Cream margarine and sugar together. Add dry ingredients (sifted together) alternately with soup. Add nuts and raisins. Bake 45 minutes at 350°. Weight watchers (note that cake contains no eggs) may choose to leave cake unfrosted. It is delicious that way, especially warm. Or, you may choose to serve the cake cut in squares and, when cool, heaped with nondairy topping. But for something truly different, try the icing below.

Raw-Apple Icing

1 c. granulated sugar
juice of ½ lemon
½ t. vanilla
1 egg white
1 large apple (peeled and chopped)

Combine ingredients in bowl and beat until mixture stands in peaks. Spread on cake.

Quick Tomato Soup Cake

1 2-layer size spice cake mix
1 t. soda
1 can tomato soup
½ c. milk
2 eggs

And, yes, there is a spin-off made with a mix. Good, too! Just use spice cake mix, adding soda, tomato soup diluted with milk, and eggs. Combine these ingredients and add to the mix. Bake as directed on package. For this why not try the following frosting?

Cream Cheese Frosting

1 3-oz. pkg. cream cheese
1 T. milk
2½ c. powdered sugar
1 t. vanilla
dash salt

Blend cream cheese, milk, and powdered sugar. Beat vigorously and add vanilla and salt. Spread on cake.

Brownie Cake

2 c. flour (sifted and measured)
1/2 t. salt
2 c. sugar

2 sticks margarine
3 T. cocoa
1 c. water

2 eggs (well-beaten)
1/2 c. buttermilk
1 t. soda
1 t. each cinnamon and vanilla

Sift together flour, salt, and sugar and set aside.

Bring the margarine, cocoa, and water to a boil and pour over flour and sugar mixture. Stir.

Whisk together eggs, buttermilk, soda, cinnamon, and vanilla. Pour over above mixture and beat well. Bake in greased and floured shallow pan (15″ x 18″) 20 minutes at 350°.

Five minutes before cake is done make:

Minute Buttermilk Icing

1 stick margarine
3 T. cocoa
6 T. buttermilk
1 box (2 c.) powdered sugar
1/2 c. chopped pecans (or walnuts)
1 t. vanilla

Mix margarine, cocoa, and milk in saucepan. Use low heat so mixture does not boil. Remove from heat and add sugar, nuts, and vanilla. Mix well. Remove cake from oven and frost immediately. Cut into squares and leave in pan if taking to picnic, potluck, etc. If serving at home, remove squares by slipping spatula beneath each piece and lifting onto plate. Makes 2 doz. "servings" or 4 doz. "brownies."

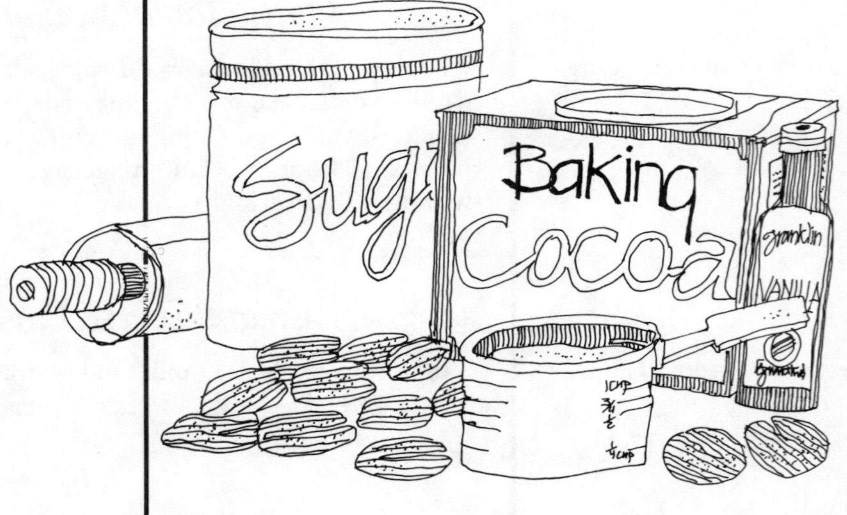

Better-Than-Grandma's Jam Cake

1 c. cooking oil
2 c. sugar
4 eggs
3 c. sifted flour
1 t. each soda, salt, allspice, and cinnamon
1 c. buttermilk
1 c. jam (preferably berry with seed in)
1 c. chopped nuts

Filling:
1 No. 2 can pineapple
1½ c. sugar
¾ stick margarine
1 T. flour
1 c. chopped nuts of your choice
1 c. coconut

Combine oil and sugar. Add unbeaten eggs one at a time and beat after addition until fluffy. Add sifted dry ingredients, alternating with buttermilk, beating after each addition. Add jam and nuts. Bake at 350° about 25 minutes. Test with toothpick for doneness.

Allow layers to cool before removing from pans. Use a spatula to loosen edges if cake does not come out immediately. Then prepare the following filling to spread between the layers and on top:

Filling

Combine first four ingredients. Cook over low heat until thick. Add nuts and coconut. Spread on cake. Next, prepare the following:

Miracle Meringue

3 egg whites
pinch of salt
1 c. marshmallow creme
1 t. vanilla

Beat egg whites and salt until whites stand in peaks. Gradually add marshmallow mix, then vanilla. Beat until very thick, then swirl over entire cake. Bake (yes, bake!) at 350° for 12 to 15 minutes or until lightly browned. Allow to cool before serving this magical treat!

Bake a Dream

When winter comes, as winters will,
And perches on your windowsill;
Just bake a dream and set it where
The world will turn and find it there;
Quite magically you may have found
The corner spring is "just around!"

Fudge Sandwich Cake

1 pkg. chocolate fudge cake mix
1½ c. cold water
½ c. sour cream (or imitation)

Filling:
2 eggs
1 8-oz. pkg. cream cheese
2 eggs
⅓ c. sugar
1 c. coconut flakes

Substitute water, sour cream, and eggs for any ingredients listed on the cake mix package. Blend these substituted ingredients into the cake mix as directed on package. Pour half of mixture into Bundt cake pan. Smooth slightly with spoon and add filling as follows:

Filling

Beat first three ingredients until smooth. Add coconut. Spoon onto first layer of batter, lightly smoothing with spoon. Cover with remaining batter. Bake at 350°. Tap bottom of pan on smooth surface to release air bubbles but do not cut through with knife (to avoid mixing filling with batter). When cake is cool, dust with powdered sugar. Do not frost.

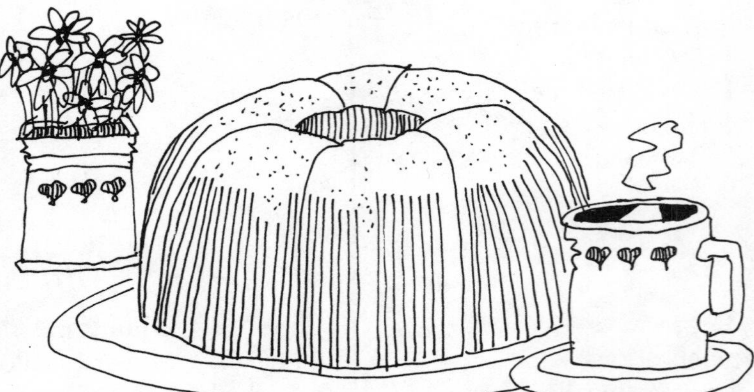

Pineapple Right-Side-Up Cake

1 pkg. white cake mix
1 lg. can crushed pineapple

Topping:
1 large pkg. cream cheese
2 c. cold milk
½ c. chopped Maraschino cherries
1 pkg. instant pistachio pudding
whole Maraschino cherries

Prepare 1 package of white cake mix according to manufacturer's directions. Bake in oblong pan (about 9″ x 13″). Remove cake from oven and, while it is hot, poke holes at 1″ intervals (use rinsed, unsharpened lead pencil). Pour crushed pineapple over cake (do not drain, but mix juice thoroughly with fruit). Allow cake to cool in pan, and make topping as follows.

Topping

Blend cheese with enough milk to form a paste. Add remainder of milk. Mix in chopped cherries. Sprinkle pudding on top. Beat until smooth and spread on sheet cake. Cut into squares and garnish each square with a whole cherry.

See-Through Gumdrop Cake
(No Eggs)
(When hens are "in the molt")

2 c. flour (sifted)
1 c. sugar
1 t. cinnamon
1/2 t. each cloves and allspice
pinch of salt
1 t. soda
1 c. sour applesauce
1/2 c. margarine
1/2 c. blanched almonds (chopped)
1 c. currants
1 c. white raisins
1 c. chopped gumdrops (no black ones)

Sift together all dry ingredients escept soda. Add soda to applesauce and set aside. Cream margarine and add applesauce alternately with dry mixture. Fold in nuts, raisins, currants, and gumdrops. Bake in greased and floured angel food cake tin about 45 minutes at 350°. Invert pan and remove cake. While still warm, drizzle with:

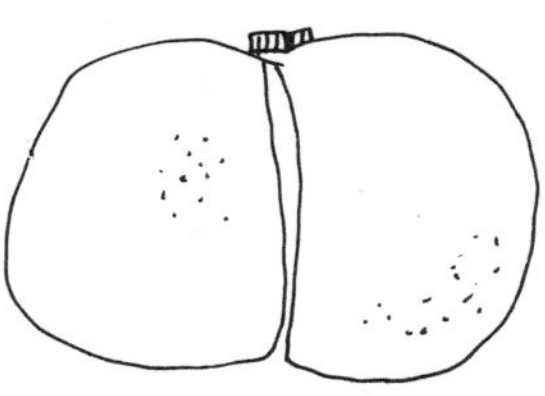

Apricot Glaze

2 c. powdered sugar (sifted)
2. T. lemon or lime juice
2 T. apricot nectar
pinch of salt

Combine all ingredients until creamy before drizzling on cake.

The creative mind dreams beautiful dreams, but it takes busy hands to make them come true.

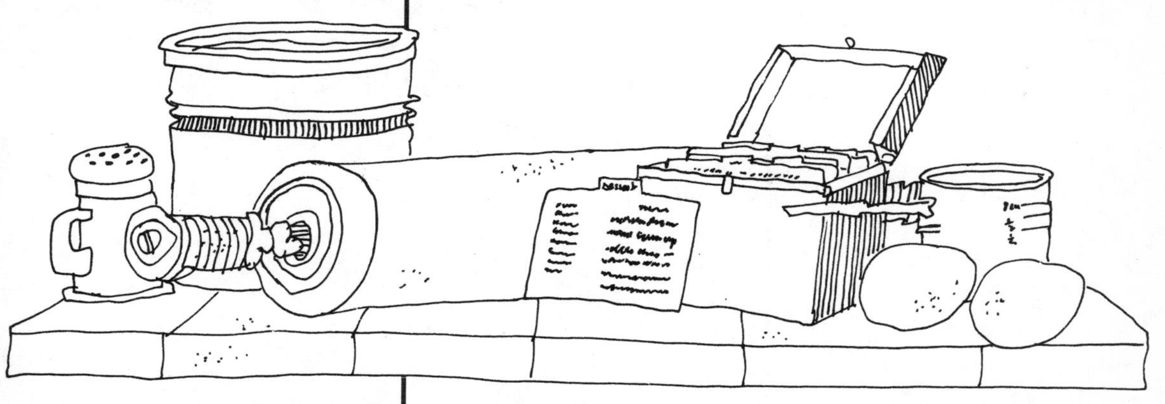

Fruit Cocktail Upside-Down Cake

1 lg. can fruit cocktail
1 T. margarine
1/2 c. brown sugar
2 eggs, separated
1/2 c. sugar
1/2 c. flour
1/2 t. baking powder
1/8 t. salt
2 T. water
1/2 t. vanilla
ice cream or nondairy topping

Drain fruit cocktail and set aside while melting margarine in a heavy skillet. Add brown sugar (sprinkle over margarine) and then arrange drained fruit on top of sugar mixture. Next, beat egg whites until they stand in dry peaks. Add beaten egg yolks and fold in until mixture is pale yellow. Gradually sift in sugar, then fold in flour sifted with baking powder and salt. Add water and vanilla. Pour over fruit and bake at 350° for half an hour. Turn onto cake plate. Serve hot with ice cream or cold with swirls of nondairy topping. Never fails!

Sausage-'n-Egg Brunch Cake

2 c. dark raisins
2 c. brown sugar
1 egg (beaten)
1 lb. pork sausage (broken apart)
3 c. flour (sifted with 1 t. each cinnamon, allspice, and soda)
1/2 t. black pepper (the pepper does the trick!)
1 c. nut meats (chopped)
1 apple (unpeeled, sliced)
sugar and cinnamon, mixed
butter

Boil raisins 2 minutes. Cool and drain off water, reserving 1 c. Beat sugar and egg together and add to sausage. Add raisin water and mix well. Fold in flour mixture and pepper; then add raisins and nuts. Pour into greased and floured loaf pan and overlap a layer of apple slices on top. Sprinkle with sugar and cinnamon. Bake at 350° about 2 hours. Test for doneness. Serve hot with butter.

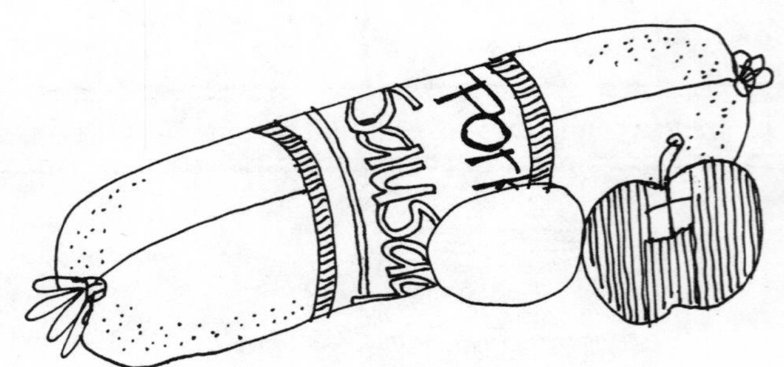

Toasted Marshmallow Carrot Cake

2 c. flour
2 c. sugar
2 t. soda
3 t. cinnamon
1 t. nutmeg
1 c. cooking oil
4 eggs (beaten)
3 c. raw carrots (grated)
3 t. vanilla
1 doz. large marshmallows

Sift together dry ingredients. Make a well and add oil, eggs, carrots, and vanilla. Beat well. Pour into greased and floured 9″ pan and bake at 350° for half an hour. Cover with marshmallows (spacing evenly) and bake another 10 minutes or until browned.

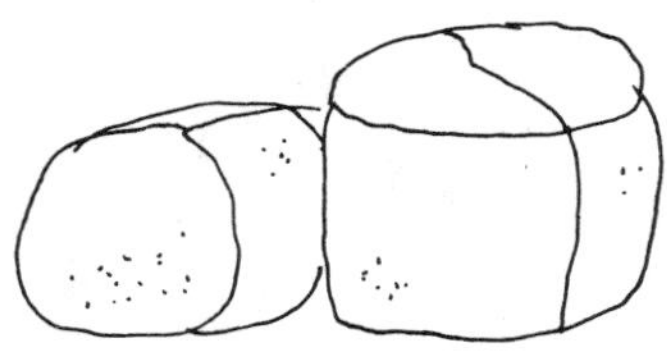

Priority

It's noontime of a busy day
And I must pause a bit,
Reflecting on priorities
Left for the rest of it:
The shopping I have left for last;
The dusting is not through;
Alas! the kitchen floor's a mess;
Too many things to do.
But, oh! this layer cake is nice,
Its frosting "sweet-tooth" high.
Who cares about the tasks undone?
My family? No—nor I!

Squash Cake

2½ c. flour
½ c. cocoa
2½ t. baking powder
1½ t. soda
1 t. each cinnamon, allspice, and nutmeg
¾ c. margarine
2 c. sugar
2 t. vanilla
3 eggs (beaten)
2 c. grated zucchini squash
½ c. milk
½ c. coconut

Sift together dry ingredients. Cream margarine, sugar, and vanilla. Beat in eggs and blend. Stir in squash and alternate additions of milk and dry ingredients. Stir in coconut. Bake 1 hour (preferably in Bundt pan) at 350°. Serve hot or cold with Lemon Sauce or Crimson Rhubarb Sauce.

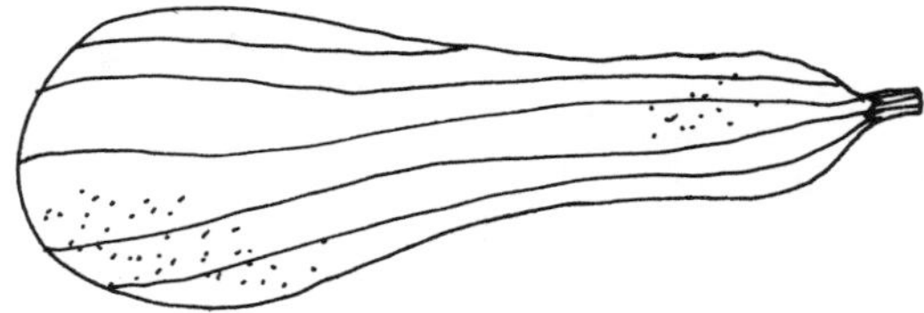

Persimmon Spice Cake

- 1/2 c. margarine
- 1 c. sugar
- 3 eggs (beaten)
- 1 t. soda (dissolved in few drops of water)
- 1 c. persimmon pulp
- 2 1/2 c. flour
- 1 t. each salt, cinnamon, and cloves
- 1/2 t. nutmeg
- 1/2 c. chopped nuts
- 1 c. dark raisins
- coconut

Cream together margarine and sugar. Add beaten eggs and beat well. Blend soda mixture and add to persimmon pulp then blend into creamed mixture. Sift together dry ingredients and add gradually to creamed mixture. Fold in nuts and raisins. Pour into floured and greased 9″ x 12″ pan, sprinkle top generously with coconut, and bake at 350° for 1 hour.

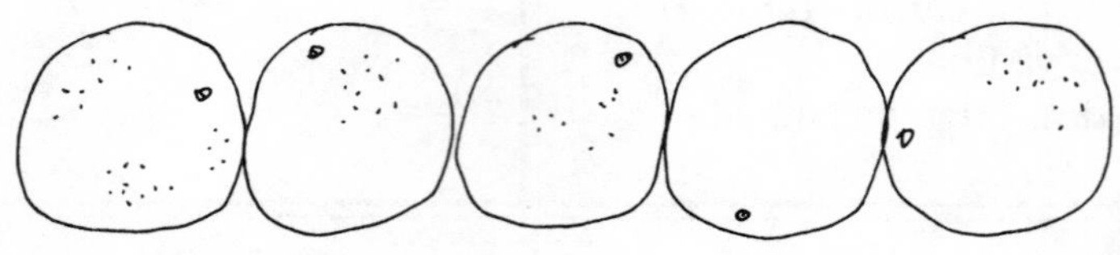

Baked-On Frosting Rhubarb Cake

- 1/2 c. cooking oil
- 1 c. brown sugar (packed)
- 2 eggs
- 1 t. vanilla
- 2 c. plus 1 T. flour
- 1/2 t. salt
- 1 c. milk
- 2 c. uncooked rhubarb (chopped very fine)

Frosting:

- 2 T. margarine
- 1/2 c. brown sugar
- 1 t. cinnamon
- 1 t. vanilla
- 1/2 c. whole pecans
- vanilla ice cream or whipped cream topping

Cream oil and sugar (mixer may be used). Beat in eggs and vanilla. Add dry ingredients (sifted together) alternately with milk. Add rhubarb last. Pour into 9″ x 12″ (or equivalent) pan and spread with uncooked frosting mixture. Press the whole pecans firmly enough into the frosting so that they go slightly into the batter. Bake at 350° for 45 minutes and serve hot with vanilla ice cream or cold with whipped cream topping.

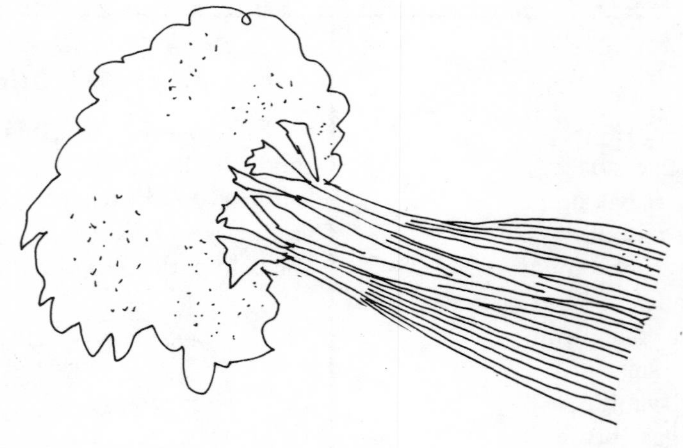

German Sauerkraut Cake

1/2 c. margarine
1 c. white sugar
1/2 c. brown sugar
2 t. vanilla
2 T. honey
3 eggs (beaten)
1 1/2 c. sauerkraut (drained and cut very fine—use kitchen shears)
1 t. soda
1 c. buttermilk
2 1/2 c. flour
1 t. baking powder
1/2 c. cocoa

Cream together margarine, both sugars, vanilla, and honey. Add eggs and beat. Mix in sauerkraut. Dissolve soda in buttermilk. Sift together dry ingredients and add alternately to creamed mixture with buttermilk mixture. Bake in greased and floured 9″ x 12″ pan at 350° for 45 minutes. Good hot or cold and keeps well.

Beet Pickle Cake

2 1/2 c. flour
1 1/2 c. sugar
1/2 c. cocoa
1 t. soda
1 t. baking powder
pinch salt
2 1/2 c. butter (melted)
2 t. vanilla
6 eggs (beaten)
3/4 c. pickled beets (drained and chopped)

Sift together dry ingredients. Make a well and add melted butter and vanilla. Mix. Add eggs and beat well, then blend in beets which have been put through food grinder. Pour into greased and floured 9″x 12″ pan. Bake at 350° about 25 minutes. Frost with favorite butter icing. Distinctively different!

Evening Prayer

Lord, let me forget to remember
Each small hurt of this day,
Remembering only the wonder
Of great things life brought my way.
Yes, let me remember the right things:
Each word, each deed, each song:
For memory's only a blessing
When I've forgotten the wrong.

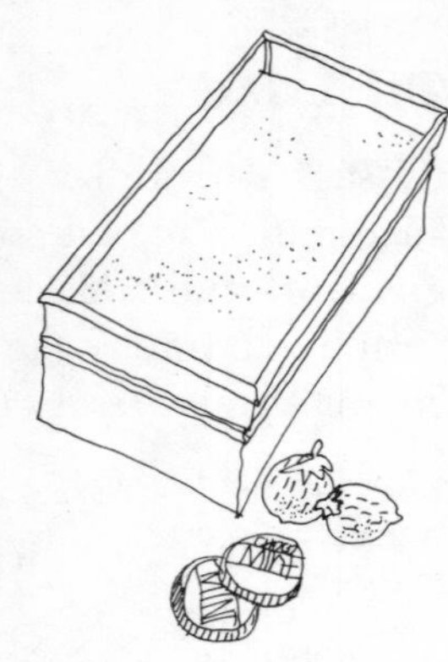

SHORTCUT-CUTS TO THE SHORTCUTS!

There comes a day when no mix will help this fix! Keep a pound cake frozen for such emergencies. Use your favorite recipe, use a mix, or purchase a bakery cake. Presto! Something wonderful like:

Minute Strawberry Shortcake

one 1-lb. pound cake (cubed)
three 3-oz. pkgs. strawberry gelatin
2 c. boiling water
4 c. ice water
cooking oil
1 carton frozen strawberries
nondairy topping

Dissolve gelatin in boiling water. Add ice water. Grease individual gelatin-dessert molds with cooking oil. Pour 1 T. separated berries in each mold. Fill molds approximately half full with gelatin and ease cubed cake into mixture, being sure that each piece is coated. Add more gelatin if necessary. Set in freezer until jelled. Unmold on chilled plates and top each serving with a swirl of topping.

Choco-Mint Treats

one 1-lb. pound cake (sliced)
chocolate ice cream
peppermint shavings or broken chocolate mints

Plan 1 slice of pound cake per serving. Toast under broiler (or in toaster set on "light") until slightly browned. Top each slice with a scoop of chocolate ice cream. Garnish with peppermint shavings or broken chocolate mints. From this you can do hundreds of your own spin-offs: pumpkin ice cream topped with canned caramel sauce, vanilla topped with coconut syrup—what do you have on hand?

Instant-Gold Bars

one 1-lb. pound cake (1/2″ slices cut into quarters)
creamy peanut butter
chopped nuts

Cut pound cake in 1/2″ slices, then cut each slice into fourths. Spread sides and top with creamy peanut butter. Roll in chopped nuts and toast at 375° until delicately browned, or spread with honey and roll in coconut; spread with cream cheese and roll in cinnamon sugar. Go on!

Pies

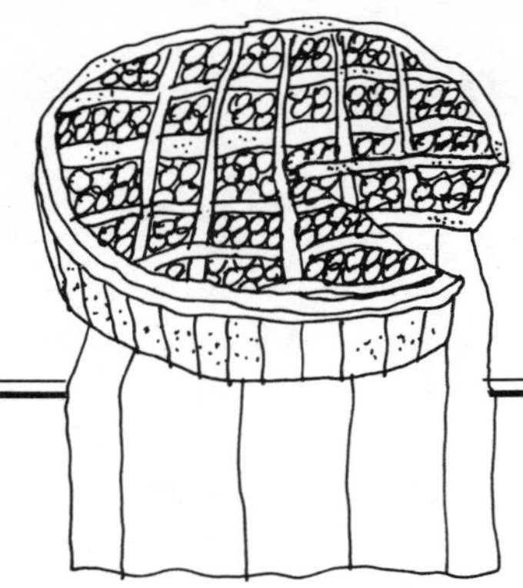

A Taste of Yesterday

"As American as apple pie!" What higher praise? Pies (apple or other varieties) are most likely our favorite dessert: fruit pies, custard pies, cream pies, chiffon pies, nut pies—the list goes on and on. And now the choice of pastry is almost as wide as the filling: baked, unbaked, crumb, meringue, double-crust, and single-crust. Most popular (and most feared) is simple pie crust.

No matter what they're made of,
No matter what their size,
It's truth to me that poetry
Lies in the shell of pies!

Stop wishing you were a "born baker." Baking skill is cultivated. It takes no special gift or secret touch to turn out a flaky crust that casts a magic spell. You need only a few simple rules and practice. In no time at all, judgment will take the place of the rules.

Generally accepted rules are: 1) make sure the ingredients are fresh; 2) use cold ingredients unless the recipe specifies otherwise; and 3) handle pastry as little as possible. But it is the wise pie maker who adds rule 4) never show pastry that you are afraid of it! Handle quickly and lightly, and hum a bit as you work!

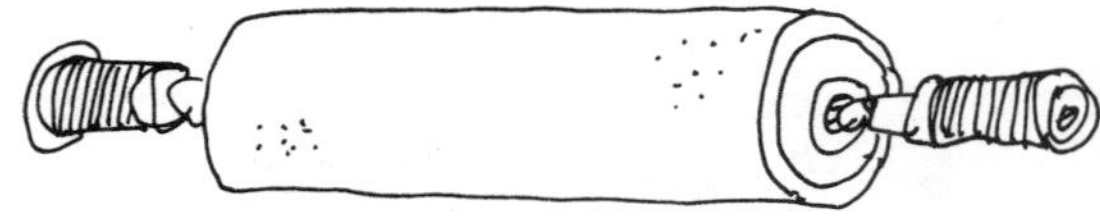

Easy-Does-It Pastry

2 c. flour
1 t. salt
1/4 c. ice water
2/3 c. shortening

Sift and measure flour. Sift again with salt. Put 2/3 c. of this mixture into a small bowl and add ice water to form a paste. To remaining flour add shortening. Cut in (with two knives) or use pastry blender till mixture is mealy. Add flour paste to shortening mixture. Mix thoroughly until dough forms a ball. Wrap in flour-dusted waxed paper and chill.

Remove pastry from refrigerator and bring to room temperature before attempting to bake. Divide in half and roll out on lightly-floured board. Place in 9″ pie plates. To bake an unfilled crust, prick bottom and sides of crust to keep it from puffing up and bake 15 minutes in a 450° oven. Then cool and fill with cooked filling. If baking the crust with the filling, follow the pie filling recipe. For the perfect finishing touch (a tempting golden glaze), brush rolled-out shells with milk or beaten egg white and sift lightly with granulated sugar.

This recipe makes enough pastry for one 9-inch double-crust pie, two single crusts, or about a dozen tart shells. (Hint: *shape pastry circles over bottoms of muffin tins for tart shells and bake with tins upside down.*)

Never-Fail Egg Pastry

4 c. sifted flour (sifted again with 1 t. salt)
1 3/4 c. margarine
1 T. vinegar
1 whole egg (beaten)
1/2 c. ice water

Cut margarine into flour mixture with knives (scissor fashion) or use blender. Pastry should be to coarse crumb stage.

Add vinegar to beaten egg. Finish with ice water. Add this mixture to the first mixture—a T. at a time, mixing lightly with a fork after each addition. Shape into a roll, wrap in wax paper, and chill until ready to use. Makes two double-crust pies or four single pie shells. (Hint: *conserve on energy—your own and the oven's—by baking all shells or pies at once. Freeze for emergencies. No room in today's oven? Then freeze pastry unbaked either rolled out and placed in pie plates or freezer-wrapped. They will keep two months.*)

The reward of a thing well done is to have done it.
—Emerson

Graham Cracker Crust (Baked)

1½ doz. graham crackers (crushed)
¼ c. white sugar
⅓ c. margarine (or butter)

Mix crumbs, sugar, and melted margarine. Pat into 9″ pie plate, pushing mixture firmly against sides with spoon. Bake in preheated oven (375°) for 10 minutes. Cool on rack. Do not remove from pan. Fill with chiffon or Bavarian-cream-type fillings.

Graham Cracker Crust (Unbaked)

1½ c. graham cracker crumbs (crushed)
⅓ c. brown sugar
½ t. ground cinnamon
½ c. ground nuts (or crumbled and toasted coconut)
⅓ c. melted margarine

Mix crumbs, sugar, cinnamon, nuts (or coconut), and melted margarine. Pat onto bottom (not sides) of 9″ pie plate and press down firmly, reserving 3 T. mixture for garnish. Chill. Fill with chiffon-type filling (not fresh fruit mixtures) and top with crumbs.

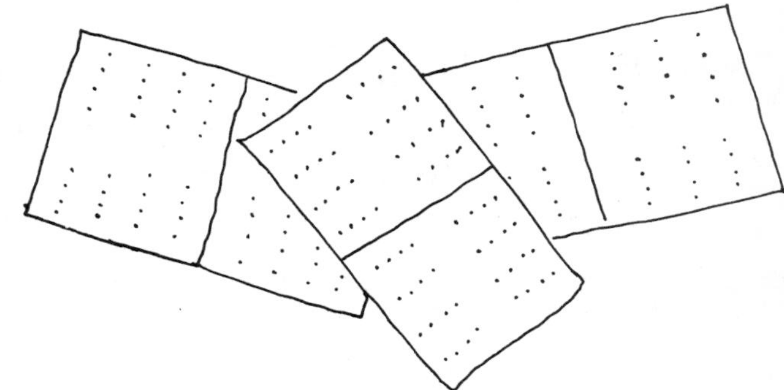

Cookie Crusts

1½ doz. chocolate wafers
¼ c. white sugar
⅓ c. margarine

Chocolate Wafer: Prepare as for Graham Cracker Crust, using chocolate wafers in place of graham crackers. Especially nice with mint-flavored filling.

3 doz. vanilla wafers
¼ c. white sugar
½ c. margarine

Vanilla Wafer: Prepare as for Graham Cracker Crust, using vanilla wafers in place of graham crackers and increasing margarine to ½ c. Especially good with cola, lime, coffee, eggnog, or any of the fresh-fruit whips.

2 doz. ginger snaps
¼ c. white sugar
⅓ c. margarine

Ginger Snaps: Prepare as for Graham Cracker Crust, using ginger snaps in place of graham crackers. Yummy with lemon filling.

FAVORITE FRUIT PIES

Great Aunt Het's "Use What You Have" Fruit Pie

1 lb. pitted, dried prunes
1/2 lb. dried apricot halves
3 c. boiling water
3 T. cornstarch
1/2 c. cold water
1/2 c. sugar
1 T. lemon or lime peel (grated)
1 t. cinnamon mixed with a pinch of salt
1/2 c. English walnuts (chopped and lightly toasted)
nondairy whipped topping

Simmer fruit in boiling water until tender (about 15 minutes). Blend cornstarch in cold water and add to fruit gradually until mixture thickens, then add remaining ingredients except walnuts.

Spread half the walnuts over bottom of baked pie shell. Pour in hot fruit and top with remaining walnuts. Cool and serve with high swirls of nondairy whipped topping.

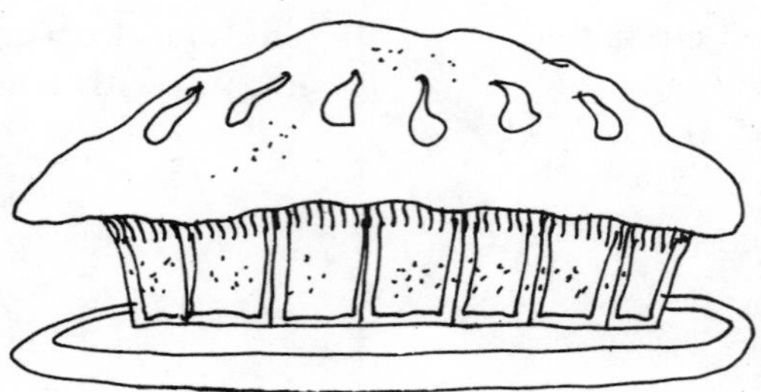

This world belongs to the energetic.
—Emerson

Glazed Strawberry Pie

1 qt. strawberries (washed and hulled)
1/2 c. water
1 1/4 c. sugar
3 T. cornstarch
1 T. margarine
1/4 c. fresh lemon juice
few drops of red food color
whipped cream or nondairy topping

Crush enough berries to make 1 c., leaving the rest whole. Combine crushed berries with water, sugar, and cornstarch. Bring to a boil and cook over low heat, stirring constantly, until clear (about 3 minutes). Remove from heat. Add margarine, lemon juice, and color.

Line baked pie shell with whole berries, piling high in the center. Pour hot glaze over berries, making sure each is covered in order to avoid "bleeding" of fruit. Cool in refrigerator. Top with whipped cream or nondairy topping just before serving.

Glaze should be prepared no more than two hours in advance. In order to avoid softening of berries, prepare fruit and bake pastry in advance, leaving glaze until shortly before serving time.

Rhubarb Tart Pies

2 c. rhubarb (cut in small pieces)
1 T. water
1 c. sugar
1 T. flour
1 beaten egg
1 T. margarine
few drops of green food color
whipped cream or nondairy topping
vanilla
cherry or toasted coconut

Cook rhubarb in water until it reaches liquid stage. Add 1/2 c. sugar. Turn off heat. Mix remaining sugar and flour together and sift into rhubarb mixture slowly, stirring constantly. Whip in beaten egg. Return to burner and cook over low flame until mixture is thick. Add margarine and food color. Pour into individual pie shells ("tarts") which have been baked previously. Cool and serve with whipped cream or nondairy topping generously flavored with vanilla. Center with a cherry or top surface with toasted coconut.

Unusual and yummy-good finale for roast pork or baked salmon!

Fresh Raspberry Pie with Pretzel Pastry

2 1/2 c. crushed pretzels
3 T. brown sugar (packed)
3/4 c. margarine
1 t. vanilla
one 8-oz. package cream cheese
1 c. sugar
1 small carton (1 c.) nondairy topping
1 T. lemon juice
one 6-oz. package raspberry gelatin
2 c. boiling water
1 qt. raspberries

Mix with fingers crushed pretzels, brown sugar, margarine, and vanilla. Pat into 9″ pie plate and press down firmly. Bake 10 minutes at 350°. Cool.

Blend cream cheese, sugar, nondairy topping, and lemon juice. Spread on pretzel mixture.

Prepare raspberry gelatin with boiling water. Stir well. Refrigerate until syrupy.

Carefully spread 1 qt. washed, drained, and chilled raspberries over cheese mixture, arranging berries evenly. Pour gelatin mixture over berries. Refrigerate overnight. Cut in squares and serve without additional topping. Delightfully different!

Loaves-and-Fishes Peach Pie

1 package lemon gelatin
1 1/4 c. boiling water
1 pt. vanilla ice milk
2 (or more!) fresh peaches

Dissolve gelatin in water. Refrigerate until almost "set." Whip ice milk with rotary-type beater (1/2 c. at a time) into gelatin mixture. Fold in sliced peaches for six servings. Chill until partly set and pour into baked and cooled pie shell.

Now! Expecting more guests? Then you will want to plan on two pies. To "double" the recipe, just use 5 large peaches!

Pineapple Pie with No-Shrink Meringue

one 20-oz. can pineapple
4 T. cornstarch
1/4 t. salt
1 c. sugar
1/4 c. water
3 egg yolks
2 T. butter
1/4 lemon (juice and grated rind)

Heat undrained fruit over hot water. Mix cornstarch, salt, and sugar with water. Add to pineapple and cook until thick, stirring constantly. Add beaten yolks, butter and lemon. Cook 2 minutes. Pour into baked pie shell and top with following:

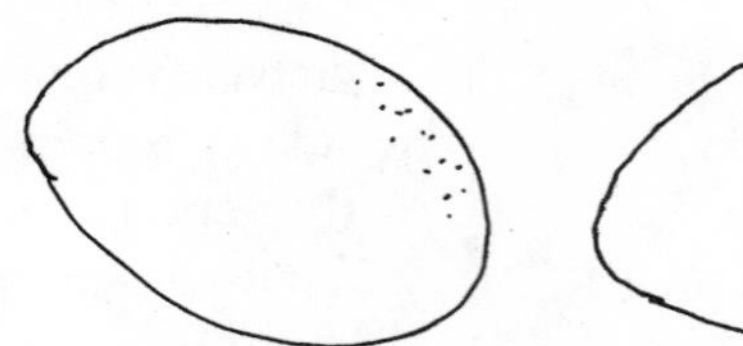

No-Shrink Meringue

1 T. cornstarch
1/2 c. water
3 egg whites
6 T. sugar

Cook cornstarch and water until clear and thick. Cool slightly. Beat egg whites until foamy. Add cornstarch mixture *all at once* and continue beating. Gradually add sugar (1 T. at a time). Meringue should be very stiff. Pile in mountain-high peaks onto pineapple pie and bake at 350° until golden brown. The perfect finish for a seafood salad supper!

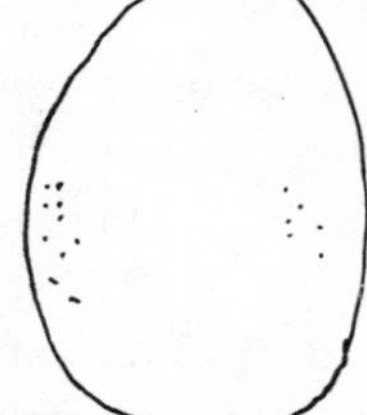

Nonesuch Orange Pie

1 c. sugar
3 T. cornstarch
pinch of salt
1/4 c. orange juice
1 T. grated orange rind
3 egg yolks
1 c. milk
2 T. butter
1 t. vanilla flavoring
1 c. sour cream

Combine sugar, cornstarch, and salt. Mix in juice and rind and beaten yolks. Add milk and mix well. Cook over low flame until thickened and smooth. Remove from burner and add butter and vanilla. Allow to cool and fold in sour cream. Spoon into graham-cracker crust. Swirl top with No-Shrink Meringue and bake in 350° oven until brown. Serves eight, as pie is sinfully rich!

For variety, try orange-snow pie. Simply fork in meringue while filling is hot but *before* adding sour cream.

Her children arise up and call her blessed; her husband also praiseth her.
Proverbs 31:28

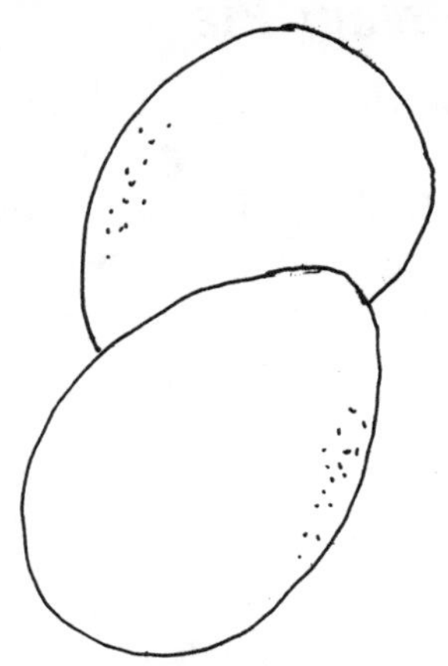

CREAM PIES AND VARIATIONS

Pies lend themselves to infinite variation. Main ingredients and flavorings love to "visit around," and for this reason pies are difficult to categorize. You will want to experiment in some instances, but it is always wise to find a few standbys from which to do your spin-offs. Grandmother would have told us that any good cook could turn out a velvety-smooth cream pie; but, of course, Grandmother knew nothing of instant mixes. Still, there is a "down home" flavor to the "from scratch" cream pie and so much you can do with it.

Basic Cream Pie

1/2 c. sugar
1/3 c. flour
1/4 t. salt
2 1/2 c. milk
4 eggs separated
1 T. margarine
2 t. vanilla
1/2 t. nutmeg

Sift together sugar, flour, and salt. Add milk gradually to the dry ingredients. Place over medium heat and bring to boil (stirring constantly). Boil only 1 minute and remove from heat. Beat egg yolks until very thick, adding 2 T. of hot liquid to them and blending well before adding to entire milk mixture. Return to low heat and stir until very thick, but do not boil. Remove from burner and add margarine, vanilla, and nutmeg. Pour into baked pie shell.

Cream Puff Pie

4 egg whites
1/2 c. sugar
pinch salt
1/2 c. cream of tartar

Beat 1/2 c. sugar, pinch of salt, and 1/2 c. cream of tartar with egg whites until stiff, pile onto Basic Cream Pie (which has been poured into a baked shell) and bake at 400° until brown.

If you prefer a meringue-in pie, simply beat egg whites (no sugar) until they stand in high peaks. Fold into hot Basic Cream Pie mixture before pouring into baked crust. Cover and refrigerate until cool. Top with whipped cream.

Butterscotch Dream Pie

Use Basic Cream Pie ingredients **but**:

2 c. milk
substitute 3/4 c. brown sugar for white
2 T. margarine
nondairy topping or meringue

Prepare Basic Cream Pie as directed except for reducing milk to 2 c. and substituting 3/4 c. dark brown sugar for white sugar. Increase margarine by 1 T. Pour into baked shell, refrigerate until cool, and top with nondairy topping (or top with No-Shrink Meringue as desired).

Banana Surprise Cream Pie

Basic Cream Pie ingredients **plus**:

4 bananas peeled and sliced
lemon juice
1/3 c. currant jelly
whipped cream

Prepare Basic Cream Pie filling as directed, cover, and refrigerate until cool. Cover bottom of baked pie crust with 3 sliced bananas. Pour cooled filling over bananas. Top with jellied bananas prepared in this way: Peel and slice 1 large banana and sprinkle with lemon juice. Arrange banana slices, overlapping them cartwheel-style, in center of pie. Heat currant jelly over hot water and glaze bananas (making sure all are covered). Serve in wedges with dollop of whipped cream in center of each piece.

Lemon Cream Pie

Basic Cream Pie ingredients **but**:

1 3/4 c. milk
2/3 c. sugar
1/4 c. lemon juice
2 t. lemon peel, grated
nondairy topping

Prepare Basic Cream Pie filling as above except for these changes: Decrease milk to 1 3/4 c. and increase sugar to 2/3 c. Add 1/4 c. lemon juice and 2 t. grated lemon peel when you add the margarine. Pour into baked shell. Cool completely and cover with nondairy topping. Garnish with grated lemon peel.

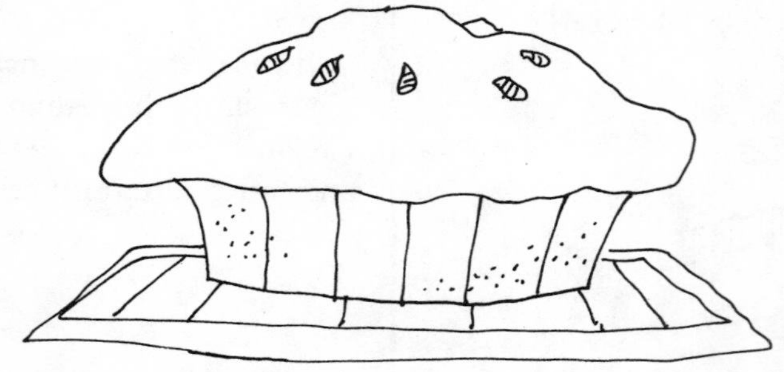

Cocoa Cream Pie

Basic Cream Pie ingredients **plus**:

2 T. cocoa
1 c. evaporated milk (substitute for 1 c. milk)
flaked coconut
nondairy topping

Prepare Basic Cream Pie filling as above except for adding 2 T. cocoa to dry ingredients and substituting 1 c. evaporated milk for 1 c. milk. Cool as directed and pour into baked pie shell which has been lined with flaked coconut. Top with another layer of coconut and a layer of nondairy topping.

Oh! Buttermilk Pie

1 c. buttermilk
3 eggs (beaten)
3 T. flour (rounded)
2 c. sugar
½ t. nutmeg
pinch of salt
½ c. margarine (melted)
1 t. vanilla
nondairy topping or vanilla ice cream

Add buttermilk to beaten eggs. Sift dry ingredients together and add gradually to first mixture. Add margarine and vanilla and beat well. Pour into two unbaked pie shells and bake at 400° for 10 minutes. Reduce heat to 325° and continue baking 35 minutes. Cool and serve plain or with nondairy topping or vanilla ice cream.

Caramel Cream Pie

½ c. flour
1½ c. sugar
3 c. milk
pinch of salt
5 eggs (beaten)
1 t. vanilla
¾ c. sugar
1 T. water

Sift flour and sugar together. Stir in milk. Add salt to eggs and beat into first mixture. Add vanilla.

Mix sugar and water. Brown in heavy pan over low heat. Pour into custard mixture and beat vigorously. Pour into baked pie shell. Top with No-Shrink Meringue if desired and bake at 350° until meringue is browned (no cooking necessary unless meringue is used). If no topping is used, serve with vanilla ice cream, nondairy topping, or marshmallow creme. Yes, it is rich!

Worthy-of-Praise Walnut Pie

½ c. brown sugar (packed)
3 eggs (beaten)
1 t. vanilla
1 c. light corn syrup
4 T. margarine (melted)
pinch of salt
1 c. walnuts (chopped)

Beat sugar and eggs together until light and frothy. Add all other ingredients (nuts last) and pour into unbaked shell. Bake at 375° about 50 minutes and remove from oven to cool. No topping necessary. Serve in small wedges, as this wonderful walnut pie is rich.

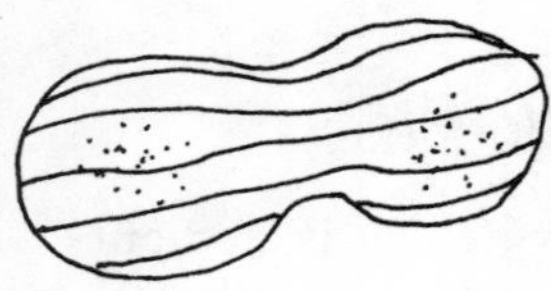

Peanut Pie

Use the recipe above but substitute peanut butter for margarine and dry roasted peanuts (unsalted) for walnuts. Spread lightly with tart jelly just before serving.

Great Aunt Het's "Poor Man's" Vinegar Pie

2 T. margarine
½ c. sugar
3 T. flour
2 T. cinnamon
1 t. each cloves and allspice
1 egg
1 c. water
2 T. vinegar

Cream margarine with sugar. Sift in flour and spices. Beat egg into water, add vinegar, and add gradually to first mixture. Cook in double boiler, stirring until thick. Pour into baked pie shell (perhaps Never-Fail Egg Pastry). Top with meringue (perhaps No-Shrink Meringue). Bake at 350° until meringue is golden brown.

California Lime Pie

1 can sweetened condensed milk
4 egg yolks (beaten)
½ c. fresh lime juice
few drops green food color

Add milk to well-beaten yolks and beat until mixture is pale yellow. Add lime juice and coloring. Beat until very thick. Pour into a baked shell and top with No-Shrink Meringue. Bake at 350° until meringue is brown.

If preferred, pour lime filling into baked graham cracker crust. Swirl with whipped cream and top with grated lime rind.

Speaking of limes, here is a sure-to-please recipe making use of the little citrus fruits.

Lime Bars

2 c. unsifted all-purpose flour
1/2 c. powdered sugar
1 c. butter or margarine
4 eggs
2 c. sugar
Dash of salt
1/3 c. fresh lime juice
Powdered sugar

Mix flour and powdered sugar. Mix in butter with pastry blender. Press mixture into 13″ x 9″ pan and bake at 350° for 20 minutes (till golden brown). Meanwhile, beat eggs until light and pale yellow. Gradually add sugar and salt, then lime juice, continuing to beat. Pour over *hot* crust and return to oven for 20 minutes more. Sprinkle with powdered sugar. Cool and cut into bars. Makes 4 1/2 dozen bars with a different tang!

Cider Pie

one 6-oz. can frozen apple concentrate
1/2 c. brown sugar
3 eggs
pinch of salt
2 T. margarine, melted
grated nutmeg
nondairy topping

Beat together thawed apple concentrate, sugar, eggs, salt, and melted margarine until smooth. Pour into baked (unpricked) pie shell. Sprinkle with nutmeg and bake at 350° for 30 minutes. Test with knife (should come out clean). Cool and serve with nondairy topping sprinkled with additional grated nutmeg.

Cherry-Go-Round Party Pie

1½ c. flour
¾ c. sugar
¾ c. margarine
4 egg yolks
1 envelope plain gelatin
2 c. evaporated milk
1 T. grated lemon rind
1 large bottle Maraschino cherries
1 c. nondairy topping

Sift flour with ½ c. of the sugar. Add softened margarine and 1 yolk. Beat vigorously or mix at high speed with mixer. Cover bowl and refrigerate several hours (or overnight). When ready to bake, press dough onto spring-bottom pan, then push up about 1″ along the sides of the pan. Bake 10 minutes at 400°. Allow to cool.

Combine gelatin and remaining ¼ c. sugar. Add milk and place over medium heat. Stir until gelatin is dissolved. Beat 3 remaining yolks, gradually adding about ¼ c. of the hot mixture. Pour egg mixture slowly into gelatin mixture, whisking after each addition. Turn heat to low and continue to cook until mixture thickens. Do not boil. Remove from heat and add ½ c. Maraschino juice and lemon rind. Refrigerate until mixture coats a spoon. Stir often to prevent mixture from sticking to sides. Remove from refrigerator, fold in nondairy topping, and pour into previously baked crust. Garnish with cherries by making circles which begin at outer edge and move toward center. Refrigerate until ready to use, then remove sides of pan. Lovely!

Black-Bottom Favorite

4 squares bitter chocolate (2 oz.)
1 envelope plain gelatin
2½ t. cornstarch
½ c. sugar
3 eggs (separated)
1½ c. whole milk
1 t. vanilla
one 9″ baked Chocolate Wafer Crust
1 T. rum flavoring
1 c. nondairy topping

Melt 1½ squares of chocolate, reserving ½ square for garnish. Set aside to cool while preparing gelatin mixture. Mix gelatin, cornstarch, and ¼ c. sugar in pan. In separate bowl beat yolks with milk until smooth, then add to gelatin mixture. Cook over medium heat until mixture thickens. Stir constantly. Remove from heat and divide into halves. Stir chocolate into one half. Add vanilla and beat until smooth. Refrigerate until mixture will hold shape in a spoon. Pile into Chocolate Wafer Crust and refrigerate. Chill second half of custard mixture until it, too, holds shape. Meantime, beat whites into soft peaks, sprinkling in remaining sugar gradually, beating after each addition. Carefully fold this mixture into cooled custard. Add rum flavoring. Pour about half of the second custard mixture on top of the pie, sprinkle on half the chocolate (which has been shaved), and refrigerate until "set." Do not refrigerate remaining custard. When pie holds shape (in only a few minutes), pour remaining custard mixture on top. Swirl on nondairy topping. Garnish with remaining chocolate curls. A special-occasion pie!

Pumpkin Chiffon Pie

1 envelope plain gelatin
3/4 t. cinnamon
1/2 t. each ginger, nutmeg, and salt
3/4 c. sugar
3 eggs (separated)
1/2 c. half-and-half milk
1 1/2 c. canned or freshly cooked pumpkin
nondairy topping
Maraschino cherries

Mix together gelatin, spices, salt, and 1/2 c. of the sugar. Beat yolks with half-and-half and stir into gelatin mixture. Add pumpkin and cook over low heat until thickened. Stir constantly. Refrigerate until cool but not "set." Beat whites to peaks, adding remaining sugar gradually. Beat until very stiff. Carefully fold into first mixture (use over-and-under motion until all traces of white disappear). Pour into Coconut Flake Crust:

Coconut Flake Crust

1 c. coconut flakes
1/4 c. gingersnaps
2 T. sugar
1/3 c. margarine (melted)

Toast coconut lightly in moderate oven. Reserve 2 T. for topping. Mix together remaining coconut, crushed gingersnaps, sugar, and melted margarine. Press firmly into bottom and up sides of a pie plate and bake at 375° until golden. Cool before filling.

Top pie with reserved coconut and swirl individual pieces with nondairy topping. Center each with a Maraschino cherry.

Coffee Cream Pie

1/2 c. percolator-grind coffee
2 c. milk
3/4 c. sugar
1/3 c. flour
pinch of salt
one 1-oz. square chocolate (shaved)
2 eggs plus 1 yolk
1 T. butter
1 t. vanilla
baked pastry shell
nondairy topping

Mix dry coffee with milk. Scald and strain. Sift together sugar, flour, and salt, and stir into milk. Cook over low heat, stirring constantly, until thick. Add chocolate and cook until melted. Beat in eggs (which have been beaten together). When thick, add butter and vanilla. Cool and pour into shell. Serve with nondairy topping when "set."

A WORD ABOUT FREEZING PIES:

- Do not freeze custard, cream, or meringue pies.
- Freeze pie shells baked or unbaked. To thaw, let stand at room temperature.
- Freeze fresh fruit pies before (or after, based on experience) baking.
- Freeze pies on cookie sheet *before* wrapping in heavy foil. Unwrap to thaw. Heat and enjoy with friends and steaming coffee!

Other Desserts

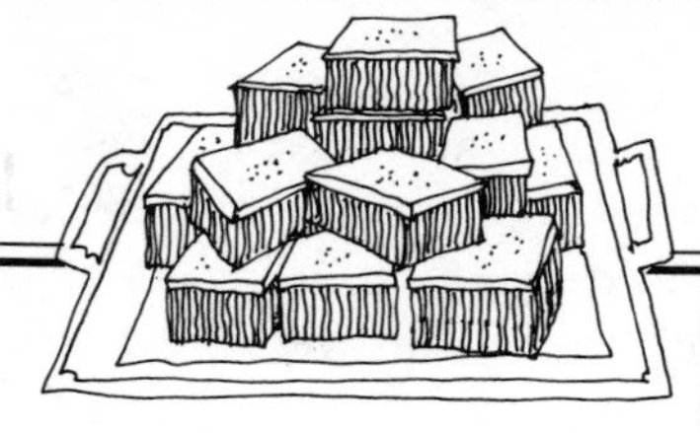

Favorite Pantry Creations

Back before green beans were stringless and Delicious apples were any color other than red, Grandmother's pantry shelves were stocked much differently from ours of today. She had to measure dry ingredients, squeeze juices, and churn the butter for recipes. Our mothers moved up to a few simple mixes, fruit concentrates, and margarine. But what a wonderful world we live in! Our grocers provide an instant mix for just about everything, and in a few minutes (with a bit of imagination) we can complete the meal it took Grandmother hours—maybe even days—to prepare. This is especially true in the area of desserts, so it is wise for us meals-on-wheels cooks to lay in a supply of time- and energy-saving packages. They will be a boon in a number of the following delightful desserts.

Did you know that apples head the list in popularity for the makings of fresh fruit desserts, followed by cherries, peaches, apricots, and berries, in that order?

With apples on the Top Ten, the wise cook is in the know about America's favorite fruit. The list of varieties is endless and it varies with the location in which one shops for fresh, local apples. It pays to study the fruit counter and ask a few questions; but for cooking, look for fresh, tart varieties (reserve Delicious for salads or eating around an open fire on chilly evenings) and make use of the Granny Smiths, Jonathans, Romes, and McIntoshes.

Small wonder apples are so popular! They serve as a base for so many fine recipes and yield to the whim of the baker. Once green apples were the scapegoat for most of children's tummy aches, but we ate them anyway even though they put our teeth on edge (providing we escaped without a call from the family doctor). Now there are green varieties on the market which make Green Apple Pie (which we once enjoyed from the forbidden fruit-in-the-raw). Just follow your regular recipe for apple pie (tarts or custards) and increase the sugar (almost doubling the amount). If you're lucky enough to have unripe-green apples, best cook them!

French Apple Pie? Sprinkle top (omitting upper crust) with a mix of 1 c. flour, 1/2 c. margarine, and 1/2 c. brown sugar (crumbled together). Apple-Cheese Pie or Tarts? Layer apples and grated cheese. Apple-Pecan? Mix 1/2 c. chopped pecans with sugar before adding to apples, then (omitting crust) spread hot-from-the-oven with glaze: 1/2 c. brown sugar, 1/3 c. chopped nuts, and 2 T. cream (or canned milk) cooked over low heat.

Finally, for that yummy-good Dutch-Apple Pie or Tart: Cover fruit with top crust, then slit liberally; 5 minutes before dessert is done, pour 1/2 c. cream into long slits, finish baking, and serve oven-hot!

Apple Yum Yum

1 stick margarine
1 package yellow cake mix
1/2 c. coconut
3 c. apples (cored, sliced, unpeeled)
juice of 1 lemon
1/2 c. sugar
1 t. cinnamon
1/2 t. nutmeg
one 8-oz. carton sour cream
2 egg yolks
grated rind of 1 lemon
3/4 c. chopped walnuts
sliced cheese

Mix margarine into cake mix until crumbly. Add coconut and pat mixture into bottom of large baking pan (about 12″ x 9″ x 2″). Bake at 350° about 10 minutes (or until brown). Arrange apples in hot crust and sprinkle with lemon juice and sugar, cinnamon, and nutmeg sifted together. Blend sour cream, yolks, and grated rind, and drizzle over top. Sprinkle with nuts. Bake about half an hour. Should be golden brown. Remove from oven. Serve hot with slices of cheese.

Yes, you *can* prepare in advance. Mix as directed and refrigerate overnight or freeze after baking. Thaw and reheat.

"Ole-Timey" Goodness Apple Dumplin's

Your favorite pastry dough
for double crust pie
fresh cooking apples
sugar
margarine
cinnamon

Syrup:
1/2 c. white corn syrup
1/4 t. cinnamon
2 T. margarine
1 c. boiling water
few drops red food color

Roll pastry dough 1/8″ thick and cut into 7″ squares (makes about 12 squares). Pare and core one apple for each square. Fill cavity with sugar. Add 1 T. margarine to top of each. Dust with cinnamon and seal pastry by moistening and bringing together pastry corners at top of apple. Place wrapped apples in a deep baking dish (they may touch) and top with syrup, made as follows:

Mix corn syrup, cinnamon, and margarine. Add boiling water. Set on burner and boil 3 minutes. Add color. Pour over dumplings while boiling hot and set immediately in previously heated oven at 450°. Bake 30 minutes. (Apple Dumplin's may be made previous day or may be made and frozen in advance. Make syrup just before baking. If frozen, do not thaw dumplin's before baking, but allow 15 minutes additional baking time. Test with fork for doneness.) Serve à la mode.

The six most important words:
I admit I made a mistake.
The five most important:
You did a fine job.
The four most important:
What is your suggestion?
The three most important:
If you please.
The two most important:
Thank you.
The one most important:
God.
The one least important:
I.

Apple Bars

1 c. flour
1/2 t. soda
1/2 t. salt
1 t. cinnamon
1/2 c. brown sugar
1 c. oatmeal
1/2 c. margarine
2 1/2 c. apples (cored, pared, sliced)
2 T. additional margarine
1/2 c. white sugar

Sift first four ingredients together and combine with brown sugar and oatmeal. Add 1/2 c. margarine and mix. Spread a layer on baking sheet, reserving some of this crumb mixture to sprinkle on top, and cover with a layer of apples (use all of fruit). Dot with margarine. Sprinkle with the white sugar. Top with remaining crumbs and bake at 350° until done (about 30 minutes).

Serve as a dessert, hot or cold, with your choice of whipped topping, ice cream, or yellow cheese. This unusual concoction becomes cookies which store well when cooled, cut into squares, and stored in a stone jar—or may be frozen instead.

Easy-As-Pie Apple Dessert

1 can apple pie filling
1 1-lb. pkg. yellow cake mix (or 1 8 1/2-oz. pkg.)
1/2 c. chopped nuts
1 cube margarine, melted
ice cream or nondairy topping

Pour 1 can of apple pie filling into ungreased dish. Top with half a 1-lb. package yellow cake mix (or one 8 1/2-oz. package). Sprinkle top with chopped nuts and drizzle melted margarine on top. Bake about 30 minutes at 350°. May be served hot or cold with ice cream or cold with nondairy topping. (Cherry, blueberry, or other fruit fillings may be substituted for variety).

Apple-Caramel Cobbler

one 29-oz. can sliced apples (drained)
1 package refrigerated caramel rolls
1/4 c. flour
1 t. grated lemon peel
pinch of salt
1/2 t. cinnamon
1/2 c. chopped nuts
one 7-oz. bottle 7-Up
1 T. margarine

Reserve 1 c. juice from drained fruit for later use. Crumble sugar mixture from canned rolls into saucepan. Add flour, peel, salt, cinnamon, and nuts. Mix 7-Up with reserved juice and mix into topping mixture. Heat until thick (being careful not to burn) and add margarine. Lay apples on bottom of a large baking dish and pour boiling liquid over fruit. Top with caramel rolls (which have been separated), pushing each gently into hot mixture until almost covered. Bake at 400° about 25 minutes or until golden brown.

Apple-Cashew (or Other Nut—Wild or Domestic) Pie

2 doz. graham crackers (crushed)
1 stick softened margarine
2 T. powdered sugar
1/2 c. finely chopped cashews
one 8-oz. package cream cheese
2 T. half-and-half
1 pkg. dry whipped topping mix
1 large can apple pie filling
cashews
cinnamon

Mix first four ingredients well and pack into bottom of 9″ x 13″ baking pan. Bake 10 minutes at 325°. Remove from oven and cool.

Beat fluffy the cream cheese and half-and-half.

Whip whipped topping mix according to directions (substituting half-and-half for whole milk). Beat into cheese mixture and pour over cooled graham cracker crust.

Top with 1 large can apple pie filling. Sprinkle with additional cashews and sift with powdered cinnamon. Refrigerate until ready to serve. Needs no additional topping.

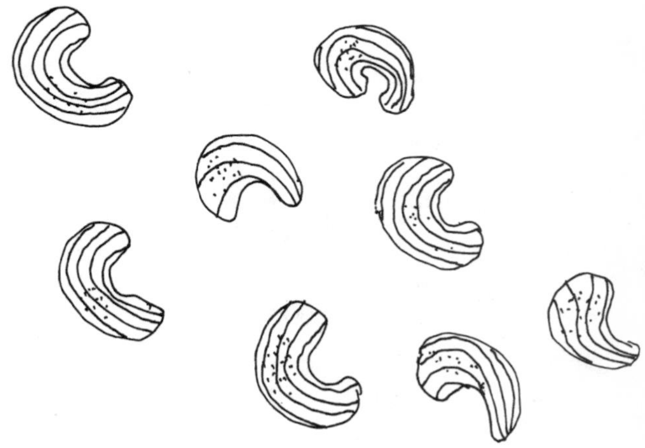

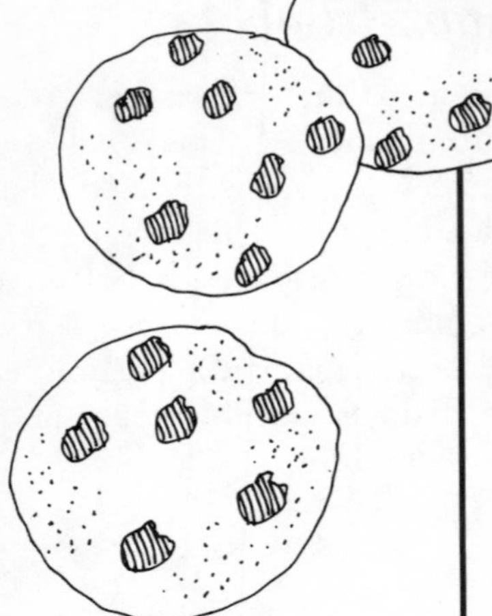

THE LIST GOES ON

Even if you are new at cooking, you've guessed by now that there is an endless string of recipes, and you very well may add to the list. Experiment with recipes in this book, then experiment with some of your very own. After all, so the story goes, Toll House Cookies resulted from an accident. Having no cocoa on hand, a long-ago cook reasoned that a chopped-up bar of bittersweet chocolate would melt as her cake baked. Well, you know the result!

And here's something equally good made from a mix:

Frosted Toll House Cake

1½ c. biscuit mix
1 egg
2 T. margarine
½ c. sugar
½ c. milk
1 t. vanilla
1 c. chocolate chips

Blend all ingredients with mixer (or by hand) except chocolate chips. Beat 4 minutes. Add chocolate chips. Pour into greased and floured pan (8″ x 8″ x 2″ or 9″ x 1½″). Bake 30 minutes at 350° and while still warm top with:

Broiled Topping

3 T. margarine
2 T. half-and-half
½ c. walnuts (chopped)
⅓ c. brown sugar
½ c. coconut
1 t. vanilla

Mix all ingredients well, but do not cook. After spreading on cake, place beneath broiler about 3″ from heat and set control at "Broil," or about 550°. Broil no longer than 3 minutes, checking frequently.

Cool and cut into squares for serving or serve hot with coffee.

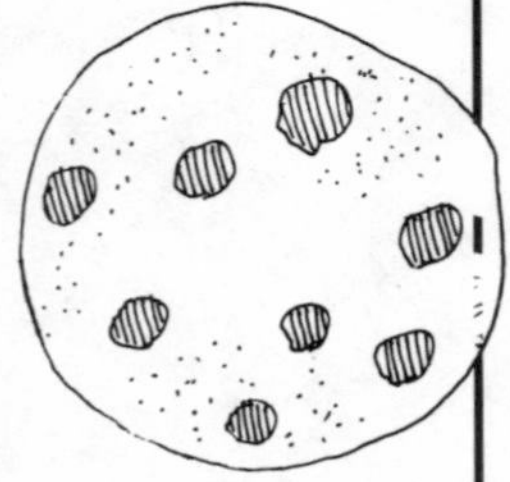

No-Bake Cheesecake
(Updated Homemade Cottage Cheese Cake)

Crust:
1/2 c. margarine
1/3 c. sugar
1 1/2 c. cornflakes (crushed)
1/2 c. walnuts (finely chopped)

Filling:
one 30-oz. can apricots
1/2 c. apricot juice
1 envelope plain gelatin
two 8-oz. packages cream cheese
1 can sweetened condensed milk
2 T. lemon juice
1 carton nondairy topping

Glaze:
1/2 c. apricot juice (from fruit)
1 t. cornstarch
5 mint leaves

Mix margarine and sugar in pan over low heat. Bring to boil and turn off heat. Add cornflake crumbs and nuts. Press all but 2 T. into 9″ springform pan. Refrigerate while preparing filling.

Drain fruit, reserving juice. Combine 1/2 c. juice with gelatin and stir over low heat until dissolved. Set aside 5 whole (or 10 halves) apricots for garnish. Blend all others (preferably in blender). Combine with gelatin mixture. Beat cheese until smooth, and add condensed milk and lemon juice. Mix well. Stir in apricot blend and fold in whipped topping (which has been thawed completely). Pour filling into crust. Make a garnish of 5 apricot "flowers" by cutting each whole apricot lengthwise into 4 pieces. Use each piece as a petal and make a 4-petal flower by arranging so that tips touch in center.

Make a glaze by cooking 1/2 c. apricot juice and 1 t. cornstarch until thick and clear. Spoon over cheesecake, then tuck a mint leaf into each flower for a stem. Refrigerate until ready to serve. Remove sides from pan and cut cake into pie-shaped wedges. This is Umm-umm good!

Mystery-Shape "Cup" Cakes

1 package yellow cake mix

Topping:
1-2 oranges
3/4 c. orange-peel slivers
3/4 c. water
3/4 c. orange juice
3/4 c. sugar
nondairy topping

Mix cake mix according to directions on package. Grease very well 10 hot-drink cups (*not* Styrofoam) and spoon batter carefully into each, filling them about 2/3 full. Place cups on cookie sheet and bake at 375° for 30 minutes. Test for doneness. While individual cakes bake, prepare topping.

Before squeezing oranges for juice, peel off a thin layer of outer rind (making sure no white clings). Cut into thin shreds. Combine with other ingredients (except nondairy topping) and boil 5 minutes. Keep warm (not boiling).

Cool cakes for five minutes, then turn each separately onto smooth surface (tapping bottom of cup before lifting it). Spoon hot topping on each cake as soon as drinking cup is removed. Refrigerate until cold. Serve with a dollop of nondairy topping on each mystery-shaped cupcake. A real conversation piece!

Early Explorers' Fantasy Dessert

one 15 1/4-oz. can crushed pineapple (drained)
1/4 c. brown sugar (packed)
1/2 c. coconut flakes
2 T. margarine
1 baked pie shell

Filling:
one 4 1/2-oz. lemon pudding mix (not instant)
1/2 c. white sugar
1 3/4 c. water
2 egg yolks (beaten)
2 T. lemon juice
1 T. grated lemon rind
1/4 c. macadamia nuts (chopped)
2 T. margarine
2 egg whites
1/4 c. sugar
toasted coconut
Maraschino cherries

Combine pineapple, sugar, coconut, and margarine. Cover bottom of pie shell with mixture (packing well) and carefully fold strips of foil around edges of pastry. Bake at 325° for 10 minutes. Remove stripping and continue baking for another 5 minutes. Set aside to cool while preparing the following filling:

Combine mix and sugar with water and yolks. Cook until thick, stirring constantly. Add juice, rind, nuts, and margarine. Remove from heat, cover with waxed paper, and stir now and then until mixture cools.

Beat 2 egg whites until frothy. Gradually add 1/4 c. sugar. Beat until mixture stands in high peaks. Fold mixture into cooled filling. Pile into pastry shell. Garnish with toasted coconut, then push Maraschino cherries at random in filling, allowing about half of each cherry to show. Chill at least 5 hours or preferably overnight. Wow!

Honey-from-the-Hive Banana Squares

1 package white cake mix (which calls for whipped-in egg whites)
3/4 c. evaporated milk
3/4 c. sugar
2 egg yolks
2 T. margarine
1 overripe banana (mashed)
3/4 c. chopped filberts
1 t. lemon juice
1 t. vanilla

Bake cake according to directions, using two square pans. While cake bakes prepare filling:

Combine milk, sugar, yolks, and margarine. Cook over medium heat about 10 minutes or until thick. Stir constantly. Add banana, nuts, lemon juice, and vanilla. Cool.

When cake is done, remove from pans and spread one layer with all of filling. Top with second layer. When ready to serve, cut into squares and top with:

Honey Whipped Cream

2 T. powdered sugar
1 t. vanilla
2 T. honey
1 carton nondairy topping
chopped filberts

Fold powdered sugar, vanilla, and honey into nondairy topping. Spread on squares and garnish with chopped filberts.

Spiced Spud Squares

- 1 c. cold potatoes (instant or leftovers)
- 1 3/4 c. sugar
- pinch of salt
- 1/2 t. nutmeg
- 3/4 c. margarine
- 3 eggs
- 1 t. vanilla
- 1 t. soda
- 1 c. buttermilk
- 2 c. flour
- 3/4 c. walnuts (chopped)
- 2 T. flour

Prepare enough instant potatoes to make 1 c. according to directions on package (or use leftovers). Sift sugar, salt, and nutmeg together and beat into potatoes and margarine. Beat in eggs. Add vanilla. Blend thoroughly.

Combine soda with buttermilk and add alternately with 2 c. flour. It is best to begin and end with a dry ingredient. Coat walnuts with 2 T. flour and stir into batter. Grease and flour a 13″ x 9″ x 2″ pan. Pour batter in pan and bake at 350° about 1 hour or until done. Allow to cool before frosting with:

Butterscotch Frosting

- 1/4 c. butter (or margarine plus 1/4 t. butter flavoring)
- 3/4 c. brown sugar (packed)
- 3 T. half-and-half
- 2 c. powdered sugar (sifted)
- 1/2 c. nuts (chopped)

Melt butter and sugar together over low heat. Cook 2 minutes. Add half-and-half and bring to boil. Cool to lukewarm without stirring. Sift in sugar and beat until smooth and shining. Add nuts and spread on cake. Cut into squares for serving (or can be frozen in pan and cut when ready for use).

Be careful how you live. You may be the only Bible some people read. Measure, sift, and sort your words carefully, following the Biblical formula.

DANDY DO-LITTLE DESSERTS

Three-Mix Torte Supreme

1 package yellow cake mix
one 4-oz. package pistachio pudding mix (not instant)
1 c. dates (seeded, pitted, and chopped)
pinch of salt
1/2 c. walnuts (chopped)
1/2 c. coconut (toasted)
2 T. margarine
1 package fluffy frosting mix
1 doz. Maraschino cherries

Mix #1: Prepare yellow cake mix according to directions and bake in two 9″ pans. Cool.

Mix #2: Prepare pudding as directed, using only 1 1/2 c. milk. Add dates and salt as mixture cooks. When thick, add nuts, coconut, and margarine, and cover with waxed paper while preparing mix #3.

Mix #3: Prepare frosting mix as directed.

Cut each 9″ cake layer in half. (Hint: Tie white sewing thread around the circumference of each layer, placing the thread halfway between the top and bottom of layer. Grasp the thread at each end and pull. The thread will divide the layer neatly in half; you'll now have a total of four layers.)

Spread pudding filling between layers, and frost top and sides of cake with frosting mix. Place Maraschino cherries on top of cake at random. Refrigerate until ready to serve in thin slices.

Peanut Butter Pudding

2 c. cold whole milk
1 c. cream-style peanut butter
one 3 3/4 oz. package instant vanilla pudding mix
1 c. sour cream
1/2 c. toasted coconut
1/2 c. chopped dates
nondairy whipped topping

Blend milk with peanut butter. Add pudding mix and beat until thick. Stir in sour cream, coconut, and dates. Chill. Top with a swirl of nondairy whipped topping. Serves six dessert lovers.

Down-Home Banana Pudding

2 eggs
one 4-serving-size package vanilla pudding and pie mix (not instant)
$2^1/_2$ c. milk
2 doz. vanilla wafers
2 large bananas (sliced)
Dash of salt
$^1/_4$ c. sugar

Separate eggs. Combine yolks with pudding mix and milk. Cook over medium heat (stirring) until mixture boils. Remove from heat. Lightly butter bottom of $1^1/_2$-qt. baking dish and arrange layer of wafers on bottom and sides. Alternate layers of bananas and pudding (beginning and ending with fruit) on top of wafers. Beat egg whites and salt until frothy. Sift in sugar gradually, continuing to beat until meringue stands in peaks. Pile on pudding (making sure edges are sealed). Bake at 425° about 10 minutes or until golden brown. A delicious quickie—good hot or cold—which rivals the kind our grandmothers "down home" used to devote a morning to making.

Pineapple Porcupine Pudding

one $^3/_4$-oz. package vanilla pudding and pie mix (not instant)
$1^1/_2$ c. unsweetened pineapple juice
1 c. nondairy topping
slivered blanched almonds

Prepare pudding according to directions on package, substituting juice for milk. Cover and cool thoroughly. Fold in nondairy topping and pile into parfait glasses. Stick almonds into pudding "quill" fashion and chill thoroughly.

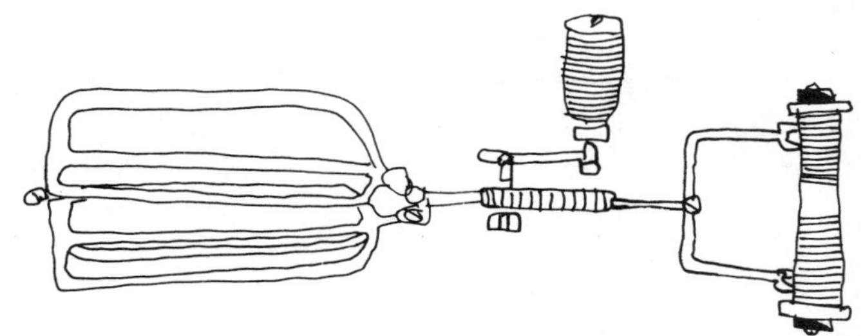

Jello Rolls

3 empty 6-oz. cans
one 3-oz. package strawberry gelatin
1 c. boiling water
$^1/_2$ c. cold water
3 medium bananas (peeled)
1 t. lemon juice

Wash cans and set aside (tops are removed with automatic opener and bottoms are left on). Dissolve gelatin in hot water. Add cold water. Mix and chill until "wobbly." Remove ends from bananas, sprinkle bananas with lemon juice, and place one banana in center of each can. Spoon gelatin around them and chill with cans upright. When ready to serve, puncture bottom of can, stand opened end on plate, and lift off can. Slice into three or four servings per can. Lovely!

Grape Poke Cake

1 package white cake mix
one 3-oz. package grape gelatin
1 c. boiling water
1 c. nondairy topping

Bake cake according to directions on package. Cool in pan 15 minutes. Dissolve gelatin according to directions on package. Poke holes in cake with soda straw. Pour half of the warm gelatin over cake and refrigerate immediately. Chill remaining gelatin until slightly thickened. Whip for 2 minutes by hand or with electric beater. Fold in topping and spread over entire cake. Return to refrigerator until ready to cut and serve in squares.

Instant Trifle

equivalent of 1 layer leftover cake
1 large ripe banana
2 T. rum flavoring
one 9-oz. carton nondairy topping
toasted coconut
Maraschino cherries

Crumble cake (butter cake is preferable to angel food). Mash banana with fork and whip into cake crumbs. Add flavoring. Fold in topping and chill until ready to serve. Keeps nicely up to a week in refrigerator and mellows with age. Scoop into parfait glasses for serving and top with toasted coconut and a Maraschino cherry.

A recipe unshared will soon be forgotten. Shared, it will live through future generations.

Quick-Trick Sundaes

favorite ice cream
favorite toppings

Tomorrow—or one week from today—is going to be too busy to serve sundaes? Wrong! Simply chill your cookie sheets and scoop servings of ice cream onto the pans. Freeze uncovered. When frozen, wrap with freezer wrap until ready to serve. Serve with your favorite homemade or deli sauces: fudge, honey, mint, raspberry jam . . . that's all there is to it!

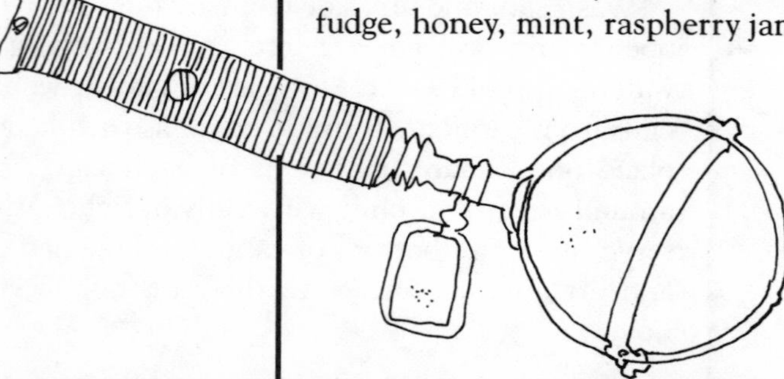

THEN THERE ARE COOKIES

A full cookie jar is a lifesaver. Children adore cookies. Adults often prefer them to more-filling desserts. And even the finicky eater will sample a cookie after saying, "No dessert for me."

Cookies these days fall into two classifications: the kind we love to bake on rainy days and store ahead, and the minute-made ones originating from mixes that challenge cookie-eaters who claim they know the difference! Here are a few favorites from which you can make dozens of spin-offs of your own.

BAKING DAY COOKIES

Coconut Dreams

Bottom layer:
1/2 c. margarine
1/2 t. salt
1 c. sifted flour
1/2 c. brown sugar (packed)

Top layer:
2 eggs
1 c. brown sugar
1 t. vanilla
1 T. almond flavoring
2 T. flour
1/2 t. baking powder
1/4 t. salt
1 1/2 c. coconut (cut with scissors)
1 c. chopped almonds

Mix margarine, salt, flour, and sugar and pat into 9″ x 13″ x 2″ ungreased pan. Press down well. Bake at 325° for 20 minutes. Remove from oven and prepare top layer.

Beat eggs. Add brown sugar, vanilla, and almond flavoring and beat until thick and light in color. Fold in flour, baking powder, and salt sifted together. Add coconut and nuts. Spread over bottom layer and return to oven and bake at 325° for 20 minutes. Cool and cut into squares. Dreamy when fresh, but freezes well and will keep indefinitely in stone jar.

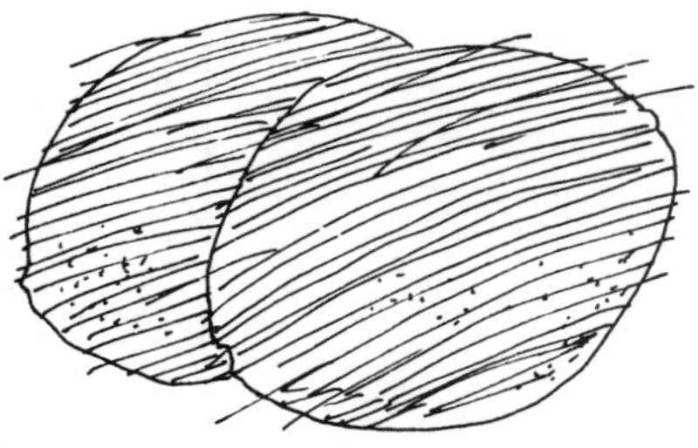

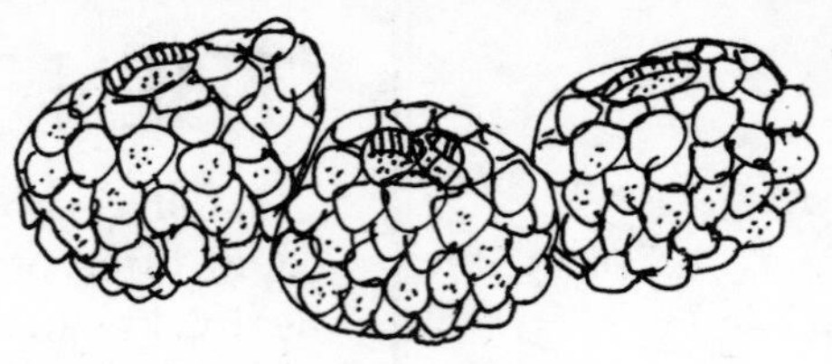

Raspberry Meringues

1 c. margarine
1 c. sugar
4 egg yolks
2 c. flour
1/2 t. salt

4 egg whites
1 c. sugar
pinch of salt
1 t. vanilla
1/2 c. chopped walnuts
1 c. flaked coconut
1 1/2 c. raspberry jam

Cream together margarine and sugar. When fluffy, beat in egg yolks, one at a time. Fold in flour sifted with salt. Spread on bottom of ungreased pan (about 11″ x 17″ x 1″) and bake at 350° for 10 minutes. Remove from oven when done. While pastry is baking prepare meringue by beating whites until foamy. Gradually add sugar and salt and beat until meringue stands in glossy peaks. Blend in vanilla. Add nuts and coconut. Spread jam on baked pastry and swirl meringue lightly over jam-covered pastry. Bake an additional 25 minutes at 350°. When golden-brown, remove from oven. Cool and cut into squares. (Be original! Substitute exotic jams.)

Cornflake Coffees

4 egg whites
3 1/2 c. sugar
3 T. instant coffee
pinch of salt
1 c. crushed cornflakes
  (measured after crushing)

Beat egg whites until mixture stands in peaks (but is not dry). Sift sugar, coffee, and salt together. Add about half the dry mixture to beaten whites, beating after each addition. Mix together the other half of dry mixture and crushed cornflakes. Fold into first mixture. Drop by teaspoon onto greased cookie sheet and bake at 275° for 15 minutes (should be slightly browned and feel dry when touched). Remove from pan while warm. Makes five dozen coffees.

Apricot Chews

2 c. dried apricots
one 15-oz. can sweetened condensed milk
2 t. vanilla
2 c. coconut flakes
1 c. walnuts (chopped)

Set food chopper on "Fine" and grind apricots. Stir into condensed milk. Dump in remaining ingredients and blend. Drop by tablespoonful onto greased cookie sheet and bake 10 minutes at 350°. Makes 3½ dozen delightful chews. (Apples, peaches, figs . . . why not?)

Surprise Kisses

1 c. margarine
½ c. sugar
1 t. vanilla
1 c. pecans (finely chopped)
2 c. flour
one 5-oz. package Hershey's Chocolate Kisses
powdered sugar

Cream margarine and sugar together until fluffy. Add vanilla. Add nuts to flour, then combine with first mixture. Make into a cylinder shape and chill. When ready to bake, slice chilled dough as for cookies. Place a Chocolate Kiss in each slice and shape into a ball. Place each "ball" on a cookie sheet (being careful that cookies do not touch). Bottoms should be flat on pan. Now carefully with fingers shape a peak on top (following shape of candies inside). Bake at 375° for 10-15 minutes (should be firm but not brown). Remove carefully from oven and sprinkle with powdered sugar while still warm.

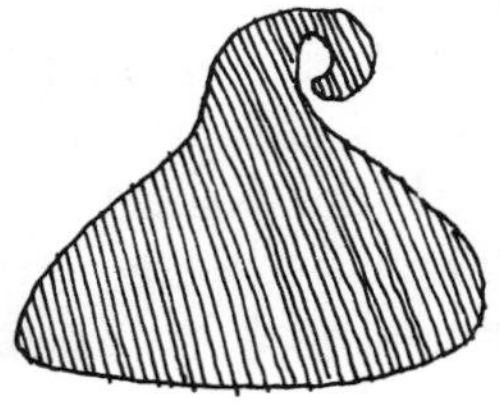

Jelly Chews

1 c. margarine
2 c. light brown sugar
2 eggs
4 c. quick-cooking oatmeal
1 t. salt
1 c. nuts (chopped)
1 c. raisins (chopped)
½ c. coconut
1 t. vanilla
1 t. black walnut flavoring
tart jelly

Cream together margarine and sugar until light in color. Beat in eggs one at a time. Mix oatmeal, salt, nuts, raisins, and coconut together, then add to first mixture. Blend in vanilla and walnut flavoring and refrigerate overnight. When ready to bake, shape into balls. Lay ball-shapes (one at a time) on cookie sheet, pressing down with the underside of a tablespoon. Cookies should not touch at edges. Make a dent in the top of each cookie and add ½ t. tart jelly (bright reds are prettier, but any color or flavor will work). Bake 10 minutes at 325°.

Forgotten Chip Cookies

2 egg whites
1 c. sugar
one 12-oz. pkg. chocolate chips
1 c. chopped nuts

Heat oven to 350° while mixing cookies. Turn off *before* putting cookies inside.

Beat whites until foamy, then add sugar gradually until mixture is stiff and glossy. Fold in chips and nuts. Place cookies in oven and leave overnight (do not open oven during "baking" time).

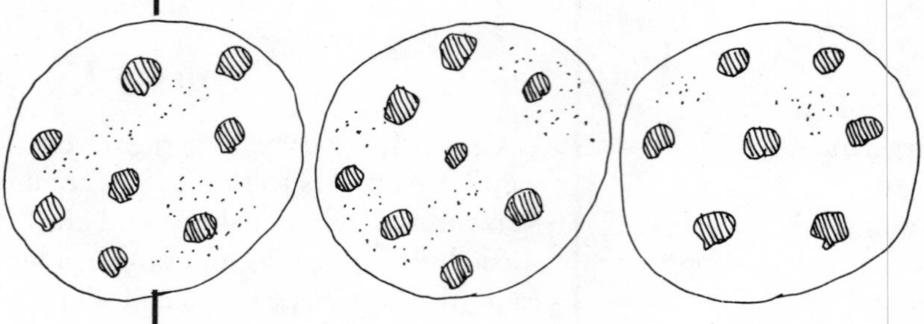

Sesame Seed Crisps

1/4 c. margarine
1/4 c. peanut butter
1/2 c. white sugar
1/2 c. brown sugar (packed)
1 1/2 c. flour
1/2 t. soda
1/2 t. salt
2 eggs
1/2 c. sesame seeds (toasted 5 min. at 375°)
1 t. vanilla
untoasted sesame seeds

Cream together margarine, peanut butter, and sugars. Blend in half of dry ingredients (flour, soda, and salt sifted together). Beat in the eggs one at a time. Add remaining dry ingredients and blend. Add toasted sesame seeds and vanilla. Drop by teaspoonful onto lightly greased cookie sheet, flatten each cookie with a fork—making a crisscross design—and top with a sprinkle of untoasted sesame seed. Sift granulated sugar on top and bake at 375° for 10 minutes.

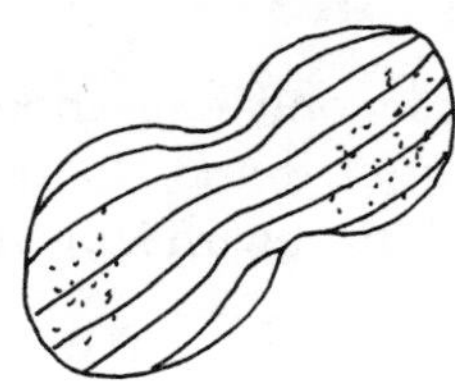

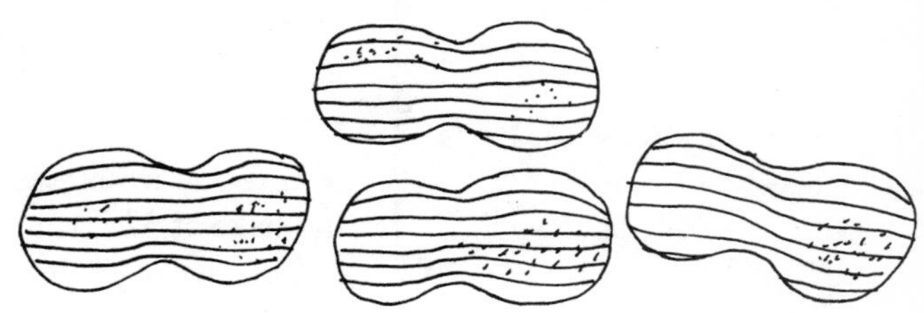

Peanut Fingers

3/4 c. margarine
1/2 c. powdered sugar
1/4 c. brown sugar (packed)
1 t. vanilla
2 c. flour
1 c. salted peanuts (chopped)

Cream together margarine and sugars. Add vanilla. Sift in flour gradually and add chopped peanuts. Shape into fingers about 3″ long and 1/2″ in diameter. Bake on *ungreased* cookie sheet 12-15 minutes at 350°. Cool and frost with:

Coffee Frosting

2 T. margarine
1 c. powdered sugar
1 t. instant coffee
2 T. half-and-half
1/2 t. vanilla
chopped peanuts

Blend margarine, sugar, coffee, milk, and vanilla. Spread Peanut Fingers with frosting and roll in chopped peanuts.

Potato Chip Cookies

2 c. margarine
1 c. sugar
1 c. potato chips (crumbled and *heaped*)
1 c. walnuts (chopped)
1 t. vanilla
3 c. sifted flour

Cream together margarine and sugar. Add potato chips, nuts, and vanilla. Sift in flour and mix well. Drop by teaspoonfuls onto ungreased cookie sheet and bake at 350° for 12 minutes (or until brown). Cookies should look rough and chips should remain crunchy.

Baby Food Squares

- 1/2 c. margarine (melted)
- 1 c. sugar
- 1 c. walnuts (chopped)
- 2 t. cinnamon
- 1 small jar strained sweet potatoes
- 1 t. vanilla
- 1 1/4 c. flour
- 1 t. soda
- 1/2 t. salt
- 1 egg (beaten)
- one 8 3/4-oz. crushed pineapple (undrained)

Combine all ingredients in any order only long enough to be sure all are blended. Pour into buttered-and-floured pan and bake at 325° for 30 minutes. Cool, frost with icing below, and cut into squares.

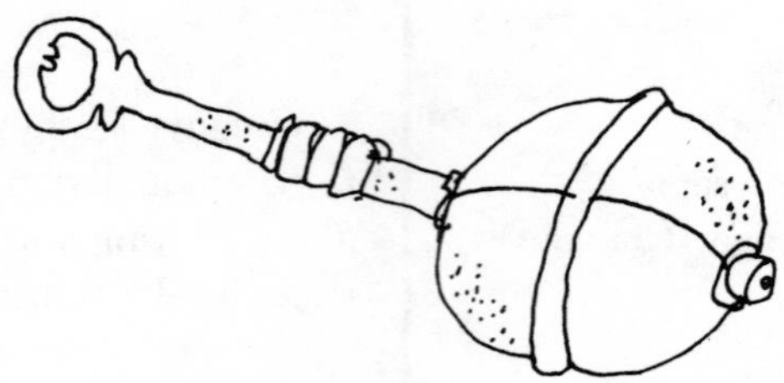

Cream Cheese Icing

- one 4-oz. pkg. cream cheese
- 1 t. vanilla
- 1 c. powdered sugar
- milk to moisten

Bring cheese to room temperature and add vanilla. Sift in powdered sugar. Add milk to form right consistency to spread.

INSTANT-MIX COOKIES

Minute-Made Macaroons

one 1-lb. pkg. shredded coconut
one 15-oz. can sweetened condensed milk
2 t. vanilla

Blend coconut into milk. Add vanilla and drop by teaspoon onto well-greased cookie sheet. Bake 10 minutes (or until crusted but not brown) at 350°. Cool 2 minutes before lifting individually with spatula.

Christmas Tree Balls

one 15-oz. can sweetened condensed milk
2 t. lemon juice
2 c. vanilla wafers (crushed to powder)
1 c. dates (chopped)
1/2 c. walnuts (chopped)
powdered sugar for coating

Blend milk with lemon juice. Add wafer crumbs. Stir in dates and walnuts. Sprinkle powdered sugar over mixture and knead. Shape into balls about the size of a walnut. Roll each ball in powdered sugar and wrap individually in saran wrap. Store in refrigerator or freeze until ready for use. Lovely makings for a gift package or an unusual idea for decorating the yule tree. Let the children or guests snip their dessert off the branches after the grand opening. Remember that the food wrap adds sparkle and keeps the cookies free from dust. For Rum Balls, simply substitute rum flavoring for lemon juice.

See-Through Bon Bons

three 6-oz. packages gelatin dessert
4 packets unflavored gelatin
4 c. boiling water
powdered sugar (sifted)

Pour water over gelatins. Mix well and pour into well-greased flat pans. Refrigerate until set. Cut into cubes and dust with powdered sugar. Make several recipes for colorful dishes.

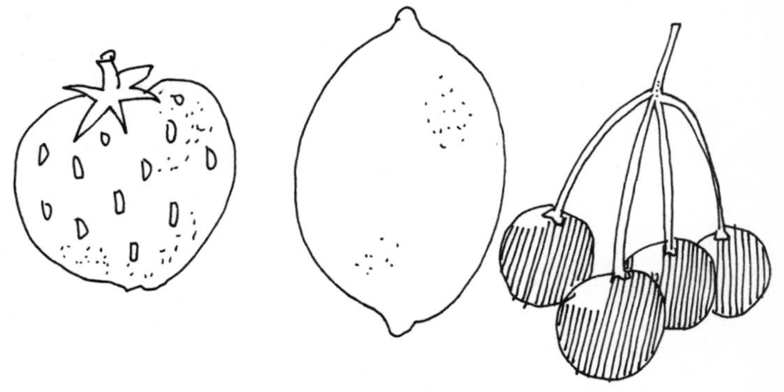

Hand-Dipped Surprises

- 4 c. cream-style peanut butter
- 1 c. margarine (melted)
- 3 c. powdered sugar (sifted)
- 1 t. vanilla

- one 12-oz. pkg. chocolate chips
- 1/4 bar paraffin
- dash salt
- 1 t. vanilla

Blend peanut butter and margarine. Sift in powdered sugar and beat. Add vanilla and shape into balls. Prepare dip.

Melt chips and paraffin over hot water. Add salt and vanilla and keep mixture over water while dipping. Do not beat.

For easy dipping, ease sharp end of a toothpick into each ball. Either dip into chocolate mixture or spoon mixture over cookie. Remove toothpick and seal hole in cookie by dipping toothpick into chocolate and smoothing dipped end over it. Cool on waxed paper.

But wait! There's more. Try dipping whole (washed, hulled, and drained) strawberries using the same method (use stem end for sticking toothpick into berries). And try chunks of peeled bananas. Refrigerate if these are to be used right away, or they freeze beautifully for that wonderful midwinter surprise!

Stir-and-Fry Date Delicacies

- 1 c. margarine
- 3/4 c. sugar
- 2 eggs
- 1 c. dates (pitted and chopped)
- 1 t. vanilla
- 2 c. Rice Krispies
- 1 c. walnuts (chopped)
- 1 c. coconut (snipped with scissors)

Melt margarine in heavy skillet over low heat. Add sugar and beat in eggs, one at a time. Stir constantly. Add dates and continue cooking until thick. Remove from heat, add vanilla, and let stand while flattening cereal by lightly rolling over it one time with rolling pin. Add to cookie mixture. Pour in nuts. Shape into balls and roll in coconut. May be frozen or stored in tight cookie jar. Fun to do and fun to eat!

Chocolate-Mallows

One 8-oz. milk chocolate bar
1/3 c. margarine
16 large white marshmallows
1 t. vanilla
1 c. flaked coconut
2 c. rolled oats

Melt chocolate, margarine, and marshmallows over hot water. Remove from heat and stir in vanilla, coconut, and oats. Drop by teaspoonful onto waxed paper and refrigerate. Yield: 3 dozen.

Handy hint: All unworthy thoughts should be well-beaten. —J.M.B.

No-Bake Peanut Butter Drops

1 c. sugar
1/2 c. margarine
1/4 c. milk
3 T. cocoa
1/2 c. peanut butter
1/2 c. dry roasted peanuts (chopped)
1 t. vanilla
1/2 c. dates (pitted and chopped)
3 c. quick-cooking oats
1/2 c. colored gumdrops (chopped)

Combine sugar, margarine, milk, and cocoa and boil over low heat 1 minute. Stir in peanut butter. Add peanuts, vanilla, dates, oats, and gumdrops. Drop by teaspoonfuls onto waxed paper. These easy, different, and delicious cookies keep well.

Shortcut Brownies

1 pkg. chocolate cake mix
1 egg (beaten)
1/4 c. water
1 c. walnuts (chopped)
powdered sugar

Mix all together and press into 9″ x 14″ pan. Bake at 350° for 20-25 minutes (these will be chewy). Remove from oven. Cut into squares and cool. Dust with powdered sugar and remove from pan.

Baked Potato-Cookies

2 c. sugar
1 c. margarine
2 eggs (beaten)
1/8 t. salt
2 2/3 c. biscuit mix
2 2/3 c. potato flakes
3 t. coconut flavoring
sugar, nutmeg, cinnamon mixture

Cream together sugar, margarine, eggs, and salt. Add biscuit mix and potato flakes, then flavoring. Stir (or blend with hands) only long enough to mix. Chill 1 hour or overnight. Roll into walnut-sized balls. Sprinkle with granulated sugar, nutmeg, and cinnamon and place on ungreased cookie sheet. Bake at 350° about 12 minutes or until slightly brown. Makes 100 fun cookies!

Hurry-Up Ginger Cookies

1/2 c. chunky peanut butter
one 14-oz. pkg. gingerbread mix
2/3 c. cold water
1/2 c. raisins

Beat at high speed for 1 minute peanut butter, mix and water. Fold in raisins and drop by teaspoonfuls onto cookie sheet. Bake 10 minutes at 350°. Serve with frosted glasses of lemonade (made from frozen lemonade concentrate, of course!).

SHARE A STARTER

Our grandmothers handed down a precious legacy. "It is good to share a recipe," they told us. "It is better to share a 'starter.' " Remember the story of how cooks shared a shovelful of hot coals for their neighbors' ovens? Later it was homemade yeast or a cup of sourdough. It is a lovely tradition—one you can keep with the two recipes to follow.

Herman Starter

The Starter:
2 c. flour
1/4 c. sugar
1 pkg. dry yeast
2 c. warm water

"Feed Herman":
1 c. flour
1/2 c. sugar
1 c. milk (room temperature)

Sift together flour and sugar. Add yeast and blend. Add warm water gradually to form a thick paste. Let stand in glass or plastic container (covered loosely) overnight. Refrigerate the following morning and leave for five days, stirring once daily.

On the fifth day it is time to "Feed Herman." Remove "Herman" from refrigerator and stir in additional flour, sugar, and milk.

Return Herman to the refrigerator for another five days. Herman is then ready to share! Measure 1 c. and give to a friend. You will have 2 c. remaining to use in a recipe (a couple will follow) and 1 c. to continue to feed in another 10 days. Allow the 10 days to pass, then feed Herman according to the Herman "Starter" recipe, except that you may share 1 c. (after feeding) and return the remainder to the refrigerator.

If you are unable to feed on the 10th day, pacify Herman with 1 t. sugar, repeating every 10 days until starter is used up or renewed.

Herman Hickory Nut Cake

2 c. flour
1 c. brown sugar
1/2 t. salt
2 t. baking powder
1/2 t. soda
1 t. cinnamon
2 c. Herman
2 eggs (beaten)
2/3 c. margarine (melted)
1 c. raisins
1/2 c. hickory nuts (if unavailable, substitute nut of your choice)

Topping:
2 t. cinnamon
1 c. brown sugar
1 c. chopped hickory nuts (or substitute)
1 T. flour
1/2 c. margarine (melted)

Sift together dry ingredients. Make a well and add Herman, eggs, and margarine. Mix well and add raisins and nuts. Pour into 9″ x 13″ greased baking pan and spread with topping.

Bake at 350° for 45 minutes. Test for doneness. Delicious hot or freezes well. When thawed for use, warm up and serve with freshly perked coffee—then share your recipe and 1 c. Herman!

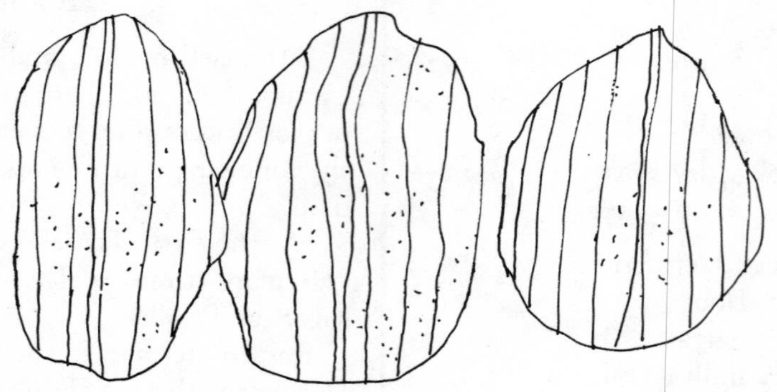

Herman Carrot Cookies

3/4 c. brown sugar
3/4 c. margarine
1 c. Herman
1 c. flour
1/4 t. each allspice, cloves, cinnamon, and nutmeg
1/2 t. soda
1/2 c. raw carrots (grated)
1/2 c. walnuts (chopped)
1/2 c. currants (chopped)
1/2 c. dates (chopped)
11/2 c. oatmeal
2 t. vanilla

Cream sugar with margarine. Add Herman (mixture will curdle). Sift flour with spices and soda. Add carrots, nuts, currants, and dates to flour mixture and sift into Herman mixture. Stir in oatmeal and vanilla. Drop onto greased cookie sheet and bake at 375° for 10 minutes. Makes 4 doz. cookies—2 doz. to serve friends and 2 doz. to send home with them!

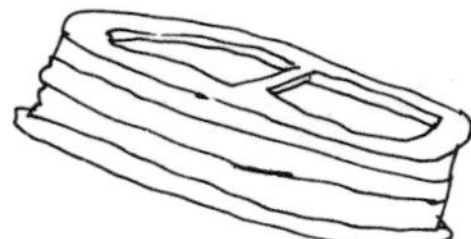

Brandied Fruit Starter

Many years ago a dear friend from East Texas shared with me a starter for this unusual formula. With it I received this written piece of advice.

This is a magic potion and must be handled with respect. There is a condition about sharing it with others. The one to whom you give this fruit must be worthy and willing to share the recipe and this admonition: You must never let the contents of this apothecary jar sink below 3 c., or fermentation will stop. Every 2 weeks you must add 1 c. sugar and 1 c. canned fruit (drained) in this order:

Pineapple tidbits (cut in halves)
Sliced peaches (canned, halved)
Maraschino cherries (halved)

You must not add oftener, but you may delay adding a day or so without disastrous results. If you delay, you will naturally have to change your calendar for later additions. Keep the calendar marked so you will remember.

When you have over 6 c. of fermented fruit, you may divide into 2 portions with at least 3 c. in each. Divide just before making another addition. You may wish to keep several jars going at once so that you can give away whenever you meet with "worthy ones." Keep jars in plain view, as they are beautiful to watch and are interesting conversation pieces. Never, *never* refrigerate. Rather, keep fruit in a warmish spot. Never, *never* put lid on tightly. Jars might explode—or so I have been told. The apothecary jars are ideal, as there is room for expansion when pressure builds up inside. Stir occasionally.

Wonderful when spooned over pound cake, vanilla ice cream, or orange sherbet—and wonderful for sharing with the "worthy ones" you call **friends**!

One secret more: *You* can start the Brandied Fruit, I found. Just follow the recipe for adding sugar and fruit and treat it with respect.

Winning Menus

Spend Some Time in an Old-Fashioned Way

So this book comes to an end with some suggestions to the hostess, ranging from a hint or two on the arrangement of the table for a sometimes-formal luncheon to the packing of a picnic basket. And there's more, for it is the wise hostess who entertains her family as guests. Then every day is a special event!

I wonder why the poets
Sing sonnets that are sad
When something is completed.
To me, they should be glad;
Sweet victory has its own notes,
So sing its song today:
You can "have cake and eat it"
On graduation day!

Recipes for some of the foods featured in the following menus appear in other sections of the book. Other menu items, identified with an asterisk, have recipes that follow the menus, so watch for the (*) sign.

In review: To serve meals which delight, satisfy, and nourish is a challenge which demands skill in shopping and preparing as well as imagination and real executive ability. Good meals should appeal to the eye as well as to the taste buds. They should present interesting contrasts of flavor, texture, color, and shape as well as a balance between substantial and light foods, and hot and cold dishes. Menu-planning should take into consideration cost, nutritional needs, help (family or outside), and the amount of time one wishes to spend in the kitchen. The hostess suggestions offered here will furnish help in daily planning. From them you can do dozens of spin-off ideas all your own.

So shed your somber habit;
Experiment, have fun—
Then write a happy sonnet
When the job is done!

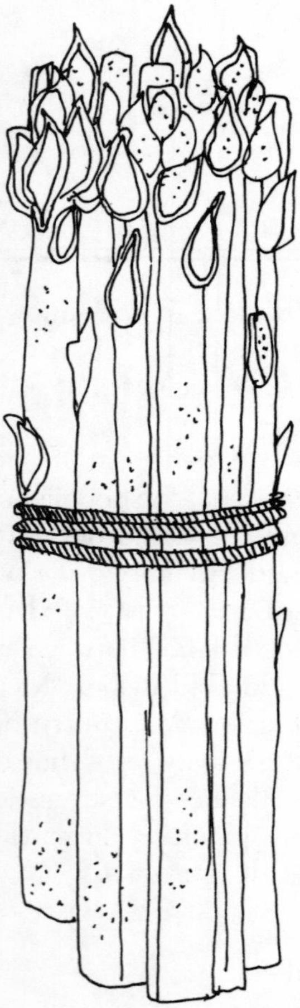

Menu Suggestion One

Informal Luncheon

An impromptu guest luncheon may be as attractive as a formal affair. Try colorful placemats and set one large table or a cluster of card tables with inexpensive but pretty dishes. Use large paper napkins in keeping with the nearest holiday or season. Omitting a hot beverage will allow you to place salad plates conveniently to the right. Place cold juice or ice water at tip of knife.

Scalloped Salmon
Orange-Cube Biscuits* Citracada Salad*
Gingerbread Squares with Molasses Whip*
Tomato Sodas*

Menu Suggestion Two

Formal Luncheon

"Formal" does not mean *stiff*! It means sitting down to a party-occasion-type meal—for example, a luncheon beginning with a light soup and ending with an elegant dessert served on your best china, with freshly brewed coffee served at the table. How about a delicious springtime luncheon with apple blossoms for a centerpiece in an heirloom crystal bowl you have longed to show your friends? Use a dainty luncheon cloth, the best silver, and Grandmother's hemstitched napkins.

Consommé
Paprika Crackers Green Olives
Grilled Sweetbreads on Toast
New Asparagus with Hollandaise Sauce
Quick Coffee Ring*
Melon Ball Salad
Fresh Strawberry Tarts*
Pastel Mints Hot Coffee

Recipes for Menus One and Two

Orange-Cube Biscuits

package of biscuits
sugar cubes
orange juice

Arrange packaged biscuits in baking pan, leaving adequate space between to insure uniform size. Press a sugar cube which has been dipped in orange juice into center of each biscuit and bake according to manufacturer's directions. Serve fresh from the oven.

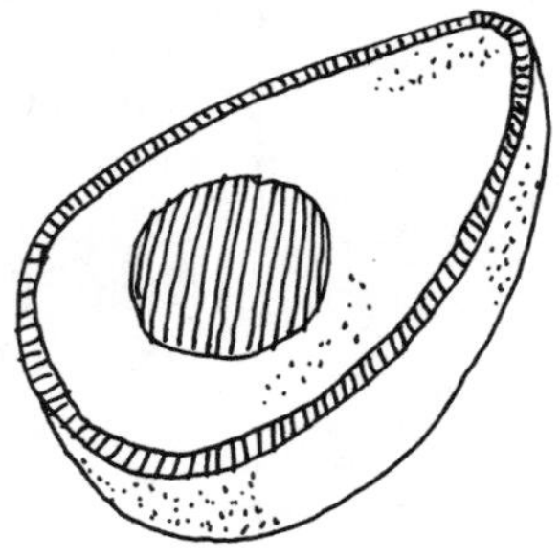

Citracada Salad

avocados
lettuce
orange wedges
coconut
lemon juice
honey

Plan on 1/2 large avocado for each serving. Cut avocados lengthwise and remove seed. Bed halves on shredded lettuce. Fill centers with orange wedges (skins and membranes removed) rolled in finely chopped coconut. Top with dressing of lemon juice and honey mixed in equal parts.

Gingerbread Squares with Molasses Whip

gingerbread squares
2 T. molasses
1 9-oz. carton nondairy topping
sugared ginger

Bake your favorite recipe of gingerbread or use a mix. Cool and cut into squares. Top with whip made by blending molasses into nondairy topping. Center with a twist of sugared ginger.

Tomato Sodas

ginger ale
lemon quarters
orange soda
orange quarters
lemon-lime soda
lime quarters
tomato-vegetable cocktail juice

Fill ice-cube tray with one of the following or make one tray of each: ginger ale (with a quartered lemon in each cube); orange soda (with a quartered orange); or lemon-lime soda (with a quartered lime). Do not peel fruit. Freeze solid and pour tomato cocktail vegetable juice over cubes in chilled glasses.

Quick Coffee Ring

1 c. golden raisins
2 c. sifted flour
4 t. baking powder
1 t. salt
1/3 c. margarine
2/3 c. milk
3 T. melted butter or margarine
1/3 brown sugar (packed)
1/2 t. cinnamon
sugar

Rinse and drain raisins. Sift together flour, baking powder and salt. Cut in margarine. Add milk and mix well. Turn onto lightly floured board and roll into rectangle about 10″ x 12″. Combine 2 T. of the butter and brown sugar, cinnamon and raisins. Spread over dough. Roll as for jelly roll. Dampen edge with water to seal the roll. Place sealed edge down on lightly greased cookie sheet. Join ends to form ring and seal ends together. With kitchen shears, cut 2/3 of the way through ring at 1″ intervals. Gently separate each section and turn it on its side so that sections overlap. Brush with remaining butter and sprinkle with granulated sugar. Bake at 400° until golden brown. Serve the ring piping hot.

In a bigger hurry? Substitute a biscuit mix and fill as directed.

Fresh Strawberry Tarts

1 qt. strawberries (washed and hulled)
1 c. sugar
1 package strawberry gelatin
1 c. warm water
one 9-oz. carton nondairy toppinng
9 baked 3 1/2″ tart shells
mint leaves

Combine berries and sugar. Let stand until sugar dissolves (about 10 minutes). Dissolve gelatin in warm water. Pour over sugared berries. Chill until mixture starts to thicken. Remove 4 T. thickened gelatin from berries and fold into whipped topping. Chill. Place layer of flavored topping in bottom of each tart shell and chill about 10 minutes longer. Cover with layer of jellied berries, pressing hull-end down gently into cream. Add smooth layer of thickened gelatin to fill tart. Top with 2 mint leaves (stem ends touching in center, leaves pointing upward and outward). Chill until completely firm. Serve without additional topping.

Menu Suggestion Three

Waffle Supper

Let waffles, baked at the table, be the feature of a supper for family or friends. There is fascination about watching the creamy waffle batter poured into the iron, waiting until—presto!—out comes the waffle, crisp, brown, and fragrant. Whether waffles are the main dish or the dessert, your guests will remember the meal.

Main-Dish Waffle Supper

Cheese Waffles with Minute Sausage*
Grilled Tomatoes
Date Sticks*
Fresh Fruit
Coffee and Milk

> *"All the miles of a hard road are worth a moment of true happiness."*
> —*Moral from Lobel Fable*

Menu Suggestion Four

Summer Dessert Waffle Supper

Waldorf Salad with Macadamia Nuts
Ebony Garlic Olives*
Hot Ham and Cheese Raisin Roll-Ups*
Summer Dessert Waffles*
Coffee and Milk

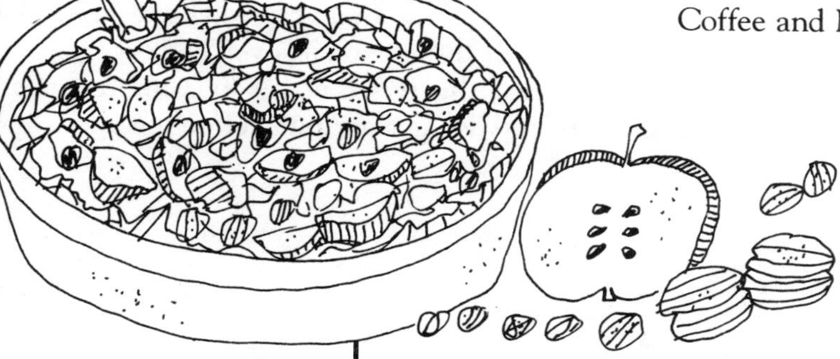

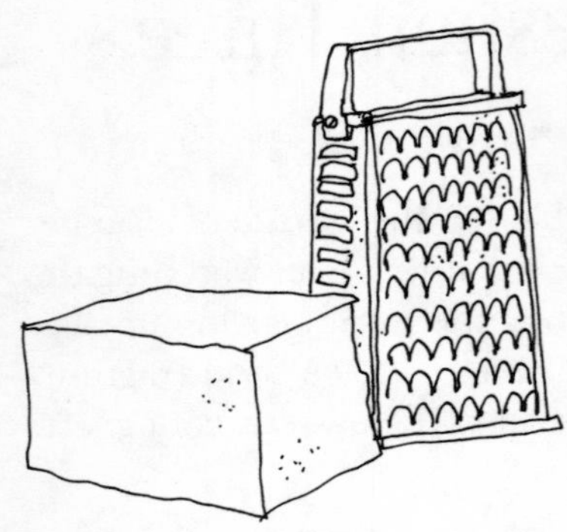

Recipes for Menus Three and Four

Cheese Waffles

2 c. sifted flour
2 t. baking powder
1/2 t. salt
3 eggs (separated)
1 c. milk
4 T. cooking oil
1 c. yellow cheese (grated)

Sift flour, baking powder, and salt together. Combine egg yolks, milk, and oil. Add to flour mixture, beating until smooth. Beat egg whites until stiff and fold in. Carefully fold in cheese. Bake in hot iron. Makes five 4-section waffles. (For variety bake on hot, greased griddle and serve as Cheese Pancakes.)

Serve Cheese Waffles with Minute Sausage. Boil little pig sausage about 2 minutes. Pour off water and drain well before refrigerating (or may be frozen). When ready to serve, brown in oven or beneath broiler. Tastier, prettier, faster, and much less fat!

Date Sticks

1 1/4 c. flour
1 1/4 t. baking powder
1/2 t. salt
1 c. sugar
2 eggs (well-beaten)
1 T. melted margarine
2 c. dates (seeded and chopped)
1/2 c. chopped nuts
1 t. vanilla
1 T. boiling-hot water
powdered sugar

Sift together flour, baking powder, and salt. Add sugar gradually to beaten eggs. Add melted margarine, dates, and nuts. Add flour mixture slowly, beating well. Blend in vanilla. Add hot water and stir quickly. Divide mixture into two greased pans, 8″ x 8″x 2″, and spread batter thin. Bake at 325° for 30 minutes. Remove from oven and cool in pan. Cut into 1″ x 3″ strips, this recipe makes four dozen date sticks. Sprinkle with powdered sugar just before serving.

Ebony Garlic Olives

one jar jumbo black olives
olive oil
garlic cloves

Pour the juice out of a jar of jumbo black olives (seed in). Replace juice with olive oil. Add several cloves of garlic (chopped). Refrigerate several days in advance of use. Shake covered jar frequently. When ready to use, skim off garlic so that none clings to olives. Lift out olives and let excess oil drip off before placing in relish dish.

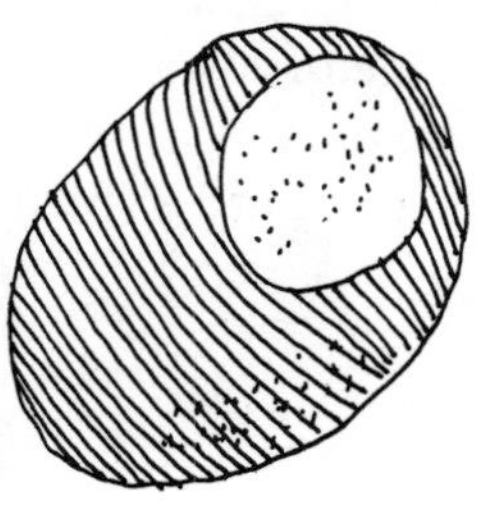

Hot-Ham-and-Cheese Raisin Roll-Ups

6 slices raisin bread
prepared mustard
boiled ham slices
Swiss cheese
margarine, melted

Flatten 6 raisin bread slices slightly with rolling pin. Spread with prepared mustard. Top each with thin slices of boiled ham and processed Swiss cheese. Roll up jelly-roll fashion. Slice each roll crosswise into 3 pieces. Skewer each with small pick. Brush with melted margarine and bake in 450° oven until toasted (about 8 minutes, being careful not to burn). Remove picks and serve hot. Makes 1½ dozen roll-ups.

Give me neither poverty nor riches; feed me with food convenient for me, lest I be full and deny thee.

Proverbs 30:8, 9a.

Summer Dessert Waffles

2 t. baking powder
$2\frac{1}{2}$ c. cake flour (sifted with $\frac{1}{2}$ t. salt)
2 T. sugar
2 eggs (separated)
2 c. milk
1 c. margarine (melted)
1 t. vanilla
$\frac{1}{2}$ c. ground nuts
powdered sugar
vanilla ice cream
fresh fruit

Measure baking powder into salted flour and sift with sugar. Combine egg yolks, milk, margarine, and vanilla. Add to flour, beating until smooth. Fold in stiffly beaten egg whites. Sprinkle nuts on top and fold in gently. Bake in hot waffle iron. Remove waffle, sprinkle with powdered sugar, and let cool at the table (or may be made in advance). Serve in sections, topped with vanilla ice cream and whole strawberries, raspberries, blueberries, or tropical fruits (mangoes, papayas, etc.).

Menu Suggestion Five

Out-of-Doors Brunch

Whether it is a brilliant May morning or a humid August day, an out-of-doors brunch casts a magic spell. Choose a bright corner on the sun porch, use the family picnic table, or set up a card table beneath the old maple tree. Use a bright drip-dry cloth and center the table with garden-fresh flowers. Watch those tired appetites snap to attention. Watch the weary diners become benevolent! Here is an easy, do-in-advance menu that lets you enjoy it, too.

Sunshine Cocktail*
Assorted Wheat Thins and Melba Toast
Breakfast Scramble with Mushroom Gravy*
Jelly Apple Rings* Hot Cinnamon Rolls
Coffee

Recipes for Menu Five

Sunshine Cocktail

one 6-oz. can tomato-vegetable cocktail juice per person
1/4 c. chilled apricot, peach, or pear nectar
dash of mace
lemon slices
mint sprigs

Combine ingredients and chill. When ready to serve, pour into frosted glasses (dampened inside and placed in freezer). Slit a lemon slice and hang on side of glass; float a single sprig of mint on top.

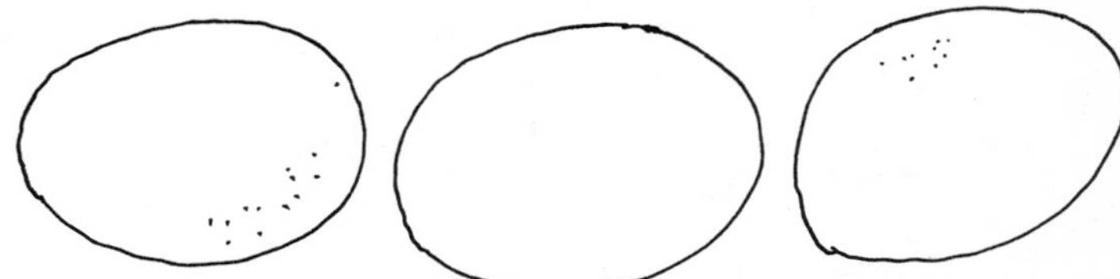

Breakfast Scramble with Mushroom Gravy

1 lb. hot sausage
6 eggs (beaten)
2 c. milk
1 t. salt
1 t. dry mustard
2 slices day-old bread cubed with crusts on
1 c. grated cheese
paprika
1 can mushroom soup/sauce

Scramble sausage in heavy skillet over low flame until browned. Drain off fat. Mix all other ingredients together and stir into sausage. Pour into greased 2-qt. casserole. Sprinkle with paprika and refrigerate overnight. Bake at 350° for 45 minutes and serve hot with mushroom gravy (canned soup heated according to directions).

Jelly Apple Rings

2 red-skinned apples (unpeeled)
2 T. margarine
1/2 c. currant jelly
1/2 t. cinnamon

Core and seed apples and slice in 1/2-inch rings. Heat margarine in heavy skillet. Add apples and cook about 5 minutes (turning often and being careful not to tear). Stir in jelly and allow fruit to remain until well-coated and jelly has been used. Dust with cinnamon.

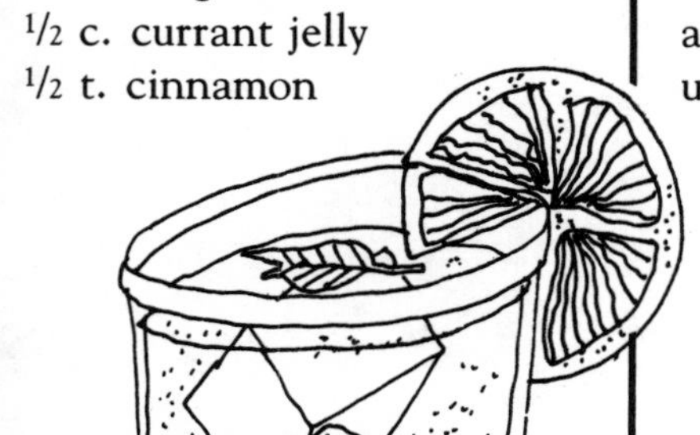

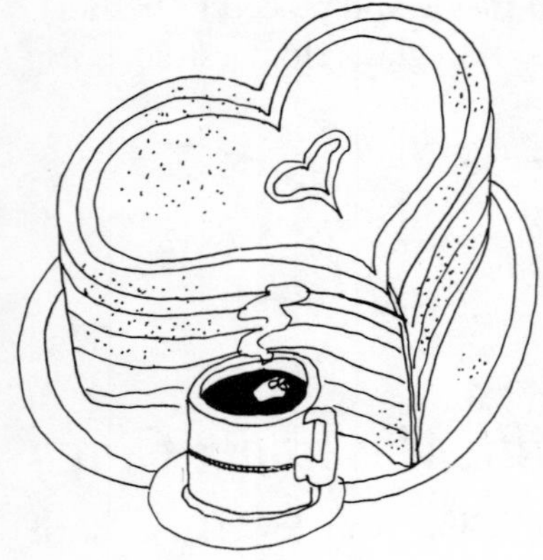

Menu Suggestion Six

Semiformal Dessert Supper

An army of butlers could hardly serve a dessert with greater dignity and beauty than can the hostess who sits at the head of her own table at a semiformal dessert supper. Dessert plates are directly in front of the hostess. Above them is an elegant dessert with serving knife and spoon. Make it simple. Make it easy. Make it beautiful with:

Raspberry Blintze Torte*

Pastel Mints — Coffee and Tea

Menu Suggestion Seven

Informal Dessert Supper

A delightful, gracious custom, and one which lends individuality to informal entertaining, is the serving of dessert (after dinner or as evening refreshments) around the hearth. Cake which may be served in a very simple way and beverage make an easy-to-serve, easy-to-eat fireside dessert. Arrange cake and beverage service on a coffee table centered with bowls of fresh fruit for those who wish; bring the cake and service in on a tray with individual fruits laid out attractively in pastel baking cups; or arrange the evenings dessert on a tea cart centered with small lighted candles and rolled in for the festive occasion. Sure to win applause!

Red Velvet Cake*

Scoops of Rainbow-Colored Sherbet on Silver Tray

Dry Roasted Nuts — Coffee and Tea

Recipes for Menus Six and Seven

Raspberry Blintze Torte

1⅓ c. sifted flour
1⅓ t. baking powder
½ c. margarine
½ c. sugar
4 eggs (separated)
5 T. milk
1 additional c. sugar
(measured separately)
2 pts. fresh raspberries
powdered sugar
nondairy topping

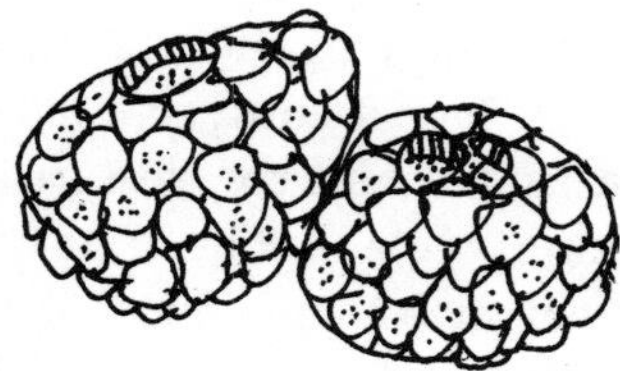

Measure previously sifted flour. Add baking powder and resift. Cream together margarine and ½ c. sugar. Add yolks one at a time, beating thoroughly after each addition. Alternate additions of flour mixture and milk, beating well each time. Spread mixture in two greased layer pans (about 9″ square) and set aside.

Now prepare the meringue by beating egg whites until foamy. Add the 1 c. sugar 1 T. at a time, beating after each addition. Continue beating until mixture stands in stiff peaks. Then spread equal amounts on top of each previously prepared layer. Bake in 325° oven for 25 minutes. Increase heat to 350° and continue baking for 30 minutes. Remove from oven and cool.

When torte is cool, spoon 2 c. fresh raspberries on top of one layer and sprinkle with powdered sugar. Lay second layer on top of the berries and spoon remainder of berries on top (reserving about 12 for garnish). Top with nondairy topping and garnish by dropping berries at random. Refrigerate until ready to serve, then cut in pie-shaped wedges.

Red Velvet Cake

½ c. margarine
2 eggs
1½ c. sugar
2 oz. red food coloring
2 T. cocoa
2½ c. flour
1 t. salt
1 t. cinnamon
1 c. buttermilk
1 t. vanilla
1 T. vinegar
1 t. soda

Cream together margarine, eggs, sugar and red food coloring. Sift together the cocoa, flour, salt, and cinnamon. Have buttermilk and vanilla ready. Mix all ingredients, alternating 3 mixtures until all are used and mixture is smooth and velvety. Now stir in the vinegar and soda.

Yield: 3 small layers or 2 large. Bake at 350° for 25 minutes. Test for doneness. Cake is bright red. An all-occasion cake or exciting on Valentine's Day. Frost with:

Rich Coconut Frosting

1 c. milk
1/2 c. flour
1 c. sugar
1 c. margarine
1 t. vanilla
1 c. slivered almonds
1 c. grated coconut
1 t. almond flavoring

Mix and cook the milk and flour until thick. Add sugar and margarine. Stir in vanilla, almonds, coconut, and almond flavoring.

Frost only between layers and on top of cake. Keeps well for several days when refrigerated.

Menu Suggestion Eight

Children's Birthday Party

Children need to learn (and adults need to review) how to relax and have "old-fashioned fun." Planning a birthday party? Nothing is more fun than a picnic, and here is one the weatherman is unable to dampen. Given a sunny day, eat out of doors. If it rains, pack everything except the dessert in a basket and let the boys and children unpack it in front of an open fire in the living room. Set up the makings of old-fashioned custard ice cream in the kitchen and let the children take turns at the ice-cream crank. And, as they picnic, center the dining table with a birthday cake, complete with candles, and lay out assorted toppings for make-it-yourself sundaes. Or buy ice cream and bake Ice-Cream-Cone Cake.

Incidentally, Grandmother knew best when she insisted that birthday parties be planned at mealtime. "Refreshments" were to be a nutritional part of the child's regular daily food intake.

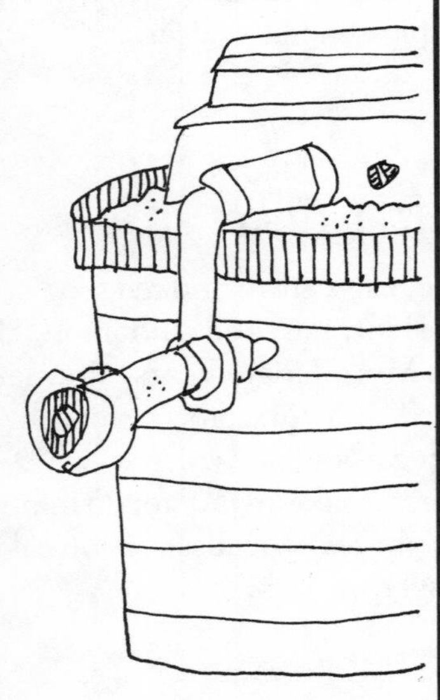

Assorted Vegetable Sticks and Fruit Wedges
Cheese Spread for Dipping
Potato Salad*
Hot Dog! Crepes*
Old-Fashioned Ice Cream*
Toasted Coconut Cake
or
Ice-Cream-Cone Cake

Recipes for Menu Eight

Hot Dog! Crepes

$1\frac{1}{3}$ c. milk
1 c. flour
4 eggs (beaten)
2 T. cooking oil
$\frac{1}{2}$ t. salt
1 t. sugar

Filling:
barbecue sauce
prepared mustard
$\frac{1}{2}$ c. sweet relish
12 wieners (toasted in oven)
chopped onion
$1\frac{1}{2}$ c. processed cheese spread
pickle slices

Combine milk, flour, eggs, oil, salt, and sugar. Mix. For each crepe, pour $\frac{1}{4}$ c. batter onto hot, lightly greased skillet. Rotate skillet slowly so that batter spreads over bottom. Test underside of crepe for brown color (using spatula). Turn once and remove from pan. Mixture should make 1 doz. crepes.

Spread each crepe with barbecue sauce, then mustard. Sprinkle with relish and lay wiener in center. Top each wiener with chopped onion. Roll up and secure each hot dog with a toothpick. Keep warm in oven until serving time, then heat cheese spread until melted. Pour over each filled crepe and top with pickle slices.

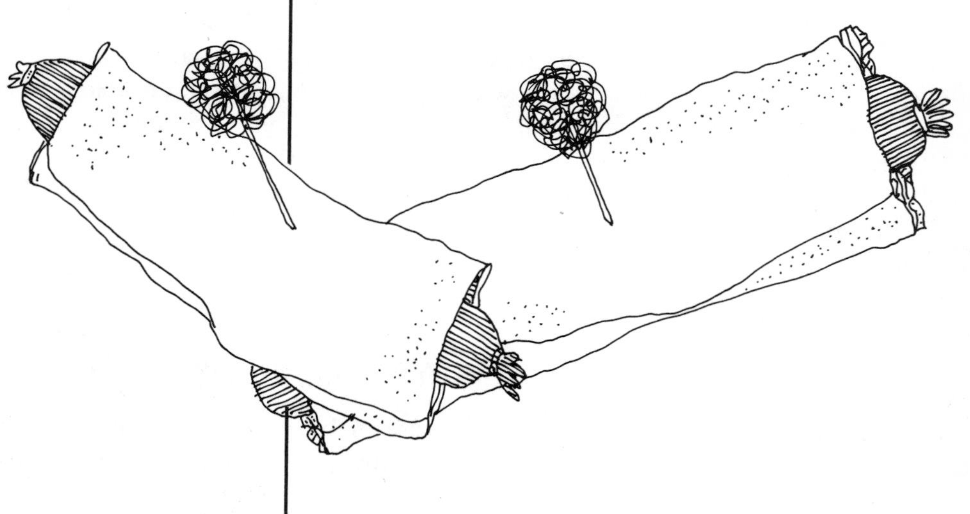

What to do with leftover love presents no problem. There is seldom enough for a satisfying first helping!

Potato Salad

6 c. potatoes (cooked, chopped)
4 hard-boiled eggs (sliced)
1 c. radish slices
1 c. chopped celery
1/2 c. sweet pickles (chopped)
1/2 c. grated onion

Dressing:
3/4 c. mayonnaise
1 t. prepared mustard
1/2 t. salt
1/2 c. sweet French dressing
1 t. sugar
1/4 t. black pepper
paprika

Boil potatoes in jackets in salted water until tender (do not overcook). Cool under cold water. Peel and chop. Combine potatoes with eggs, radishes, celery, pickle, and onion.

Make dressing and pour over salad. Toss lightly. Sprinkle with paprika. Chill.

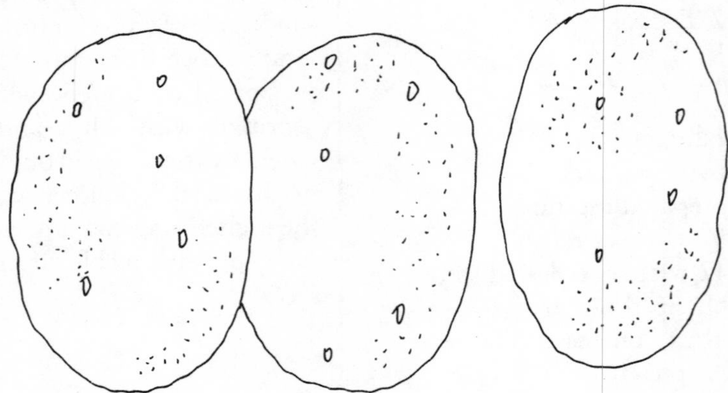

Old-Fashioned Ice Cream

1 1/2 c. sugar
1/2 c. flour
1/2 t. salt
4 eggs (separated)
1 qt. milk
2 T. vanilla flavoring
1 qt. cream

Sift together sugar, flour, and salt. Beat egg yolks and combine with milk. Add liquid to flour mixture. Cook over low heat until thick (stir to prevent scorching). Remove from heat and cool for 2 minutes. Add vanilla and fold in stiffly beaten egg whites, then chill. Stir in cream, then freeze (preferably in hand-crank freezer).

Ice-Cream-Cone Cake

batter from cake mix or favorite cake recipe
colored ice cream cones
frosting
nuts

Use your favorite birthday cake recipe or a mix for this fun idea that is sure to win applause from the younger set. Simply fill colored ice cream cones 2/3 full of batter, set cones in individual muffin tins, bake according to manufacturer's directions, and swirl tops with assorted frostings. Top with nuts, etc., if desired.

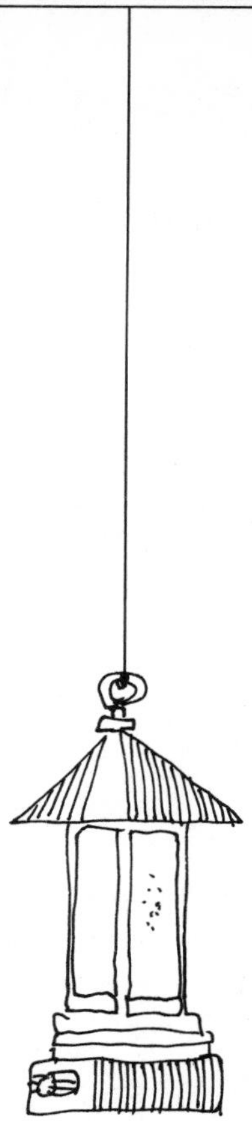

Menu Suggestion Nine

Soul Food Dinner

Those who hanker for "down-home cooking" will settle for no less. It sticks to the ribs. It nourishes the body and restores the spirit like Grandma's sulfur and molasses. We're talking about soul food—an eating experience worth trying sometime.

Plan on a bright tablecloth (oilcloth if you want to go all the way), red-checked napkins, a bouquet of wildflowers, and the soft light of a kerosene lamp.

Potato Soup
Turnips and Greens (cooked together)
Tenderloin with Cream Gravy*
Hoppin' John* Fried Okra
Sauerkraut Dumplings* Hush Puppies
Grits Cornbread Sweet Potato Pie*
Mississippi Mud Coffee
(Chicory blend—strong—served with milk)

Recipes for Menu Nine

Tenderloin with Cream Gravy

pork loin roast
flour
salt and pepper
oil
2 T. flour
2 c. milk

Plan 2 servings per person. Selected pork loin roast. Bone and slice meat (reserving bones to cook with turnips and greens—be sure to "sweeten the pot" with 1 t. sugar). Pound flour and salt and pepper to taste into loin slices and deep fry in hot fat. Drain off oil and make gravy with brown "drippings" in bottom of skillet. Add flour. Brown quickly and pour in 2 c. milk. Salt to taste when thick. Pour over tender loin slices and serve hot. Pass the hush puppies for "sopping!"

Hoppin' John

6 slices thick-slice bacon
2 c. dry black-eyed peas (cooked)
4 c. white rice (after cooking)
1/2 c. sweet chili sauce
salt and pepper to taste
1 large onion (chopped)
2 c. green beans (tenderized)
1 T. Worcestershire sauce
1/2 t. cayenne
fresh tomato wedges

Cut bacon in small strips and fry slowly until lightly browned. Drain on paper towel. Combine other ingredients, then fold in bacon. Pour into casserole and place in 400° oven long enough to heat through and give flavors a chance to blend. Garnish with tomato wedges.

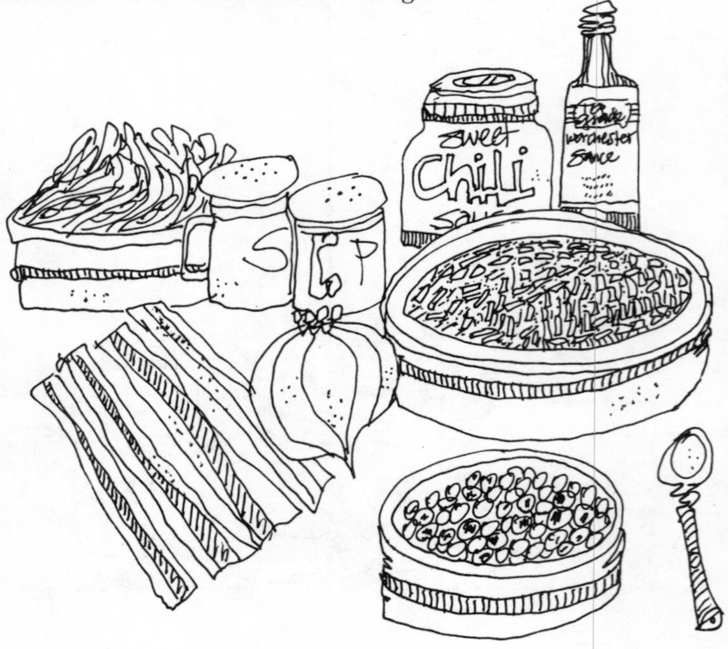

Sauerkraut Dumplings

4 c. sauerkraut (reserve juice)
1 hot, red pepper (chopped)
4 T. sugar
2 green onions (chopped)
biscuit mix
paprika
melted butter

Mix first four ingredients and pour into Dutch oven or Crock Pot. Add enough water to sauerkraut juice to cover (no more). Use biscuit mix (follow directions for biscuits) to make dumplings. Drop by teaspoon on top. Sprinkle with paprika. Cover and steam at low heat until dumplings are done. Serve hot, drizzling melted butter over top just after dishing up.

Sweet Potato Pie

1 c. mashed sweet potatoes (or yams)
1/3 c. butter (melted)
1/3 c. rich milk
1/2 t. baking powder
1 t. each nutmeg, cinnamon, vanilla
2 eggs (beaten)
1 c. sugar
pinch of salt
whipped cream
coconut, toasted

Combine all ingredients except last two and pour into unbaked pie shell (made with lard). Bake at 400° half an hour. Serve this golden oldie with generous mounds of whipped cream topped with toasted coconut.

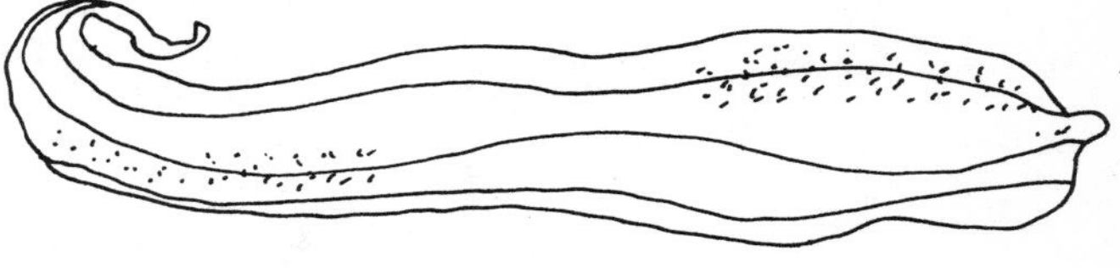

Menu Suggestion Ten

After-the-Holidays Buffet

There is a time between the Christmas festivities and the preparation of income tax returns when a change of pace is in order. The refrigerator bulges with leftovers you dare not discard. Yes, it is time for an After-the-Holidays Buffet Supper!

Such get-togethers can be as formal or as informal as you choose. Center the serving table with your sterling candelabra, lay out the matching silver or heap apples in the center, and roll the silverware in individual paper dinner napkins. Whatever the mood, the menu should be planned so that everything is on the table at once and the service and food grouped in a way that allows guests to make an orderly journey around the table. The atmosphere should be so relaxed that they feel free to return to the table again and again.

Buffet Supper

Hot Turkey Salad*

Ranch-Style Biscuits* — Corn Fritters

Assorted Fruit Wedges and Dip

Pimento Cheese-Stuffed Celery — Cherry-Cake Pie*

Coffee, Tea, Milk

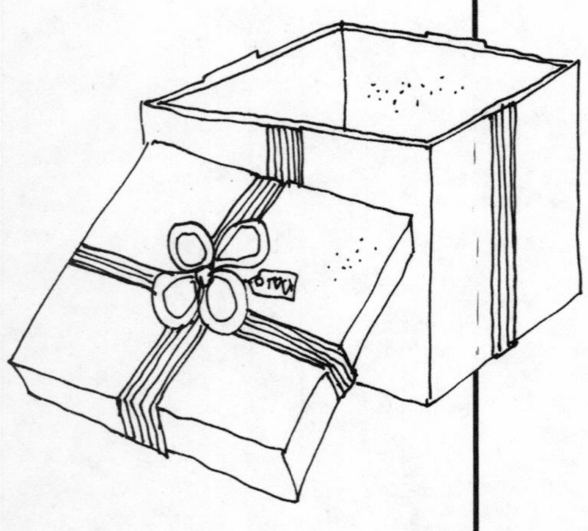

Recipes for Menu Ten

Hot Turkey Salad

- 2/3 c. mayonnaise
- 2 T. vinegar
- 1 T. sugar
- 1/2 t. salt
- 4 c. chopped cooked turkey
- 1 c. diced celery
- 1/2 c. slivered almonds
- 4 boiled eggs (sliced)
- 2 T. chopped pimento
- 2 T. chopped onions
- 1/2 c. chopped sweet pickles
- 1 c. white raisins (plumped in hot water)
- 1 can chicken soup
- 1/2 c. coconut

Combine mayonnaise, vinegar, sugar, and salt. Set aside while mixing all other ingredients except coconut. Pour dressing over salad mixture and mix only until ingredients are covered. Put into a greased casserole dish, top with coconut, and bake about 25 minutes at 350°.

Ranch-Style Biscuits

- 6 c. flour
- 1/2 c. powdered milk
- 1/4 c. baking powder (really!)
- 1/4 c. sugar
- 2 t. cream of tartar
- 2 t. salt
- 2 c. margarine
- 1 2/3 c. cold water
- sugar sprinkles

Mix together all dry ingredients. Soften margarine and blend in with pastry blender. Stir in water last (but do not beat).

Knead on floured board only until smooth, then roll into rectangle (about 3/4″ thick). Cut lengthwise, then crosswise, to form squares. Brush each square on top sandwich-style. Press down slightly. Sprinkle with sugar and lift onto cookie sheet, making sure that biscuits have room to grow! Bake about 20 minutes until golden-brown at 400°.

And good news! If you wish to use only half, do not divide recipe! Make the entire recipe and freeze squares on sheets until ready to use. Keeps up to 90 days.

Magic Cake and Cherry-Cake Pie

Begin by making the following Magic Cake (magic because the batter can be refrigerated until you are ready to use it for one of the fresh-baked ideas that follows):

Magic Cake

$4^2/_3$ c. sifted cake flour
$4^1/_2$ t. baking powder
$^1/_2$ t. salt
1 c. margarine
2 c. sugar
4 eggs (beaten)
$1^1/_2$ c. milk
2 t. vanilla
cherry pie filling
vanilla instant pudding mix
powdered sugar
nondairy toppoing

Sift together sifted flour, baking powder, and salt. Cream margarine with sugar; beat in eggs until light and fluffy. Alternate additions of milk with flour mixture, beating each time. Add vanilla. Divide batter in half. Cover one half and refrigerate. Pour the other half into two greased 8″ pans (or their equivalent) and bake at 375° for 25 minutes. Cool.

Cherry-Cake Pie

Spread one of the Magic Cake layers with a layer of cherry pie filling followed by a layer of vanilla instant pudding mix. Place second Magic Cake layer on top and press down just enough so that the cherry filling runs out to show color on sides. Sprinkle with powdered sugar and refrigerate. When ready to serve, cut into squares and top each square with nondairy topping. Nice for Washington's Birthday and Valentine's Day as well.

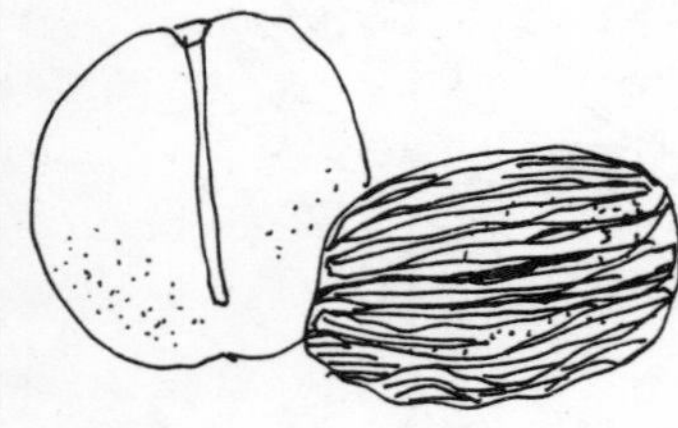

And you can use the other half of the Magic Cake batter for this delicious cake:

Apricot-Prune Upside-Down Cake

Magic Cake batter (half)
6 large dried prunes (cooked)
13 dried apricot halves (cooked)
4 T. margarine
$^1/_2$ c. brown sugar (packed)
nondairy topping

Halve prunes. Seed. Bring to a boil. Turn off heat. Cool and drain. Follow the same procedure with the apricot halves. Melt margarine in 8″x 8″x 2″ pan over low heat. Add sugar. Arrange fruit on top, cut-side-up, alternating prunes and apricots. Pour over half Magic Cake batter. Bake at 350° for about 30 minutes or until cake springs back when touched. Loosen cake from sides with spatula and invert pan, bringing it down with force onto cake plate. When cool, cut into squares and garnish with nondairy topping.

Menu Suggestion Eleven

After-the-Egghunt Dinner

Easter bunnies have tireless legs. Not so with the cook. The menu below is planned especially so that you can enjoy the beauty of the season with your family and friends with a little planning ahead.

Baked Virginia Ham
Scalloped Potatoes
Cornbread Sticks (use mix)
Tomato Bisque
Tossed Green Salad (choice of dressings)
Pickled Eggs
Fruit and Cheese Tray
Spiced Rhubarb Squares*
Coffee and Juices

Recipes for Menu Eleven

Spiced Rhubarb Squares

Magic Cake batter (half)
2½ T. molasses
½ t. each cloves and nutmeg
1 t. cinnamon
nondairy topping

This is another spin-off from the Magic Cake. Add molasses and spices to half Magic Cake batter and stir well. Turn into greased 8″x 8″x 2″ pan. Cover and refrigerate until ready to use. Bake in 350° oven half an hour or until cake springs back when touched. Cool, cut into squares, and top with Crimson Rhubarb Sauce. Swirl with nondairy topping.

Crimson Rhubarb Sauce

2 c. rhubarb (washed and cut in ½″ pieces)
2 c. strawberries (washed, hulled, and cut)
½ c. water
1 c. sugar
few drops red food coloring

Combine ingredients and cook until fruit is tender.

Spiced Pecan Cupcakes

Topping:
1 T. margarine
1/4 c. pecans (chopped)
2 T. brown sugar (packed)
1 t. cinnamon

Follow directions for Spiced Rhubarb Squares. Pour into individual muffin cups (use muffin tins and line with paper baking cups). Bake at 375° for about 20 minutes. Just before removing from oven, spread with topping and bake 2 more minutes. Cool in pans (do not remove papers). Makes about 2 dozen. Nice for picnics!

Menu Suggestion Twelve

Merry-Christmas Dinner

What could be more appropriate than offering a Christmas menu as a final suggestion? How, you wonder, can you make the festive meal different and yet keep it in line with tradition? Several weeks (or even months) before you deck the halls, why not plan a Christmas Plum Pudding and let it play a main role in the holiday meal? The following menu includes one which is fun to make, exciting to wrap, and oh! such fun to flambé at the table! You will want to bake the Cherry Pound Cake ahead for mailing or as little take-home gifts to those who share the special day with you.

Chilled Grapefruit and Tokay Grape Juice
Roast Turkey with Cornbread Dressing
Fluffy Mashed Potatoes   Giblet Gravy
Seven-Layer Green Salad
Baked Squash with Marshmallow Topping
Creamed Onion   Celery, Pickles, Olives
Cranberry Ice
Christmas Plum Pudding*
Cherry Pound Cake*
Candies   Nuts   Demitasse

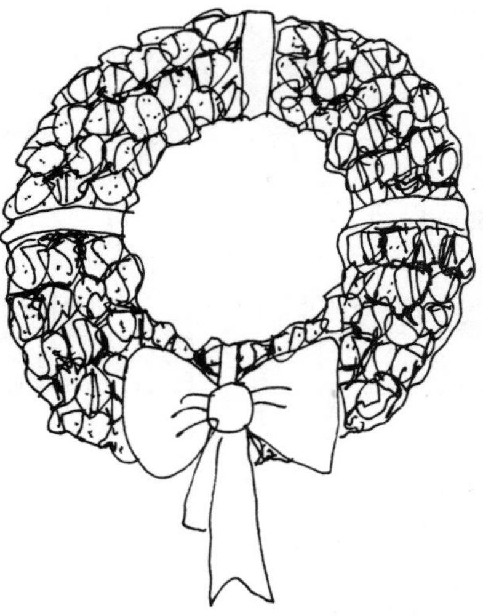

Recipes for Menu Twelve

Christmas Plum Pudding

1/2 c. apple (chopped)
1/2 c. suet (chopped)
1/2 c. molasses
2 eggs (beaten together)
1/2 c. milk
2 c. sifted flour
1/4 c. figs (chopped)
1/2 c. currants
1/4 c. candied cherries (quartered)
1/2 c. raisins
1/4 c. citron (sliced)
1 T. candied orange peel (chopped)
1/4 c. almonds (chopped)
2 t. baking powder
1/2 t. each salt, soda, cinnamon, and nutmeg

Combine apple, suet, molasses, eggs, and milk. Sift flour, measure, and mix 1/2 c. with dried fruit and nuts. Combine remaining flour with baking powder, salt, soda, cinnamon, and nutmeg. Add to apple mixture. Add floured fruits and nuts. Turn into decorative greased molds, filling 2/3 full. Cover and steam 3 hours. Cool. Wrap. Freeze until ready to use.

Serve cold with hot hard sauce, whipped cream, or flambé at the table. Use your favorite mixture for flambé or simply dip sugar cubes in lemon extract and light. In any case, surround with holly and sprigs of mistletoe.

Cherry Pound Cake

1 c. margarine
1 c. sugar
3 eggs
2 c. flour
1/2 t. salt
1 c. red candied whole cherries
1 c. green candied whole cherries
2 t. grated lemon rind

Preheat oven to 300°. Grease miniature foil cake tins and dust with flour.

Cream together margarine and sugar. Beat until light and pale yellow. Add eggs (one at a time), beating thoroughly after each addition (mixer may be used).

Blend and sift together flour and salt. Add gradually to creamed mixture, blending thoroughly.

Fold in cherries and lemon rind.

Bake 45 minutes at 300° and test for doneness. Continue baking until straw comes out clean. Cool in tins. Wrap in waxed paper and freeze. When ready to use as gifts, gift wrap and include your recipe!

Potpourri

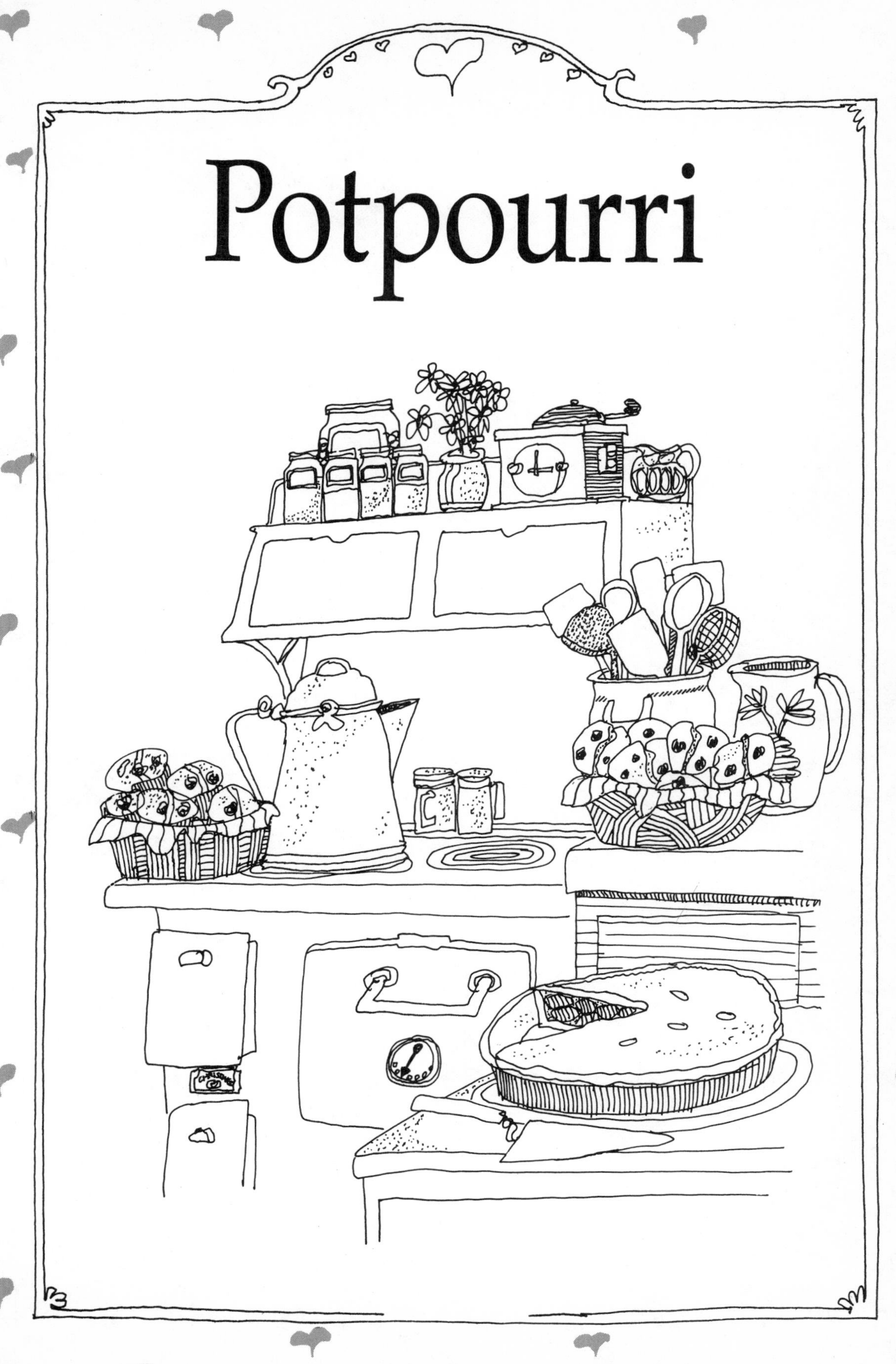

SUBSTITUTION—MOTHER OF INVENTION!

Bearing in mind that it is unwise to tamper with the basic ingredients of most recipes, there's a lot of room left for creative experimentation, substituting of nutritional ingredients, and the cutting of corners in time and money spent in meal preparation.

- Try oat flour in place of regular flour in a favorite cookie recipe. It's better for you and adds a nutlike flavor.
- Use oatmeal for thickening gravies. No oatmeal on hand? Substitute instant potato mix.
- Be kind to your figure and add nutritional value to recipes by using yogurt in place of sour cream. Try fruited yogurt in pancakes for a Wow! flavor.
- Save liquids from canned (or freshly cooked) vegetables and fruits. Vegetable liquid is delicious in gravies and casseroles. Fruit liquid is excellent in gelatin desserts, meat loaves, etc.
- Humor your budget by saving leftover coffee for a mousse, the liquid in dark breads, and would you believe in some gravies?
- Use Jerusalem (or ground) artichokes in place of water chestnuts in casseroles; or substitute peeled radishes in salads calling for chestnuts.
- Cut down on salt by using cloves, garlic, lemon, etc. Try cinnamon in coffee or tea if you are cutting down on sugar intake.
- Save seed from children's jack-o-lantern. Toast in the oven for TV munching in place of sweets or salted chips.
- Use 1/2 c. all-bran to replace equal amount of flour in pancake, muffin, and fruit-bread recipes. For your "roughage," you know!
- Chocolate baked goods calling for the real thing work well with cocoa with this formula: 3-4 T. cocoa plus 1/2 T. additional fat.
- No buttermilk? Just add 1 T. vinegar, lemon juice, or cream of tartar per c. of milk called for in recipe.
- You have buttermilk but need sweet milk? Neutralize buttermilk with 1/2 t. soda per c., remembering that each 1/2 t. soda replaces 2 t. baking powder in recipe.

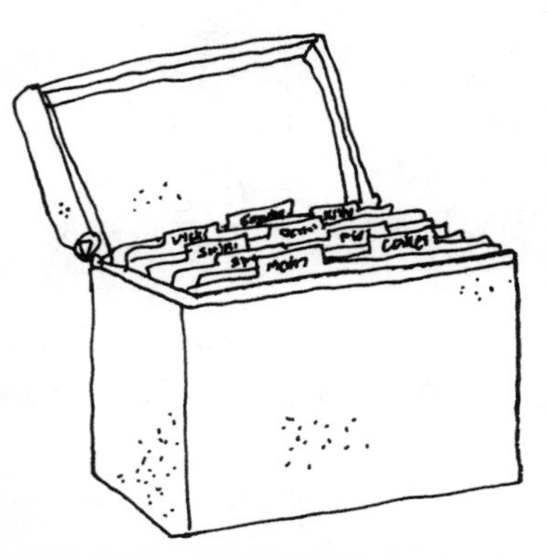

• In canned fruit pies, reserve juice, chill it, and substitute it for cold water called for in pastry recipe. Add unexpected zip!

• In need of cake flour for that special cake? For each cup of cake flour, you can substitute 1/4 c. cornstarch and 3/4 c. regular flour, sifted together. Smooth as silk.

• Custards calling for 1 whole egg will work with 2 yolks; and baking (cookies, etc.) will work with the 2 yolks plus 1 T. water.

• Recipes calling for honey respond to substitution of 3/4 c. sugar plus 1/4 c. liquid for each cup of honey. Just as sweet but changes flavor a bit. Consider additional flavoring.

Add your own ideas to the list. Maybe you'll come up with a great invention!

Invention is the talent of youth as judgment is of age.
—Jonathan Swift

(And we add: Combine the two!)

BUYING ON A BUDGET

Going shopping? Be wise. Economize! Maybe these reminders will help.

1. Check newspapers for specials (check on mileage, too!) and compare.
2. Keep a shopping list and stick to it. Avoid impulse buying.
3. Make use of store's brands (why should you pay for advertising?)
4. Consider dry milk for cooking (and drinking, if counting calories).
5. Experiment with lower-cost cuts of meat. Make use of your microwave oven, pressure cooker, or extra hours at home. Try some of the tenderizers on the market, sprinkle with lemon juice, or make overnight marinades work for you.
6. Buy fresh fruits and vegetables in season or those which are grown in your own area. Notice that frozen and canned goods also drop in price as a season ends. Bargain-counter items are often good buys, but know which to choose. A slightly damaged package of dry mix is probably fine, but avoid dented or bulging cans.

Just about the time you can make ends meet, somebody moves the ends!

7. Day-old bread? Why not? Remember that bread for this morning's toast was baked yesterday! Marked-down cakes, etc. (for emergency items in your freezer) are a good investment.
8. Buy the size of package that is right for you, and check prices carefully. Sometimes the "big economy size" actually costs more per ounce! Remember, too, that it is false thrift to buy a too-large package of a perishable item and have to discard the unused portion.
9. Stock up on protein-helpers (dried beans, peas, etc.), which furnish needed nutrients and are very kind to the budget.
10. Compare prices of meat and meat substitutes. (Reminder: It is wise to plan the main dish first, bearing in mind that you need either lean meat, cheese, eggs, dried beans, peas or lentils, or peanut butter.)

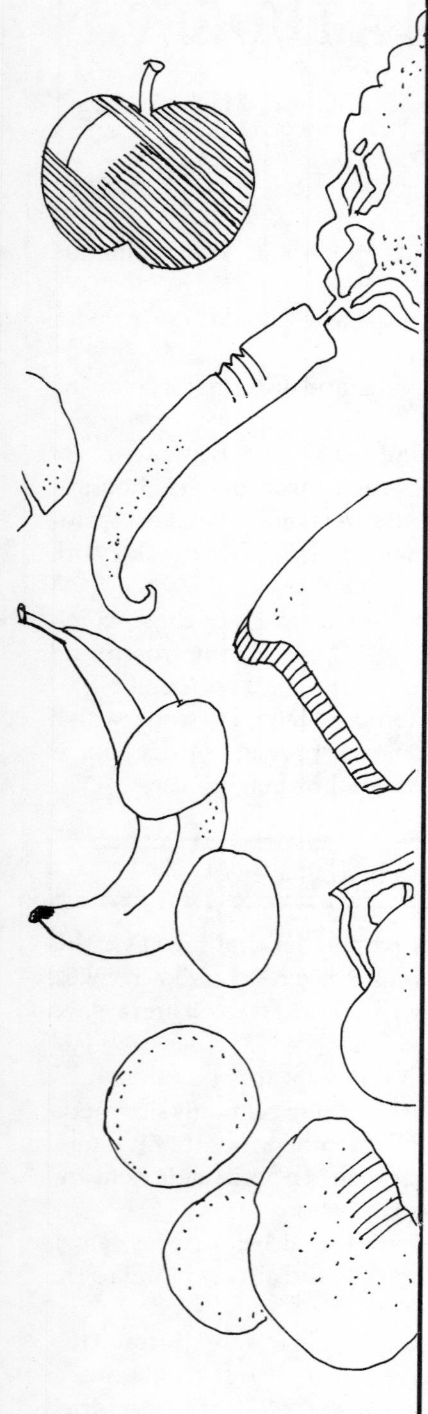

COUNTING CALORIES

Sorry! There is no magic formula for reducing weight—no chart, crash diet, or even counting alone will do the job. There is only one rule: *Take in fewer calories than you burn!*

There are ways that you can help yourself to a slimmer, more healthy, more beautiful you, however. And the beauty of it all is that you do not have to starve. You want to stay fit, above all. So: 1) Have a medical checkup and get your doctor on your side; 2) look for good-tasting, hunger-satisfying protein main dishes; 3) study the basic food groups and include them in your daily diet; 4) take no seconds other than undressed salads; 5) learn to substitute low-cal goodies for high-calorie ones, which add nothing but another layer of fat; and 6) say as little as possible to others about your diet. Why should they know until the New You emerges?

Yes, you need to know something about calorie content of every food. Yes, you need to exercise common sense in balancing food intake and exercise. And, yes, you need to know that in many—in fact, *most* cases—calorie content of a particular item is less the enemy than the hidden salts, oils, sugars, dressings, etc., tacked on. Half an avocado, for example, contains less than 100 calories. Drown it in dressings and you more than double the caloric content. Potatoes (about 90 calories per medium-size) and pasta in themselves are good friends of your figure and furnish essential carbohydrates. French fry the potatoes and dip them in catsup or cover the pasta with rich sauce and top it with grated cheese, and you're in the firing line!

So learn the approximate number of calories in the foods you ordinarily use (never mind the A-Z content of the others). Substitute here and there with dressings, etc., and above all else learn what constitutes a proper meal—and *thin is in*!

Here are a few calorie-counting helpers. From them develop your individualized list (spin-offs, you know). Here also are a few sample menus for starters if, say, you restrict yourself to a 1000-calorie diet (*caution:* with your doctor's approval).

You use up 100 calories in any one of the following:

Apple, 1 large
Bread, 1/2″ thick slice
Cabbage (eat it!), 4-5 c. raw
Carrots, 1 2/3 c. (yes!)
Crackers, 4 soda
Eggs, 1 1/3 (keep them plain)
Fish, lean (size of 2 chops)
Peanut butter, 1 T.
Sugar, white, 2 T.
Banana, 1 medium
Butter, 1 T.
Cantaloupe, 1 medium
Celery, 4 c. (yes!)
Cream, 1 T. (watch it!)
Grapefruit, 1/2 large
Milk, 5/8 c. (try buttermilk)
Potatoes, 1 medium
Pizza, 1/8 of a 14″ pie (no!)

Breakfast

1/2 medium grapefruit or one 8-oz. glass tomato juice
1 Ry-Krisp or 1 slice whole grain bread
1 T. margarine or 1 t. unsalted peanut butter
1 egg (poached or boiled)
coffee or tea (black)

Lunch

shredded cauliflower and lettuce salad
melba toast (1 slice)
1 apple or banana
buttermilk or skimmed milk (8-oz. glass)

Dinner

sliced tomato or beet salad
1 medium baked potato (1 T. margarine)
1 slice turkey or lean beef
green beans (1 serving)
1/2 medium cantaloupe or 1 scoop sherbet
coffee or tea

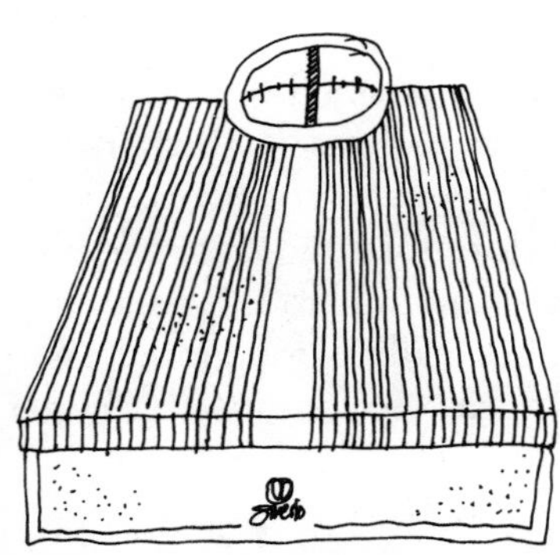

HELPFUL HINTS

Boil eggs in salted water. Improves flavor and makes peeling a breeze. (Always hold eggs under cold water while peeling.)

• Use a piece of egg shell to corner that pesky bit of yolk that falls into separated whites and eludes a spoon.

• Cooking oil gone rancid? Halve a white potato and fry it in the hot fat before reusing. Discard the spud. Save the oil!

• No time to soften butter or margarine for a recipe? Grate it.

• A lettuce leaf will remove some of the fat from a too-rich stew. A slice of raw potato will do the same for oversalting.

• Roll lemons, limes, or oranges between your palms or with your palm on a hard surface to make squeezing easier.

• Citrus fruits are easier to peel when plunged into boiling water 1 or 2 minutes, removed, and peeled immediately.

• "Sweetening the pot" improves almost any vegetable except white potatoes, but be as discreet with sugar as Grandmother was with face powder.

• Onions have you weeping? Dry your tears by chewing on the stem end of a stick match. Nobody knows why it works. It just does!

• For fluffy mashed potatoes, beat in powdered milk in place of the regular amount of milk called for. Too dry? Add more *hot* water.

• Add a few grains of salt or a tiny pinch of cream of tartar (baking powder will work) to boiled frosting recipes to prevent sugaring.

• For perfect meringue, make sure egg whites are at room temperature. They will whip faster with a pinch of salt added and higher with a pinch of cream of tartar. Allow pastry and filling to cool before spreading on meringue. Otherwise, topping will shrink.

• Form the habit of lifting whole cooked vegetables onto serving dishes with tongs. You can arrange them neatly without piercing or breaking off pieces.

• Save lemon and orange rinds for grating. Grate them up immediately after squeezing and store in plastic bags (refrigerator or freezer). Use in recipes calling for grated rind; sprinkle in ice cubes for special occasions; or mix with butter and sugar for spreading under-the-broiler morning toast.

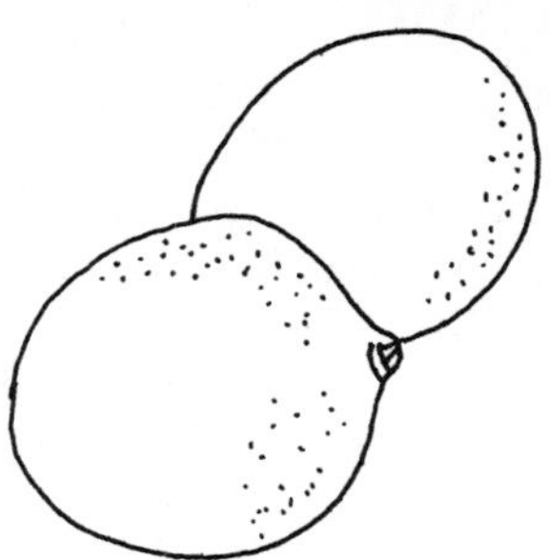

• Remember that limes can do anything lemons can do: Tenderize meats, clean stains from pots and pans, enhance salads, freshen the bathroom, garnish dishes, rinse your hair "squeaky clean," make sauces, and prevent scurvy!
• In reducing recipes, be exact! For 1 egg, beat the whole egg, measure, and divide.
• When doubling a cake recipe, add 1 minute extra beating time.
• Mother told us to store sachets, empty perfume bottles, and bars of scented soaps in our lingerie. But have you tried tucking them among your dishcloths and cup towels? Morning fresh!
• Save dabs of leftover marmalade as a glaze for ham or baked chicken.
• Those broken potato chips and taco shells make handy toppings for casseroles and salads.
• Color coconut simply by storing it in a covered glass container and adding a few drops of food color.
• To make candle holders or miniature vases for a special cake, try tucking large macaroni subtly here and there in the frosting.
• Quick-cool angel food cake by inverting pan over a tray of ice cubes.
• When doubling a recipe, taste before doubling seasonings.
• *Most important: Write down your own spin-offs as discovered!*

SOME DATES TO REMEMBER

Holiday-of-the-month times are naturals in planning company meals or even family meals, especially for such special events as birthdays and wedding anniversaries. Even the most ordinary meal becomes extraordinary at the smell of spice or the sight of red-white-and-blue bunting! So use your imagination with these dates.

Month	Flower	Birthstone	Holidays
January	Carnation	Garnet	New Year's Day, 1
February	Violet	Amethyst	Lincoln's Birthday, 12 Valentine's Day, 14 Washington's Birthday, 22 Ash Wednesday, last Wednesday
March	Jonquil	Aquamarine	St. Patrick's Day, 17
April	Sweet pea	Diamond	April Fool's Day, 1 Palm Sunday, Sunday before Easter Passover (Maundy Thursday) Good Friday Easter Sunday Secretaries' Day, 21
May	Lily-of-the-valley	Emerald	Mother's Day, 1st Sunday Memorial Day, 31
June	Rose	Pearl	Flag Day, 14 Father's Day, 3rd Sunday
July	Larkspur	Ruby	Independence Day, 4
August	Gladiolus	Peridot	Friendship Day, 1
September	Aster	Sapphire	Grandparents' Day, 2nd Sunday Jewish New Year Yom Kippur
October	Calendula	Opal	Columbus Day, 11 Boss's Day (Sweetest Day), 16 Mother-in-Law's Day, 4th Sunday
November	Chrysanthemum	Topaz	Veteran's Day, 11 Thanksgiving, 3rd Thursday
December	Narcissus	Turquoise	Hanukkah Christmas, 25

Anniversaries are a time for sentiment. The finest gift is remembering, a synonym for *love*! The following guide may suggest ideas for presents, but it can also be helpful to the hostess in planning a motif for a small dinner or a large party. For instance, *paper* suggests colored streamers or paper roses (find out the color scheme used at the wedding!); *cotton* suggests red-checked tablecloth and napkins (and wouldn't a bouquet of cotton burrs with cotton intact be nice?); then, when the gems become the symbol, use your best china, silver, etc., or reflect sapphires and emeralds in the color scheme. Get the idea?

ANNIVERSARY SYMBOLS

First, paper
Second, cotton
Third, leather
Fourth, fruit/flowers
Fifth, wood
Sixth, candy/iron
Seventh, copper/brass
Eighth, bronze
Ninth, pottery/willow
Tenth, tin/aluminum
Eleventh, steel
Twelfth, silk/linen
Thirteenth, lace
Fourteenth, ivory
Fifteenth, crystal
Twentieth, china
Twenty-fifth, silver
Thirtieth, pearl
Thirty-fifth, coral/jade
Fortieth, ruby
Forty-fifth, sapphire
Fiftieth, gold
Fifty-fifth, emerald
Sixtieth, diamond

BIRTHDAYS

Give a special birthday party sometime. Find out the *day* as well as the *date* and work around this theme:

Monday's child is fair of face,
Tuesday's child is full of grace.
Wednesday's child is loving and giving.
Thursday's child works hard for a living.
Friday's child is full of woe,
Saturday's child has far to go.
But the child that is born on the Sabbath Day
Is brave and bonny, and good and gay.

—Old Nursery Rhyme

TERMS IN GRANDMOTHER'S COOKBOOK

A *handful* equals one cup
A *double handful* is twice as much
A *sift* is one shake
A *dab* equals 1 teaspoon
A *pinch* is less than a dab
A *lump* is the size of an egg
A *small lump* is the size of a walnut
To pan means right-size utensil
Sprinkle equals several shakes
Crumble means the size of peas
Well-done varies
Smoking skillet means hot
To taste means not too much or little
Heaping means running over
Scant means not full
Devil means peppered
And her *sage advice*: "Cook so that folks know you followed the recipe. Walk so they know you read your Bible."

EQUIVALENTS, WEIGHTS AND MEASURES

Cheese
1 lb. = 2 2/3 c. (cubed)
Cocoa
1 lb. = 5 c.
Coffee
1 lb. = 5 c. (ground)
Cornmeal
1 lb. = 3. c.
Cornstarch
1 lb. = 3 c.
Crumbs
23 soda crackers = 1 c.
15 graham crackers = 1 c.
Eggs
1 egg = 4 T. liquid
4-5 eggs = 1 c.
7-9 whites = 1 c.
12-14 yolks = 1 c.
Flour
1 lb. all-purpose = 4 c.
1 lb. cake flour = 4 1/2 c.
Lemon juice
1 medium = 2-3 T.
5-8 medium = 1 c.
Lemon rind
1 lemon = 1 T. (grated)
Orange juice
1 medium = 2-3 T.
3-4 medium = 1 c.
Orange rind
1 = 2 T. (grated)
Shortening
1 lb. = 2 c.
Sugar
1 lb. brown = 2 1/2 c.
1 lb. cube = 96 regular,
= 106 small cubes
1 lb. granulated = 2 c.
1 lb. powdered = 3 1/2 c.

And, like Grandmother told us: "Happiness divided is happiness multiplied!"

3 t. = 1 T.
4T. = 1/4 c.
5 1/2 T. = 1/3 c.
8 T. = 1/2 c.
10 2/3 T. = 2/3 c.
12 T. = 3/4 c.
16 T. = 1 c.
2 c. = 1 pt.
4 c. = 1 qt.
4 qt. = 1 gal.
16 oz. = 1 lb.
32 oz. = 1 qt.
8 fl. oz. = 1 c.
1 fl. oz. = 2 T.

A Real American

She never paid taxes or donated to charities, because she owned no property and earned no income. She never examined the terms of the Constitution or educated the nation's young because she could not read. She never voted, because she was not allowed to. And yet, she was the greatest American I have ever known.

Our mutual love and respect goes back to my cradle days. We gave her the title of "Auntie" and she chose her own surname—ours. Nobody knew her lineage. She was the last of her clan that "belonged to the land." She selected the Fourth of July as her birthday.

Auntie's ankle-length apron always smelled of gingerbread, and our house smelled of honeysuckle when she entered. Those homey smells and her wide, warm lap lulled me to sleep. Man probes the mind and questions; a child sits in the lap of America and understands.

I learned about hospitality from her. Only the "how" counts.

In the kitchen, her busy hands shaped loaves and molded butter to feed the hungry backpack peddler when others were too busy. Dinner might be greens and buttermilk, but "Come on in, y'hear?" Auntie would say. "They's a-plenty. De Lawd dun promised us a new earth!" Through her eyes I saw it—America the Beautiful, the Promised Land.

Auntie's garden was a mixture of peas, corn, and tropical American herbs, with cantaloupes running wild. "Dey's all got to larn gittin' along. Elsewise dey's no hope fer us humans." Dear Auntie—the voice in the wilderness of her desegregated garden!

The great lady and her singing were one. She sang while she beat biscuits. She crooned to croupy children. She "shouted out the glory" in the canebrakes, and her treatment of patriotic songs would have moved their authors. Folklore? Legend? I choose to call it wisdom—the kind that gave purity to the white stripes in our flag.

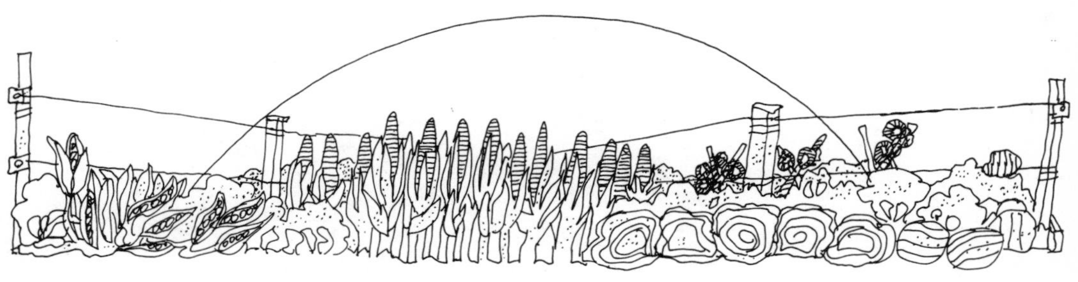

Index

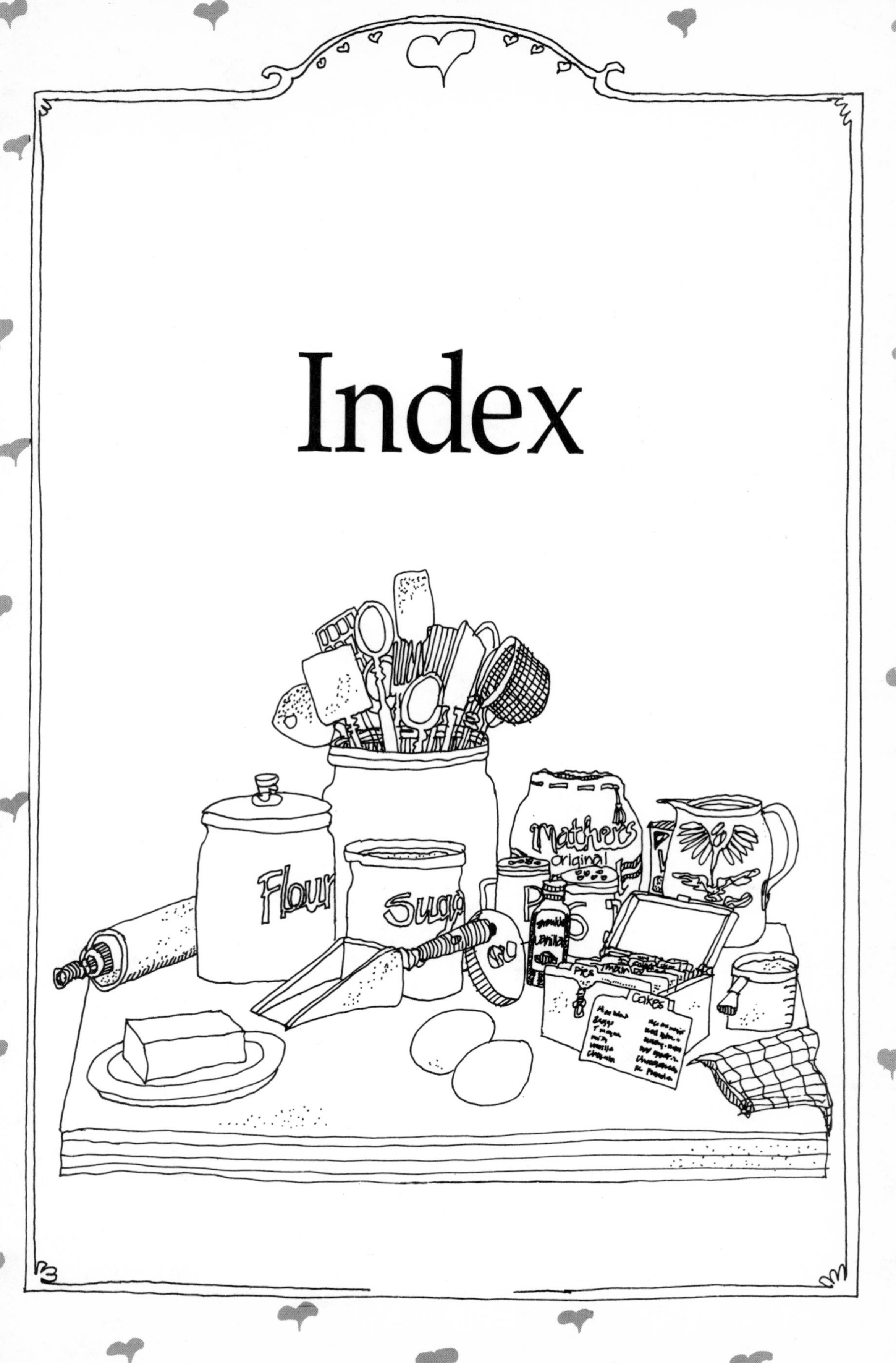

INDEX

MEMORABLE BOOKS
by June Masters Bacher

The Love Is a Gentle Stranger Series

An adventurous saga of the American frontier and a young woman's quest to find a new beginning.

Book 1 *Love Is a Gentle Stranger*
Book 2 *Love's Silent Song*
Book 3 *Diary of a Loving Heart*
Book 4 *Love Leads Home*

The Journey To Love Series

The continuing story of Rachel Buchanan and Colby Lord along the Frontier Trail to Oregon.

Book 1 *Journey To Love*
Book 2 *Dreams Beyond Tomorrow*
Book 3 *Seasons of Love*
Book 4 *My Heart's Desire*

The Love's Soft Whisper Series

Courtney Glamora is sent to the rugged Columbia Territory where she becomes a pawn in a family feud.

Book 1 *Love's Soft Whisper*
Book 2 *Love's Beautiful Dream*
Book 3 *When Hearts Awaken*
Book 4 *Another Spring*

Quiet Moments—A Daily Devotional for Women
The Quiet Heart—A Daily Devotional for Women
The June Masters Bacher Country Cookbook

Contact your local bookstore or Harvest House Publishers for more information about books by June Masters Bacher:

Customer Service
Harvest House Publishers
1075 Arrowsmith
Eugene, Oregon 97402